THE
HEART
OF THE
CHRISTIAN
MATTER

THE HEART OF THE CHRISTIAN MATTER

AN ECUMENICAL APPROACH

JOHN CARMODY

Abingdon Press • Nashville

The Heart of the Christian Matter:
An Ecumenical Approach

Copyright © 1983 by Abingdon Press

Library of Congress Cataloging in Publication Data

CARMODY, JOHN, 1939–
The heart of the Christian matter.
Bibliography: p.
Includes index.
1. Theology, Doctrinal—Popular works. I. Title.
BT77.C235   1983   230   82-13921

ISBN 0-687-16765-5

Scripture quotations are from the Revised Standard Version of the
Bible, copyrighted 1946, 1952, © 1971, 1973 by the Division of
Christian Education of the National Council of the Churches of
Christ in the U.S.A. and are used by permission.

MANUFACTURED BY THE PARTHENON PRESS AT
NASHVILLE, TENNESSEE, UNITED STATES OF AMERICA

For Bob and Sydney Brown

CONTENTS

PREFACE

This book is meant to be an ecumenical introduction to Christianity. In attempting to present the living center of Christian faith, I have drawn from whatever sources—Protestant, Catholic, or Orthodox—seemed most helpful. I have treated the distinctive contributions of each of the three Christian families to the whole Church, and I have argued that the heart of the Christian matter—Jesus, Loving God, and Loving Neighbor—provides a basis for substantial ecumenical agreement.

There is a venerable Christian maxim: "In necessary things, unity; in doubtful things, liberty; in all things, charity." I believe that Jesus and the twofold commandment supply all that is strictly necessary. I believe that we may approach other more doubtful aspects of Christian faith or tradition with great liberty. And I believe that Jesus' Spirit of love urges us to overcome the division that Christians still indulge, by getting on with necessary things and letting doubtful things take care of themselves.

I have in mind an audience of college level, whether enrolled in formal courses or self-educated, and I have tried to be relatively simple, concrete, and brief.

My thanks to the Confessing Faith in God Today group; to the many students who have tested materials like these over the years; to my wife, Denise, for good counsel; and to Karla Kraft for her very efficient typing.

INTRODUCTION

Stanley Rother

In the spring of 1981 I attended a lecture on Central America, sponsored jointly by the American Friends Service Committee, Kansas peace groups, and the Religion Department at Wichita State University. After the lecture I went to lunch with the speaker, Phillip Berryman, and a few others who were eager to continue the discussion. A tall, quiet, bearded man joined us. It turned out that he, like Berryman, had worked as a missionary in Guatemala. In fact, he had only recently returned to his native Oklahoma since learning that his name was on a right-wing hit list. His "crime" seemed to be that he had labored to improve the lot of the poverty-striken Cakchiquel Indians. He had been ministering to them for thirteen years.

I did not catch that missionary's name, but I did catch a quiet strength, especially when he said that he hoped to return to Guatemala when things quieted down. At the end of the summer, flying back to Kansas from a visit to the East Coast, I was thumbing through *Time* magazine. There, under the title "Requiem for a Missionary," was a picture of the man who had joined us at lunch. He was Father Stanley Rother, the first American slain in the Guatemalan turmoil. The steady eyes seemed to deepen, the picture to take on a frame of martyrdom.

The early Christian martyrs earned their name because their deaths were the supreme witness *(martyria)* to faith in Jesus Christ. They were willing to die for what they had found in that Jewish man from Galilee. There are parallels in many religions. Jews, Buddhists, Muslims, and other believers have died for their faith, as have adherents to causes less clearly religious. In each case, the central treasure on which the dying person's heart was set must have gained more significance in the beholders' eyes. It meant more than daily life, and so it must have challenged daily life.

For the past month, since I came upon his picture in *Time*, Stanley Rother has been challenging my daily life. Like those of a Byzantine Christ blazing forth from a thousand-year-old icon, his eyes have made me sober about this *Heart of the Christian Matter*. However valid my original notion of writing a synthesis that might be useful in college courses, this project has become more than academic. People continue to die for clinging to the Christian "matter." They continue to sell all they have (Mt 19:21) and give themselves to the poor, such as the Cakchiquel Indians. When those people are quiet, kind, and strong, like Stanley Rother, they make Christian faith something prudent teachers do not trifle with.

The same is true of less dramatic confessions of Christian faith. If it is possible to disparage much of the "electronic church" that dominates Sunday morning television because the preachers seem to make few demands for social justice and many demands for money, it is not possible in good faith to disparage the quiet confession of millions of churchgoers whose weekday lives are honest and loving. Insofar as honesty and love are at the center of what we mean by admirable human maturity, they advise us to look carefully at such people. Insofar as such people link their honesty and love to Christian faith, they advise us to look carefully at Christian faith.

I assume that you, the reader, are willing to look carefully at Christian faith because you are on the lookout for human maturity. I assume that you want a life-way that helps you to grow wise and fruitful. If so, you will not be deaf to a Stanley Rother or to a Mary Q. Public who manifests an unusual goodness, an unusual integrity.

Past Christian ages called such people saints.[1] Now they are more apt to be called enigmas, but the meaning is much the same. Such people remind us that we do not live by bread alone. They tell us that a good table and a good bank account are not our full measure. And by such reminding, such telling, they do us a great favor. Though we may not initially like it, they challenge us to define *our* humanity, the way *we* are going to spend a lifetime.

Despite all the problems it raises, all the confusion it calls forth, this challenge is at the nub of being human. Therefore one would think it should be at the nub of liberal education. Avoiding the temptation to discourse on why it often is not at the nub of liberal education, let us simply agree that this exercise in theology will be a search for wisdom and fruitfulness. Let us simply agree that we will take people like Stanley Rother seriously.

Collegeville

During the summers of 1979, 1980, and 1981, I worked with a group at the Institute for Ecumenical and Cultural Research in Collegeville, Minnesota, on the topic "Confessing Faith in God Today." The group was drawn from the full span of Christian denominations: Eastern Orthodox, Roman Catholic, Episcopal, Methodist, Presbyterian, Evangelical, Lutheran, Quaker, and more. It included blacks and whites, men and women, rich and poor, all committed to reaching outside the borders of their own denominations, if that would make Christian faith more vital. We must have spent more than a month together, over the three summers, and most of that time was inspiring. For here were people who greatly valued others' witness to Christianity's current relevancies and failures. Here were people speaking from the heart about the implications of their own faith.

Speaking from the heart, from personal conviction—this is what the group meant by "confessing faith." Our major medium was the written word. First to one another and then to the broader public, we wrote out the beliefs we could stand behind.[2] Whether those beliefs were traditional (staples of faith from the Christian past) mattered less than whether we ourselves stood behind them. For we would be convincing to others, it was agreed, only if we dealt with home truths, principles we actually had staked our time, money, and careers upon.

Perhaps the most trying and certainly the most rewarding periods during those three years were the days we worked alone, burrowing down to our deepest convictions. Almost always, in fact, our discussions were only as deep as the burrowings that had preceded them. But Collegeville provided a good atmosphere for burrowing. The institute sits at the edge of St. John's University, which houses the largest community of Benedictine monks in the world. Tracing their way of life back to the father of western monasticism, Benedict of Nursia (c. 480–550), the monks at St. John's have established a quiet environment where private reflection and communal liturgy *(public worship)* can prosper.

Our group lived in small apartments beside a peaceful pond. Snatched from busy lives in parishes or colleges, we found this more reflective atmosphere quite stimulating. Stray thoughts queried during the past year returned for a thorough hearing. Vague misgivings previously felt now solidified into either valid worries or false alarms. The result was an exacting series of exchanges. Indeed, early on, each of us had prepared a personal creed—a personal expression of Christian faith that cut to the heart of the matter. The creed I composed has stayed with me since, furnishing the structure for this book: "Moved by the paradoxical congruence of our human experience and the life, death, and resurrection of Jesus of Nazareth, I confess that the prime treasure and command of human existence is to love God with my whole mind, heart, soul, and strength, and to love my neighbors as myself."

Today the first phrase embarrasses me. "Paradoxical congruence" is theological jargon, not very helpful outside the academic ghetto. What I meant to convey is that I believe Jesus of Nazareth fulfills our deepest human hopes and clarifies our deepest human fears, but somewhat strangely. For he takes our hopes far beyond what most of us consider realistic, telling us that we can live forever with God; and he brings our fears into an almost punishing light, telling us that we can utterly ruin ourselves and our world by loving badly.

Thus Jesus' life makes our lives dramatic. Like a story that soon will reach its climax, our time grows tense when we stretch it on Jesus' frame. The more intimately we know Jesus' life, the more it turns our significance, our lives, into a reflection of his death and resurrection. What are we dying for, what are we choosing against? What will we rise to, how shall our last numbers tally? When Jesus burst upon the Israelite scene, he laid down this most forceful challenge: "The time is fulfilled, and the kingdom of God is at hand; repent, and believe in the gospel" (Mk 1:14). I believe he continues to lay down this most forceful challenge wherever we allow him onto our scene.

So for me, the motive of Christian faith, its cause and source, is the power or allure of Jesus himself. What about the content of Christian faith? I found, in my ponderings at Collegeville, that I could boil it down to Jesus' own twofold command. The prime treasure and imperative of human life, Jesus said (Mt 22:36-40), is to love God utterly and to love our neighbors as ourselves. From this summary teaching, both the obligations and the opportunities of human life organized themselves before me. Both the contemplative life, pursuit of God in study and prayer, and the prophetic life, pursuit of social justice, gained a new clarity. The rest of this book consists of my effort to explain that creed as later discussion and reflection have refined it.

1/JESUS

If Jesus is the motive for Christian faith, we should reflect on Jesus most seriously. An appealing line of recent Christian reflection views Jesus as God's metaphor, God's poetry. In his flesh shines forth the richest word we have received from divinity about both itself and ourselves.

As we study Jesus' poetry, we find that above all, he was concerned with his God. That parental source was the mysterious fullness he strove to express, the mysterious fullness Christians believe he incarnated.

The story of Jesus' fate—how he fared at the work of incarnating God's Word—is the central concern of the Gospels and also of later Christian tradition, for it is the story of our salvation, of the life that can make our lives free.

For Christian faith, our lives are richest when they blend into Jesus' life to make an organic unity like that of branches with their vine.

The best way for human branches to abide in the divine vine, and so prosper, is to follow the program Jesus laid down, his essential twofold command.

CHAPTER 1. *GOD'S METAPHOR*

First Appearances

In the Metropolitan Museum of Art in New York there is a portrait titled "Head of Christ," attributed to Rembrandt. It shows a man of perhaps thirty, with dark hair, a heavy beard, and heavy brows. He has a full nose and full lips. A cord around his neck, or the fringe of his collar (it is hard to tell which, in reproductions), sparkles as though it were made of fine cloth. But it is Jesus' eyes that draw one's attention. They gaze a little to the side, half-abstracted and a bit sad. The overall impression is of a man who might be powerful and energetic, were he not so sensitive, so aware. He might be a captain of war or industry, were he not possessed of the soul of a poet, attuned to human suffering.

Rembrandt, who lived in the seventeenth century, exercised considerable license by painting Jesus in this way, because there is no authoritative canonical portrait of him. Christian sources say nothing about Jesus' height, weight, or appearance. Their descriptions run rather to his character. He was the sort of man who could blaze with anger at injustice, as when he drove the money changers from the temple (Jn

2:13-22). He was the sort of man who would weep for a dead friend and the family, touched by their tragedy (Jn 11). Above all, he was the sort of man who was filled with a sense of mission. Jesus had a message to deliver, a work to carry out, a destiny to fulfill that was his meat and drink, his consuming passion. So he must have appeared both sensitive and serious. He must have tended more to sadness or endurance than to high spirits. While the Gospels do not portray him as morbid or morose, neither do they show him much at laughter. The times were ripe, the reign of God was at hand, amusement and distraction had little place.

The distance from Rembrandt's seventeenth-century Netherlands to twentieth-century America is quite far in terms of intellectual history, but not far at all in terms of the average person's religious imagination. Most Christians in the United States probably would find the "Head of Christ" to their expectation and liking. Perhaps a more interesting voyage, culturally, is from twentieth-century America to twentieth-century Japan. I, at least, have found the contemporary Japanese novelist Shusaku Endō's biography of Jesus quite fresh and provocative.[1] Impressed by the difficulty Christianity has had in taking root in Japan, Endō tries to draw from the New Testament a Jesus more to Asia's liking than most western portraits have been. This leads him to stress Jesus' love—above all, Jesus' almost maternal love of the poor and suffering. Japanese religious sensibilities, no doubt for reasons rooted in Japanese family structures, traditionally have preferred feminine imagery for God. Since the Japanese father-figure has been fearsome—aloof and potentially punishing—it is maternal figures such as Kwannon, a Buddhist bodhisattva overflowing with mercy, that have been most beloved.

On full reflection, Endō's portrait of Jesus is less
novel than one might first suspect, since a close
reading of the Gospels supports his stress on Jesus'
love for society's marginals. Similarly, a close reading
supports a stress on Jesus' humanity, both in the sense
that the Gospels clearly portray a true man, one of our
own species, and in the sense that they underscore his
awareness, tact, and finer feelings. Perhaps, then,
Endō's viewpoint, rooted in his Japanese cultural
outlook, is closer to the original Christian impression
of Jesus than are many western viewpoints.

In many western eras, including those close to the
present, Jesus has been not so much human as divine.
There are historical reasons for this stress on divinity,
of course, including the western reaction to the Arian
heresy (fourth century and following) that denied
Jesus' divinity. Part of that reaction, for instance, was a
liturgical style that stressed the distance between
Christians and their incarnate God. This was expressed
in the medieval Latin mass, when people who
worshiped in the large cathedrals stood far removed
from the eucharistic *(sacramental)* action going
forward at the altar, seeing only the priest's back,
hearing only a few of his most important words, and
frequently not even understanding the Latin. It is
partly because of this sense of distance from God that
Francis of Assisi and other later medievals wished to
stress the Child Jesus and that Christmas became the
most popular Christian festival. The Babe in the
manger and the young Madonna were so much less
threatening, so much more approachable, than the
heavenly Son and Judge that the common people
greatly preferred them.

At any rate, it is a safe bet that Jesus appeared to his
contemporaries as an attractive, intriguing, somewhat

enigmatic character. Clearly he was full of a compelling urgency, and clearly he was sympathetic to the common person's difficulties. He would not entrust himself to people easily, even those who professed great enthusiasm (Jn 2:23-25), and his center, his core motivation, seems to have lain outside politics or any other species of human ambition. This has always made him especially attractive to independent, truly religious people.

Parables

In suggesting that Jesus has been attractive to independent, truly religious people, I am trying to slip a slow curve by on the outside corner. Surely an admirer of Jesus should be forthright, though, so let me make the pitch right down the middle. The religion I see Jesus encouraging is one that creates independent and mature human beings. It leads them away from such false gods as money, status, or even respectability and asks that they set their hearts only on the kingdom of heaven (Mt 6:33). The kingdom of heaven, God's reign over human affairs, was Jesus' own treasure. It was the central burden of his preaching; it gathered together his most important intuitions of the changes the times were groaning to bring forth. Whereas previous prophets spoke of a future deliverance of Israel from its sufferings, Jesus said that the hour was now. Whereas previous prophets spoke of an anointed king *(messiah)* who would usher in the new day, Jesus said that he was that man. His words, his vision, his person were the focus and instrument that would enable God to establish a new state of affairs. In him, God was making all things new.

We shall dance variations on this theme in the next chapter, for Jesus' preaching of the Kingdom cannot be separated from his relation to and his conception of his God. Here let us attend not so much to substance as to style (though of course the two go together, especially with great seers). It was Jesus' peculiar style to speak his most important thoughts in parables. Parables are little stories, usually with an unexpected twist. So there is the parable of the prodigal son (Lk 15), in which an ungrateful scion who has gone off to squander his inheritance in loose living is welcomed back as though he were a conquerer, because he "comes to himself" (realizes his ingratitude and repents of it), and because his father (who represents Jesus' God) loves him unreservedly, no matter what his faults.

The parable is drawn from commonplace experiences. Jesus could assume that his hearers knew callow youths not above biting the hand that had fed them. He could assume that they knew sibling rivalry like that between the spotty younger son and his dutiful, humorless, elder brother. The two novel ingredients were the repentance of the younger son and the largess of the father.

The repentance of the son was motivated by his personal sufferings—a point not to miss. Having wasted his inheritance, he warded off starvation by working as a swineherd (a job especially abhorrent to people who considered the pig unclean). But to give him his due, the son finally came to himself. He was willing to turn his psyche around, admit the mess he had made of things, and go back to ask his father's forgiveness. So he wins from the hearer a certain admiration: It is heartening to see someone grow up.

The father is novel and admirable at a much higher

level. Willing to give the son his inheritance prema-
turely, granting the son the freedom to sow his wild
oats, the father is so good, so beyond keeping records
or bearing grudges, that he takes the very appearance
of the son on the horizon as title to a complete
forgiveness, a complete restoration to the bosom of
the family. When the elder son protests the home-
coming party, the father gives himself away: "It was
fitting to make merry and be glad, for this your brother
was dead, and is alive; he was lost, and is found" (v. 32).

That was the way Jesus thought of God: as a Father,
prodigal, unmeasured, with his love. That was the way
Jesus thought of the Kingdom: as the time, the era,
when such love stood ready to reset all human
relationships. And that was the way Jesus spoke about
God and the Kingdom: in striking stories that often
overturned his hearer's expectations. Emphasizing
such an overturning of ordinary human expectations,
recent literary analysts of the New Testament have
clarified something of the independence and true
religion of Jesus himself. The sort of person who
speaks parabolically possesses an unusually acute
sense of the difference between the magnanimity of
God *(the divine Mystery that holds all life)* and the
petty-mindedness that human beings so regularly
display.

With such a sense, the parabolic person must try to
communicate indirectly, angling around the flat-
footed, unimaginative minds that can only comprehend business as usual. He or she must be challenging, alluring, puzzling, so as to shake people from their
usual torpor. And, in Jesus' case, parables also were a
way to hint at the *otherness* of the true God, the true
God's transcendence of moralism. The true God is as
far from legalism as the heavens are from the earth;

even when our hearts condemn us, the true God is greater than our hearts (I Jn 3:20).

Robert Funk has summarized the revelations implied by Jesus' parables:

> [Jesus'] message can only be understood as something designed to precipitate the loss of the received world of Judaism in favor of the gain of the world of the Kingdom. The world in which the scribes and Pharisees were at home was shattered upon a new world designed for the poor and the destitute, the tax collectors and sinners. The righteousness of the Pharisees was devalued as confederate paper.[2]

Denunciations

The Pharisees were a group especially concerned with exact religious observance. In their eyes, the God who had made the covenant (contract) with the Jews through Moses on Mount Sinai wanted the people to follow very closely a quite detailed set of religious laws. The Pharisees promoted a number of loftier spiritual attitudes, and overall they deserve a better reputation than the New Testament alone supplies, but there is little doubt that they opposed Jesus' sense of the Kingdom and, ultimately, Jesus' sense of God. For those who wrote the Gospels, the Pharisees therefore were antagonists. As the Gospels unfold the drama, the opposition of the Pharisees mounts, clarifying the cause that was at stake in Jesus' gospel (glad tidings). For Jesus' followers, the cause at stake was the acceptance or the rejection of God's offer to change the human condition by moving religion and social intercourse toward a basis of merciful love.

Jesus himself apparently saw enough threat in the Pharisees, and in the other members of the religious establishment, to attack them vigorously: "Woe to you, scribes [religious lawyers] and Pharisees, hypocrites! for you are like whitewashed tombs, which outwardly appear beautiful, but within they are full of dead men's bones and all uncleanness. So you also outwardly appear righteous to men, but within you are full of hypocrisy and iniquity" (Mt 23:27-28). Why were the scribes and Pharisees, who were among the most observant religious Jews, so abhorrent in Jesus' eyes? What can we learn about Jesus and his gospel from such denunciations?

Martin Luther, the father of the Protestant Reformation, was a fine scholar of Scripture, and many Lutherans in his train have done yeoman work in scriptural studies. Frequently they have more or less knowingly applied the key Lutheran idea of justification by faith (reaching a right relationship with God only by opening oneself to God's love) in their interpretations of New Testament passages. The power of this idea is manifested in Joachim Jeremias' interpretation of Jesus' quarrel with the Pharisees. Jeremias believes that Jesus implicitly accused the Pharisees of not taking sin (separation from God) seriously. By its casuistry and its idea of merit, Pharisaic Judaism rendered sin innocuous:

> Casuistry views the individual sin in isolation. Sin, it is said, consists in transgressing one or more of the 613 commandments or prohibitions of the Torah [Jewish Law], or the prescriptions of tradition, the Halakah. Gradations are made of conscious or unconscious sins, greater and lesser sins. The main thing is not to commit any greater sins. The result of

this casuistry is that sin is not seen as rebellion against God.[3]

Jeremias' interpretation of merit runs in the same vein. The Pharisees believed that good human deeds could compensate for sins, as though God entered sins and good deeds in two columns of a ledger. The result was that those who regularly performed meritorious deeds came to feel complacent before both God and other members of the Jewish community:

> This self-assurance, in Jesus' view, destroyed the whole of a man's life. The man who thinks too well of himself no longer takes God seriously. Because he is sure of God's positive judgment on his life, he only asks what men think of him. All his piety is directed to the one sole purpose that others should regard him as pious. It thus becomes hypocrisy (Matt. 6.1-18). Similarly, the man who thinks too well of himself no longer takes his brother seriously. He believes himself to be better, and despises him (Luke 15.25-32; 7.39).[4]

In contrast to this Pharisaic tendency, Jesus moved on an entirely different plane. For him the great sin was closing oneself to God, refusing to accept God's offer of love and forgiveness. A person's heart was much more important than his or her outward actions. Jesus felt God renovating his own heart, filling him with enormous love. The legalistic spirit of the Pharisees seemed to stop this love at its source, cutting off all the potential change it contained, all the potential improvement in human beings' lot. To quench God's love by blind observance of detailed laws that prescribed what not to eat, what not to do on the sabbath, was to oppose all that *God* meant to Jesus. The result was a sort of holy war, begetting the fiercest denunciations that Jesus, so obviously a man of compassion, so obviously "slow to anger and quick to forgive" (like Yahweh), ever mustered. Seeing the enemy, he named it forthrightly. The enemy was hypocrisy!

Recently a popular newspaper columnist gave her Hypocrite of the Year award to a Senator who left the hearings on abortion to vote against banning the distribution of an infant formula in third-world countries (where it seems to cause many deaths). The columnist was incensed that a professed pro-lifer should act in such a blatantly pro-death manner. Something similar must have motivated Jesus' anger. Seeing religious leaders add to people's burdens when they were supposed to bring them God's solace, he lashed out at their false piety. The sabbath was made for human beings, not human beings for the sabbath. God was a healing physician, not a lawyer who counts transgressions.

Healings

Out of his union with a healing God, Jesus performed many cures. The Gospels are full of scenes in which people brought their sick and deranged, that he might alleviate their bodily or spiritual suffering. Insofar as these are descriptions of miracles, with Jesus supposedly interrupting the natural course of a disease by a simple act of his will, they present twentieth-century westerners with a considerable problem. We do not ordinarily witness miraculous healings, though from time to time we do hear of cures that boggle the medical establishment. (For example, there are a number of cases documented at Lourdes—the shrine to Mary, mother of Jesus, in France—that medical science as we presently know it cannot explain.) Still, the burden of proof lies with any report of a miraculous healing—all the more in the case of a religious wonderworker whose followers regularly ascribe extraordinary effects to their leader's teaching or person.

It is well, therefore, to set the accounts of Jesus' healings in the broader context of his entire ministry. First, Jesus healed just as he preached and suffered—in the framework of the coming kingdom of God. If his touch seemed to carry a special power, as his words seemed to carry a special light, it was as a sign, an almost inevitable overflow, of the growing presence of God in his hearers' midst. Second, Jesus asked the same response to his healing powers that he asked to his preaching: faith. God's kingdom could become effective for Jesus' hearers only if they opened their hearts to it. Since God was not a God of compulsion but of freely offered love, that kingdom had to be accepted freely.

Third, a number of psychosomatic changes become possible when one opens oneself in deep faith to another person or to an idea, and no doubt Jesus' physical influence on people often was based on these psychosomatic changes. Finding him to be a man of powerful vision and extraordinary goodness, people would lay all their psychic energy at his disposal, committing the great amounts of willpower that hope can summon. This does not deny that Jesus may indeed have worked physical miracles, but it takes into account the general change of mind *(conversion)* that his ministry regularly achieved.

For, fourth, the goal of Jesus' entire labor was the new state of affairs called for in the Kingdom. Whereas previously, people had felt distant from God, unable to accomplish the behavior the Law demanded, in the Kingdom, God himself would draw people close to him. Whereas previously, people often were sick physically, emotionally, and in their social relationships, in the Kingdom, God would work actively to heal their ills. At every level of life, therefore, the Kingdom implied a new beginning, a new set of possibilities. Open to me and my message, Jesus said, and the power of God that originally made the world will remake your whole situation.

It is this comprehensive healing that I would stress. Jesus' therapies apply to our entire human situation, private and social, spiritual and physical. But since the crux of our social situation is the justice and love we do or do not show one another, and the crux of our private situation is the order or disorder in our hearts, it is fitting that Jesus' primary healing pointed in the direction of social justice and personal order.

Social justice is perhaps the hallmark of the Old Testament God.[5] The way to worship Yahweh is to show justice to one's neighbors. Jesus sharpened the point of this message by paying special attention to those on the margins of his society. The neighbors who most drew his heart were those whom the social structures of the day ignored or depreciated: the poor, the sick, the ignorant, "sinners," women, and children. They were much more likely to draw the attention of the compassionate healing God of the kingdom than were the complacent, prosperous Pharisees. And they were much more likely to be open to this healing God, because every day, life told them they were of little account. They needed a new start.

A modern analogy is not hard to find. Recently the United States government reported that about 13 percent of its population was below the poverty line. This means that about thirty million people were suffering marked deprivation. If Jesus' own behavior is any index, those thirty million people are prime objects of God's healing concern.

Jesus' ministry of healing and solace went beyond bandages and bread. The good news of the Kingdom would call fortunate people to a spirit of generosity so that they would share their wealth with the less fortunate; but even more, it would assure the downtrodden that they mattered in the final scheme of things, that God remembered them more as society cared for them less. Thus we come to Jesus' beatitudes: "Blessed are the poor . . . Blessed are those who mourn . . ." (Mt 5:3-4). The healing of the Kingdom cut to the marrow of society and the individual soul, replacing injustice and despair with justice and hope.

Humanity as Metaphor

The blessings that Jesus pronounced on society's marginal people expressed God's compassion in rather dramatic terms. Responding to some of the deepest instincts of the human heart, Jesus preached that God overturns many human expectations. Like a deeply sensitive mother, God loves the beleaguered runty child even more than the successful handsome one. This "humanity," this exquisite humaneness of Jesus and his God, are close to the center of Christian revelation. Speaking through the kindness, the wisdom, the love of Jesus, God told all who could hear that there is a better justice, a more beautiful reckoning, than the tilted treatment most people receive. For those who were not scandalized by this deep attack on worldly values, Jesus' flesh became the best indication of the nature of the biblical God, the biblical God's attitude toward human beings.

The Gospel of John, written after Matthew, Mark, and Luke, meditates on this revelation at a deeper level than the other Gospels. From the outset, in his "prologue" (Jn 1:1-18), the author muses upon the idea that Jesus' flesh is the very embodiment of God's Word. As a consequence, this Gospel is especially symbolic; almost all the words and actions of Jesus carry several levels of meaning. Some reflect the life of the early Christian church, especially its liturgical life centered in the Eucharist. Thus the stories of changing the water into wine at Cana (Jn 2:1-11) and of multiplying the loaves and fishes by the Sea of Tiberias (Jn 6:1-14) carry eucharistic overtones. So too, the discourses between Jesus and the other Jews reflect the controversies between the early church and the Jews about the status of Jesus—controversies especially acute for the communities that produced the Johannine literature.[6] Thus in John, the Jews dispute Jesus' statement that he will give his flesh for the world like bread (Jn 6:51-52).

This perspective of the author of John leads directly into the early Christian conviction that Jesus was the Word, or Son of God incarnate. From earliest times, Christians took the person and life of Jesus as the key revelation of their God. God so shone forth from this Man that he must have been wholly of God, must have been divine. Applying the Old Testament notions of

God's Word and Wisdom, early Christians looked on Jesus as God's eternal self-expression come into time, God's own offspring in human form. Wholly a man, wholly one of us, Jesus yet transcended ordinary humanity, was also, in substance, divine.

The Pauline epistles to the Colossians and the Philippians agree with this incarnational theology. For them, too, Jesus was a man with a heavenly prehistory, one of us humans living "below" in time, but possessed of a divine life "above," outside time. These are difficult notions, of course, and Christian theology has struggled for two thousand years to clarify (not to remove) the mystery at their core. We do not know how an infinite God can express him- or herself in a finite human being. We do know that the early Christians who produced the New Testament believed with all their hearts that God had done just that in Jesus of Nazareth. Because of Jesus' extraordinary humanity —his unearthly goodness, mercy, power, and love— the early Christians called him God's very Son.

There are several corollaries to this incarnational faith that it might be well to make explicit at this point. First, as the report on Johannine theology suggests, in the New Testament there are no direct photographs or recordings of Jesus, but there are a number of interpretations of his identity and work.[7] While the parables give us some suggestion of the way Jesus himself spoke, most of his words have been filtered through the experiences of early Christian communities that had lived for some time in the belief that he was God's central revelation.

Second, the twofoldness in the New Testament interpretations of Jesus—the insistence that he was both fully human and so much more that he must have been divine—became part of dogmatic Christian faith *(the faith officially declared by the church's teachers)* in the solemn assemblies of bishops that dealt with heresies in the fourth and fifth centuries. In addition, it supplied subsequent Christian reflection with a special approach to the study of human nature, for if Jesus had been fully human, yet filled with God's Word, full humanity itself must have a certain openness toward God, a certain capacity to fulfill itself by moving beyond limited space and time to the unlimited life of God's eternity. Eastern Orthodox Christianity built this approach into a theology of *theosis,* divinization. For Eastern Christianity, Jesus had transformed our destiny from mortality to immortality, taking the nature he shared with us up into the very life of God.

Third, these variants of incarnational theology combine to give the Christian believer a peculiar outlook that might be called a humanistic realism. Taking Jesus as God's privileged revelation, the Christian considers human flesh to be the point where God's influence in our world is most intense. It is to human beings, with all their grandeur and all their dirt, that we should look first to see what God is like, what God is doing. It is humanity that is God's main metaphor.

CHAPTER 2. *JESUS' GOD*

Elusive Presence

As modern biblical scholars have increased their knowledge of Jesus' life and times, they have narrowed the division between "Old" and "New" Testament that Christians had developed over the centuries. Without denying that Jesus created a new moment in Jewish religious history, modern biblical scholars have come to realize the Jewishness of Jesus' own ethics and theology. For all that Jesus was innovative in stressing an ethic of self-sacrificing love, he built on the previous Jewish concern for heartfelt observance. For all that he leaped to a new level of intimacy with God, treating God as a completely trustworthy parent, he built on the long tradition that God was espoused to Israel in covenant. Recently Samuel Terrien, a distinguished Protestant biblical scholar, has combined the basic theology of both Testaments under the guiding motif "elusive presence."[8] Both prior to Jesus and afterward, biblical theology explained God as being present with humans, self-expressive through the metaphor of humanity, but ever elusive, ever beyond human control.

I think it will be useful to develop Terrien's notion as a backdrop for our study of Jesus' conception of God and also as a chastening reminder that we should never think that our words and ideas, however orthodox or clever, remove the intrinsic mystery of God. If Jesus prayed to his God as to One who takes precedence over all, we do well to remember that any real understanding of the word *God* depends on an experience that God himself must initiate. (As too many Western Christians do not know, Eastern Christianity always has had great respect for a negative theology which stresses God's necessary overspilling of our little vessels of understanding.[9] This section affords us the opportunity to emphasize this negative tradition.)

Paradoxically enough, God's elusive presence was a presupposition of the biblical theology that stressed Jesus' flesh. The incarnational theology of John's prologue concludes with the verse, "No one has ever seen God; the only Son, who is in the bosom of the Father, he has made him known" (Jn 1:18). It was a staple of Old Testament theology that no one had ever seen God. Again and again the prophets and historians and sages emphasized the fundamental religious humility that God—the true God of Abraham, Isaac, and Jacob—was, at most, heard in the words of remarkable leaders or experienced as a fellow traveler, a sharer of Israel's pilgrimage through time. The crucial third chapter of Exodus, in which Moses asks for God's name, is a pillar of this negative theology of the Hebrew Bible. There God gives no clear picture or image of divinity, no finite container. Over time, the Israelites will learn who God is, through living with God in covenant. God will be as time and shared experience show him or her to be. God will be present and reliable, but elusively so, according to divine, rather than human standards.

A considerable part of the misunderstanding between Jesus and the other Jews of his time turned on the interpretation of this negative theology, as did a considerable part of the controversy between Jews and Christians in the first centuries of the Common Era (A.D.). The Jews believed that Jesus was compromising the mystery of God, and thus God's uniqueness. Since the uniqueness of God was at the heart of Jewish faith, cried out each day in the *Shema* (the prayer based on Deut. 6:4-5: "Hear, O Israel: The LORD our God is one LORD"), this was a most serious charge, equivalent to blasphemy. Jesus thought that God's mystery and uniqueness were patent to all and that when he proclaimed the Kingdom, just as when he interpreted God or expressed God in a privileged way (for example, by forgiving sins), he only focused God's mystery more effectively than did prevailing Jewish religion. Even the later Christian depiction of Jesus' divinity, which we find in the earliest New Testament literature, strove mightily to preserve God's mystery and unity. Neither the theology of the Incarnation nor the theology of the Trinity *(God as Father-Son-Holy Spirit)* were meant to detract from what the early Christians called God's monarchy, God's unique power and rule.

We shall have more to say about these matters later, but the point should be kept in mind. To speak of Jesus or of humanity as God's metaphor is not to render God more known than unknown, let alone render God subject to the control of human beings. Theology and faith move by metaphor, symbol, or analogy because the frail light these offer is the best that human intelligence can muster. God has left us enough traces to get us through, but God cannot give out sheets of information any more than instamatic pictures, because the true God simply exceeds human perception. We must open ourselves to the sort of presence God offers according to Jewish and Christian experience, riveting especially on Jesus if we are to follow his way, but we must let God make of this presence what he or she wishes. God seems pledged not to disrupt biblical and church tradition, but that too is a negative norm. The first word for God's presence is always *elusive*, because the true God always remains free.

Abba

All the more remarkable, then, is the God Jesus discovered. In his human experience of God, his religion, Jesus was drawn to conceive of the Mystery that had created the world, that had formed Israel, as a living parent, an intimate father *(abba)*. Without denying that God was the sovereign Lord, the Master of the universe and Commander of all nations' fates, Jesus declared that there was a better name for God, a better theology. At the very least, God made his rain to fall, his sun to shine on just and unjust alike. At the most, God offered intimate love like that of a parent wholly captivated by a small child, utterly unable to do anything but stand with the child. The parable of the prodigal son we discussed previously is perhaps the most beautiful exposition of this view, but Jesus' whole bearing displays it. There is his prayer: "Our Father . . ."; the extension of this prayer, in John's profound meditation (Jn 14–17), takes us into the bosom of the divine life, where Jesus specifies all his being by his relation to the Father. There is his self-abnegation in the Garden of Olives, where Jesus gives himself over to whatever the Father wishes for him, no matter how bitter.

Now consider the things that become possible if God is a loving parent, always standing with his offspring. First, the world may run by principles that, without denying justice, take justice to a higher level. Possessed of a love that knows all, God can forgive almost all: even when our hearts condemn us, God is greater than our hearts. Relying on this, placing his center not in human justice but in God's love, Jesus became free to love unrestrictedly, opening himself to all he met. Obviously Jesus could not completely overcome human limitations—he became tired, hungry, discouraged. In speaking of "the disciple whom Jesus loved" (Jn 13:23), the New Testament even suggests that Jesus had human preferences, that his love was not universal in a bland, indiscriminate way. But again and again he broke the easy, instinctive preferences most of us develop: for the attractive over the unprepossessing, the rich over the poor, the healthy over the sickly, our own kind over strangers.

In dealing with the Samaritans, for instance, Jesus was offering contact with people whom Jews hated as heretical ethnic foes. In dealing with women, he was violating the sexual segregation that a rabbi of his time was supposed to observe. So too concerning tax collectors, prostitutes, lepers, and other despised groups. Raising social justice to a new level, Jesus told all those people that they were part of God's citizenry. In the eyes of his God, no one was marginal.

Second, if the obverse side of Jesus' bearing was a universal love, the reverse side was a lack of self-protection. Most of us, not possessing a hopeful view of God, protect ourselves much more than Jesus protected himself. Most of us keep our defenses high at all but the rarest of times. Jesus seems not to have needed an elaborate set of defense mechanisms.[10] God was so real to him, and so good, that he could cast his bread upon the waters without fear that it would sink. Then considering the lilies of the field, how they grow, Jesus could find a lesson in blessed indifference. If God so cares for the flowers and the birds, for the grass that is here today and gone tomorrow, how much more will God care for us? How much more should we refuse to worry? Considering the ways of human beings, evil as they are, Jesus still could find a lesson in hope. Which human parent when approached by a child for bread will give the child a stone? What human father or mother is so debased that when asked for an egg, he or she will give a child a viper? If even debased humanity shows these deep streaks of decency, must not God be utterly trustworthy? Can we predicate less of God than we would predicate of a nursing mother, a patient patriarch?

Jesus obviously could not predicate less, so he taught, third, that she who seeks will find, he who knocks will have it opened unto him. In other words, he taught that God requires only our faith, our openness, our goodwill, to show us that divinity is on our side. Once again, he taught this by analogies. Lacking bread, we can go to a friend, even in the middle of the night, and expect that if we bang on his door long enough, he will rouse and save us from our hunger. Wanting redress, an abused widow who pesters an unjust judge long enough, worrying him with her suit, can expect that the judge finally will give in, from exasperation if not from virtue, and grant her petition.

As with the previous analogies, the argument is: "If

with humans . . . how much more with God?" God must be at least as decent, as aware, as easily persuaded by what is right, as are ragtag human beings. God must have at least something like the milk of human kindness. Were we but to open our hearts to the good news, turn away from our calculation and give the Kingdom a chance, we would find in the world a cornucopia of blessings. No matter the evil and pain life carries. No matter the injustice and death. We shall deal with these later, but here we can note that for Jesus, evil and pain are much more the doings of human beings than of God. In Jesus' experience, God had freely chosen to be our loving parent, our father, our mother, our kin.

Grace

This free choice by God is the substance of the state that the New Testament, interpreting the general effect of Jesus' life, calls grace. Because of the way Jesus lived, died, and was raised from the dead, Paul and the other New Testament authors said that where sin previously had abounded, grace now abounded more (Rom 5:12). Once and for all, God had shown himself to be a divinity of mercy rather than of judgment, a divinity of love rather than of wrath. Although our human obtuseness and evil had given God more than grounds for writing us off, God showed in Jesus that she never would. Like a nursing mother, a woman moved to the quick by the child she had carried, God never would abandon the human race. As the rainbow was a pledge to Noah that God never again would let the world come to the brink of destruction by water, so the person and message of

Jesus were a pledge that God always would stand with us, always fight the evils that threaten to drown us.

Among contemporary theologians who have reflected on the meaning of this grace, Karl Rahner the prolific Roman Catholic author has delineated perhaps the most profound consequences.[11] For Rahner, Jesus' conception of God implies a universal state of affairs called the supernatural existential. By existential, Rahner means *conditioning, shaping, all people's existences.* By supernatural, he means *going beyond anything to which human beings have a strict right, into the realm of God's own inner life.* The supernatural existential, then, attempts to describe a marvelous situation, a condition both wonderful and surprising. If Jesus told the truth, all human beings are invited by God to be his friends, because God has revealed to all who will hear them the secrets of the divine heart.

When Christian theologians of the past meditated upon Jesus' revelation of God's grace, they sensed something of the universal outreach Rahner emphasizes. Thus Acts 10:34-35 indicates Peter's break with ethnocentrism: "Truly I perceive that God shows no partiality, but in every nation any one who fears him and does what is right is acceptable to him." Thus I Timothy 2:4 stresses God's desire that all persons be saved and come to the knowledge of the truth. When they speculated upon the effect of God's grace, the early church Fathers used Greek philosophy to spotlight the changes in being that grace brought about. Indeed, from New Testament texts such as II Peter 1:4, they developed the notion that ontologically *(in its being),* grace means that one shares in God's own nature. Rahner simply has used the stimulus of our current global situation, in which we are much more conscious of the proportions of the human race than were previous centuries, to clarify the way God offers himself in love to all human beings.

The offer is person-to-person, heart-to-heart. Assuming the view mentioned previously, in which the Incarnation illumines the capacity of human nature to receive something of God's fullness, we can say that *grace* is the result of God's choice to be the very "horizon" of human consciousness. By that we mean that our indistinct notion of God, against which our human awareness locates particular things, the "universe," or the "totality," becomes precise through Jesus' description of God's self-giving love. Specifically, our indistinct sense of God as the "totality" or "mystery" to which our consciousness reaches out becomes the presence of Father-Son-Holy Spirit, the presence of Jesus' God dealing with us from the "inside," from the personal love that Jesus himself found so compelling.

Such an inside, personalist view of God helps us to make sense of passages in the Johannine and Pauline literature of the New Testament in which the Spirit is said to labor on our behalf as a special advocate *(paraclete)*; where we are exhorted to abide in Jesus' love; where the Spirit is said to make the deepest prayer in our depths, with sighs too deep for words. In inner-directed portions of Scripture such as these, *grace* seems to denote the community, the shared life, that God wants to enter into with us. The ultimate favor Jesus reveals is that God has an almost romantic desire to espouse humanity so that divinity and humanity may enjoy one family life.

There are overtones of this desire in the Hebrew Bible, where Hosea depicts God's love for Israel as being like the passion of a husband who is even willing to suffer his beloved's infidelities. The Johannine,

Pauline, early-church, and latter-day theologians of grace such as Rahner have orchestrated these overtones and have emphasized even more the clear notes that Jesus himself gives forth, combining them into a symphony of God's nearly incredible generosity. Through the promise of Jesus—above all, through his resurrection and the sending of the Spirit—we can say that God has accomplished the divine desire to espouse humanity, the divine desire never to leave humanity in desperate solitude. For the Spirit is God both given and received, the divine love not only offered and potential but accepted and actual (fully in Jesus, partially in most other people). Moved by the Spirit, Paul can say that for those who love God, all things work together unto good (Rom 8:28). Sensing the complete goodness of God and the completeness of God's identification with those who love him, Paul can find the world replete with grace.

Evil

The supernatural existential implies that God has offered the world the one thing necessary for its peace and joy. So too does the gospel imply the glad tidings that God's reign over human affairs is breaking forth. But what about the many evidences that the world is without peace and joy? What about the evil that makes the gospel and the Kingdom almost a mockery? In the next chapter we shall deal with Jesus' role in the Christian understanding of evil, relating his function as Savior to the victory of grace over sin. Here, though, it seems well to reflect on the relation between the wholly positive view of God implied in Jesus' preaching and the common human experience that many things are out of joint, sometimes to the point that evil seems to prosper.

There are several rather reasonable responses to the problem of evil, and Christianity has dutifully developed them in the course of its long ministry to troubled humanity. One response, targeted toward physical evils such as earthquakes and cancers, notes that in order to maintain a world of innovation, of evolution by the laws of statistical probability, even God must allow for interactions which produce effects that are painful to human beings. Thus those who revolt against God because of the physical suffering of innocent children seem to neglect the processes by which those children came to exist at all. In other words, the price for the splendid complexity of our brains and eyes is the possibility that chemicals may misfire, genes may fail to encode properly. Similarly, the price for a Yosemite Valley or a Lake Tahoe is an occasional earthquake or forest fire that may, incidentally, bring great human suffering.

A second response, targeted toward moral evils such as war, torture, and crime, is that in order to maintain a race of free persons, even God must allow choices that result from selfishness or maliciousness. The great evil of the recent genocides, in which Nazis tried to wipe out Jews, or Turks tried to wipe out Armenians, or followers of Pol Pot tried to wipe out fellow Cambodians, or one African tribe tried to wipe out another, is entirely a human affair. God is responsible only in the sense that God made human beings free. If they are to be capable of love, fidelity, art, science, cooperation, healing, or any of the other good things for which we bless humanity, they must also be capable of mind-boggling evil.

Much the same holds true for such phenomena as

starvation in a world of plenty, unemployment in a nation with countless pressing tasks, and the greed, racism, sexism, and other forms of ill will that we can discern beneath starvation and unemployment. If nature is bountiful enough to feed the world's population and human beings are inventive enough to farm and engineer, then the malnutrition that stalks a quarter of the current world population is a human responsibility. If the United States has sufficient resources and requirements so that all its citizens may enjoy a decent standard of living and useful work, then the dysfunctions of our economy and society are the responsibility of Americans. God bids us be mature, this response argues. God tells us to open our eyes and use our hands, cleanse our hearts and share our wealth.

I think these responses carry enough force to disarm the village atheist and put the responsibility for the evils that most madden human beings right where it belongs—with men and women, rather than with God. On the other hand, I think healthy human intuition can resist these responses as not touching the heart of the matter, not really vindicating God. For if the presence of evil brings one to question the entire worth of Creation, including the creation of beings like ourselves, then it may bring one to question the wisdom, goodness, or even the existence of God. And it is not hard to imagine that evil can bring one at least close to this point—think of the parents of the five-year-old who was raped and slain by a madman, the parents of the Vietnamese children whose eardrums the Communists pierced with chopsticks. There is a disorder, a diabolical malice, a scale of injustice possible in our world that does indeed seem to implicate the Creator. How could a good God, an Abba and Source of grace, produce a world sometimes so brutal? How could such a God allow life to be so hard for so many?

To these questions, I think, there is no simply notional, untested answer. The only answers that really carry weight are fraught with experience, like the silence of Job or the cross of Jesus. For the silence of Job is actually God's restatement of the question: Have you the right to denounce the scheme of Creation when you glimpse only such a paltry fraction? Can you ever hope to be wise if you stand off like an independent being when your every breath depends on my giving?[12] And Jesus' cross is actually God's counterindictment of human evil, God's almost hyperbolic expression of divine love. So much do I stand with you, God says from the cross, that I myself will suffer your evil, if that is the only way to tear out its root. I myself will become despised, rejected, a Man of sorrows and acquainted with grief, so that after Friday's blackness, you may awaken to Sunday's light.

Light

First John 1:5 says, "God is light and in him is no darkness at all," meaning that Jesus' God suffers no Friday blackness apart from us, is in himself all Sunday light. As Jesus dealt with God as a loving father and thus implied divinity's total trustworthiness, so the Johannine images of God's light, life, and love imply something totally positive. When later Christian theology developed these New Testament confessions, it refused to allow God to possess any evil or limitation. The Christian God was totally good and totally accomplished, lacking all evil and lacking all limits. In the philosophical terms that developed from the age of the councils to the time of the medieval scholastics, God was Pure Act, infinite existence, absolute independence and freedom. In his being as well as in his action, his intellect as well as his will, God was perfect. For that was what one meant by "God." Stepping back from the experiences of Israel and Jesus and from the human tendency to picture God in human garb *(anthropomorphism)*, Christian philosophers developed and refined the intuitions of classical Greek thinkers such as Plato and Aristotle into a theology that made God not a being, but unlimited Being.

This Greek strain always has been in some tension with the Semitic biblical strain of Christian theology. As modern philosophy discovered some of the weaknesses of the medieval Christian worldview—notably its inadequacies concerning history and the concrete human being—the tension was made to seem antagonistic. The Protestant Reformers inadvertently contributed to this impression by their enthusiasm for biblical categories, and for some centuries now the Western church has found it difficult to coordinate revelation and reason. (The Eastern church, for which the theology of the church Fathers of the first centuries has remained the basic authority, only recently has begun to suffer the full impact of modernity.) Lately, however, what some scholars call postmodern studies of history, personalism, and symbolism have opened the possibility of reconciling biblical theology and the philosophy of Jesus' God.

The careful construction of a full-scale reconciliation would be an enormous enterprise, but we may make a few observations—enough to express the slant of this book. First, as indicated by the text from I John and other biblical reflections on God, Jesus' theology probably assumed God's utter perfection. Evil or darkness or limitation surely had no place in his picture of his Abba. Second, the passages in Scripture in which God is presented as imperfect, in either character or power, must be read in the context of this basic assumption of God's perfection. Thus the wrath or vindictiveness occasionally attributed to God in the Hebrew Bible, or the implication that God suffers from human infidelity or evil because these exploit some divine lack, is to be taken as a figure of speech, an effort to indicate God's deep involvement with human history, rather than an effort to discourse formally on God's nature.

Third, this realization should lead to a rather careful handling of Scripture, in an attempt to avoid two dangerous extremes. The one extreme is fundamentalism: reading the text so literally that one ignores its frequently symbolic character and the limitations (in intellectual control) of the human writers who fashioned it. The other extreme is critical reductionism: relishing the logical skills developed since the Enlightenment so much that one dictates what "God" can or cannot be, can or cannot do, on the basis of what one thinks "reasonable." Fundamentalism usually stems from undereducation, and critical reductionism usually stems from overeducation. Virtue here, as in most cases, lies in the middle, the central point of balance. It is very unlikely that God told the Israelites to slaughter their enemies or that he gave any of the other brutal prescriptions of biblical "holy" war. On the other hand, the biblical picture of God as passionately concerned with justice, to the point of fighting on the side of right, probably carries an important symbolic truth—namely, that God is not inert, detached, "care-less," but stands with the victims of evil against the perpetrators of evil.

Fourth, although the picture of God we can draw from the Bible and the best of human reflection is precious, it remains but a pencil of light shining into the divine immensity. God is not unreasonable, but suprareasonable—beyond, richer than, anything our finite minds could ever grasp. For this reason Christian tradition has declared that even in the "beatific vision" of heaven, God will remain a mystery.[13] For this reason the classical Christian mystics spoke of a "dark night of the soul" and a "cloud of unknowing," through which those who come to the most intimate union with God learn experientially, in their very marrow, how utterly God transcends human imagination and conception. Never, though, do mystics such as John of the Cross impute any evil or lack to God. Never do they question that God is Light, in whom there is no darkness at all. Like Jesus, the saints who have come closest to God say that God is everything and that they themselves are nothing, that God must increase (in our estimation) and that our egocentricity must decrease.

CHAPTER 3. *THE SAVIOR*

Sin

A good link between our discussion of Jesus' God and the Christian belief that Jesus is humanity's Savior is found early in the Johannine prologue: "The light shines in the darkness, and the darkness has not overcome it" (Jn 1:5). For Christian faith, humanity apart from God wanders in destructive darkness. It is only due to God's great favor that light enough, love enough, to make our way still remains. Insofar as we conceive Jesus as being God's signal revelation, Jesus is the light of the world, which all our human evil cannot extinguish. Insofar as we focus on the struggle between light and darkness, in faith that God, in Jesus, has decisively conquered the forces of night, we focus on soteriology, *the understanding of salvation.*

The root meaning of *salvation* is *making healthy.* Its overtones suggest that much human darkness stems from disease, so that Jesus (light from divine light) is not only God's revealer but humanity's healer. By his stripes, we are healed. And if the word for God's dispositions to work our healing is *grace,* the word for our disposition to need such healing, let alone to resist such healing, is *sin*. God offers light, life, and love, but sinful humanity veers toward darkness, death, and lovelessness. God is goodness that pours itself out, but sinful humanity is petty malice that shuts God out. It refuses to love God with whole mind, heart, soul, and strength, and it refuses to love neighbor as self, so sinful humanity careens through history, leaving a trail of corpses and garbage. Salvation expresses Christianity's hopeful conviction that in Jesus, God has shown that divinity is greater than human carnage and pollution, more gracious than human sin.

The reverse image of the twofold commandment, *sin* entails an ignorance or a contempt of God and an abuse of our fellow human beings. It is not hard to verify this image in any period of history—ancient, medieval, modern, or contemporary. It is not hard to verify it in every part of the globe. The Egyptian text "A Dispute Over Suicide" testifies to the social evil rampant in the interval between the Old and Middle kingdoms around 200 B.C.E.[14] The reports from Latin America during the 1980s C.E. suggest equally ample grounds for despair—torture, rape, butchery. Most of the in-between eras and areas show legions of skeletons out of the closet, countless demonstrations of malice and stupidity. Seen in panoramic vision, heard in stereo, human history is cause for a dreadful loss of heart. As many theologians have opined, the one Christian doctrine hard to controvert is the doctrine of original sin.

Somewhat later we shall counterbalance this gross view of human history; we will take a cue from faith to look more closely and discover humanity's many winsome gestures of nobility, many struggles to at least try to be good. But some version of original sin is so close to the Christian conception of human nature and Jesus' work that first, we should probe the meaning of such sin. Essentially, it is a privation or disorder of love. In Augustine's terms, sin is love of self that has grown into contempt of God. In other Christian theologians' views, it is a turning away from God, rebellion against God, which leads to the vices Paul detailed in Romans:

> And since they did not see fit to acknowledge God, God gave them up to a base mind and to improper conduct. They were filled with all manner of wickedness, evil, covetousness, malice. Full of envy, murder, strife, deceit, malignity, they are gossips, slanderers, haters of God, insolent, haughty, boastful, inventors of evil, disobedient to parents, foolish, faithless, heartless, ruthless. Though they know God's decree that those who do such things deserve to die, they not only do them but approve those who practice them. (1:28-32)

In our day, original sin shows up in such basic disorders, such rampaging irrationalities as the arms race, the economic disparity between rich nations and poor, and the pollution of the earth's ecosystems. Without getting into judgments on particular policies or individuals, one need only stand back and discern the large-scale patterns of humanity's current behavior to verify the intuition of original sin—something is horrifyingly amiss. A screw is loose, a gyro is warped, so the center does not hold. People who should bless God are shouting, like Lucifer, "I will not serve." People who should love one another are causing one another unspeakable misery. People who should husband the earth are raping it for base profit. Seen from the moon, the lovely blue and white earth houses a master race of madmen. The good we should do, we do not, and the evil we should not do, we do. Unhappy people that we are, who will deliver us from our bondage to profit, lust, pride, and power? Who will save us from ourselves before we turn the earth to cinders?

If you follow any of the logic that leads to these questions, if you concur with any of the passion, you, too, are on the lookout for a savior. However unexplicitly, you are seeking a wisdom, a goodness, a power that might turn things around, offer a counter-basis for hope. Jesus' symbol for such a power was the kingdom of God. The early Christians' symbol was Jesus himself, as Lord and Savior.

Death

Jesus became the countersymbol to original sin through his death and resurrection. Although the first Adam, the first of the human race, led a people captive to sin as though some primordial disobedience had warped the whole human enterprise, Jesus, the Second Adam, led his people out into freedom. Adam's disobedience had led to death, which itself died on Jesus' cross: "Dying he destroyed our death, rising he restored our life."

Through such dialectic and paradox, the early Christians meditated on Jesus, their Savior from death. His weakness had been made into supreme power by God. His love had overcome the hate of sinners. When Jesus went down into the grave, Satan's power was buried. When he arose, a new light-bearer *(Luci-fer)* came to ascendancy. To and fro, up and down, the early Christians played with the divine poetry. The metaphor of Jesus' flesh, grown gravid with history, became a major drama in three acts: life, death, and resurrection. But in contrast to the great dramas of classical paganism which brooded on the tragic fate of mortal humanity, the Christian drama was a divine comedy, the good news of humanity's passover to God's own deathlessness. In light of Christ's resurrection, Adam's sin became a happy fault.

Western history has been different from Eastern history largely because of this divine comedy. No matter how dismal a given epoch, Jesus' death was there to stare down all earthly terrors. So the Cross became a holy rood, a tree of life, a new center of the world *(axis mundi)*. To be sure, many authors and eras indulged a morbid fascination with death. Thomas à Kempis' *Imitation of Christ,* for example, seems almost to forget that Jesus preached a light and life. But the overall Christian stance-in-the-world defanged many of death's terrors. As Scripture and sacrament taught week after week, Jesus did not go to his death uselessly. Those who followed after him could hope for more than rigor mortis.

It is perhaps a moot point whether our time retains this hopeful attitude toward death and so is, at root, hopeful about life. Many estimable western artists, having (with great help from unimpressive Christians) washed away much of the Christian veneer, now probe human motivation with considerable sobriety, considerable depression from mortality. So, for example, Walker Percy's *Second Coming* pivots on a middle-aged man's memory of his father's suicide, and Shirley Hazzard's *Transit of Venus* frames its protagonist's passage between her parents' fatal accident and her own.[15] Mortality is at the marrow of both these fine novels, exerting a steady pressure, as if the writers were out to display philosopher Martin Heidegger's analysis of human existence as being-unto-death.

For Percy, the gyrations of human beings through their little span are rather comic. Only his deranged people, who confront the absurdity of most human affairs, seem sane and respectable. His sane and respectable people, who run the churches and holiday inns, seem deranged, spouting an incredible jargon and doubletalk. For Hazzard, who appears less informed by Christian aesthetics, the mood is sadder. Her voice is tender toward vulnerable humanity, but little lit by hope. The transit of the planets gives small license to smile, much less guffaw as at a comedy.

Watching my father die slowly of cancer, I certainly found no license to guffaw, but I did find cause to smile. Despite an impressively fatuous crew of doctors and priests, he went to his death peacefully, even joyously. In fact, his face on that first day of January bore a sweet smile, as though he were welcoming much more than a new year. Although timeworn like that of an El Greco saint, it gave off a clear Greek light. It was so consoling that I was shaken. Never had I expected such a legacy, and never have I feared death since. A shriveled man, more failure than success in the eyes of the world, told me that the blood I carry is stronger than any carcinogens, because for centuries it has mingled with Christ's blood.

So the "law" of Christian salvation is a law of the Cross. Jesus liberated humanity of death and sin by suffering death and sin on the cross: He conquered death by dying and rising; he conquered sin by not striking back. "Do your worst," Jesus said. "Come to me, all human destruction, and I will give you rest." And the Father backed his statement. Permitting his very Word to suffer evil, the Father destroyed evil's vicious circle, broke its cycle of tit-for-tat. Where the Song of Songs in the Hebrew Bible had glimpsed a wonderous love strong as death, the Christian gospel could behold a love stronger than death, a love that destroys the evil on which death breeds. Happy fault indeed.

Resurrection

For a variety of reasons (persecution by Christians through the centuries high among them), many Jews have had a visceral aversion from the crucifixion. Yet as Chaim Potok's moving novel *My Name is Asher Lev* suggests, the crucifixion shows humanity at its utter limits of anguish and dereliction. Arms outstretched, Jesus seems to take to himself all the millennia of human travail. Thus the young artist Asher Lev, working his way more deeply into the depiction of the suffering of his own Jewish people, finds himself, against massive taboos, painting crucifixions. Deeply aware of the irony, deeply pained by the hurt it will cause his parents, he still approves of himself as "an observant Jew working on a crucifixion because there was no aesthetic mold in his own religious tradition into which he could pour a painting of ultimate anguish and torment."[16]

Nonetheless, it is doubtful that Jesus' crucifixion would have become the premier symbol of human suffering had not Jesus emerged triumphant. All the accounts we now possess were written in light of Jesus' triumph, so they all invite the reader to contemplate the death of a more than ordinary man. What we now call the resurrection was the decisive manifestation of

Jesus' more-than-ordinariness. If his unearthly goodness and love did not convince those who beheld him
during his lifetime (and it seems they did not), his
breaking of the bonds of death and his reappearance
to the disciples did convince them. That is the only
plausible explanation of the disciples' transformation
from shallow cowards to witnesses so steadfast that
they spent themselves unto death.

The resurrection, then, is central to the New
Testament, crucial to the establishment of the Christian faith and church. From the early observations of I
Corinthians 15 to the late ponderings of the Gospel of
John, the resurrection is the event and symbol of Jesus'
Lordship. Jesus is believed to have conquered Satan,
to have seized control of history, because the Father
raised him from the dead. The Father took Jesus across
the chasm that separates mortality from divine
deathlessness, established Jesus as the head of a
people destined to share the qualities that make God
God. To the Greek mind, nothing made God God
more than athanasia (deathlessness). Thus later Eastern Christian theology thought of grace in terms of
being divinized, being refashioned into deathlessness. For the Hebrew mind, complicated by the many
overtones that Messiah, Lord, and resurrection bore in
Jesus' day, the resurrection demanded a quantum leap
beyond the usual interpretation of the categories
hitherto available.[17]

So in the New Testament, in which the Hebrew mind
prevailed, we find no clear, tidy portrayal of the
resurrection. The accounts of the different authors do
not completely square, the atmosphere is rather
confused, and the general sense is of a mystery the
authors do not understand. Jesus appears to Mary
Magdalene, to the apostles, to the disciples on the

road to Emmaus, and to others. He bids Thomas put a finger in his side and invites the fishermen to breakfast on the shore. There is enough continuity with his previous manner of being, his earthly life, for those who knew him then to recognize him now, but he is changed, transformed, freed. His appearances and the scene of his ascension tell us that ordinary human limitations no longer bind him, that he has passed over to a unique union with God.

Ruminating on all this, the early Christians who were theologically minded, such as Paul and John, projected Jesus' unique union with God back before his birth. For John, then, salvation begins with the Incarnation, since the very entry of God's Word into human flesh, to the full measure it attained in Jesus, was the radical conquest of mortality and sin. The Evangelists brought their ruminations to bear on Jesus' birth, suggesting in the infancy narratives that, from the outset, Jesus' life was that of the Messiah and Lord. Thus the very matrix of the New Testament, and so of Christian faith, is the revelation, the salvation, the grace issuing from Jesus' death/resurrection. In Christian terms, that compound act is the exact hinge of all human and cosmic history, because there God has accomplished once and for all the conquest of death and evil and the union with divinity for which all creation has been longing.

For the members of my small liturgy group, the grass-roots community that constitutes my local church, the resurrection has proved every bit as large a stumbling block as it was to those who first heard it preached by the apostles. We are not much given to accrediting such stuff, even when it illumines and fulfills our deepest longings. Not only does it not happen on Broadway and Forty-Second Street, it is too good to be true. Well, maybe. But consider how good Jesus said his God was, and how good Jesus himself proved that humans can be. Consider the absolutely pure love Jesus expressed on the cross, especially his "forgive them for they know not what they do," and think about whether it would not be in character for the God on whom Jesus relied so completely to raise him, to take him and all whom he loved into the divine deathlessness, the divine fullness of life.

The Spirit

As the writers of the New Testament portrayed Jesus under the influence of the Spirit, led into the desert and anointed to proclaim good news to the poor, so they portrayed the disciples' transformation as an act of the Spirit. At Pentecost, fifty days after Passover, the Spirit fired the ecclesia *(gathering)* of Jesus' followers into the Church Courageous. Retrospectively, John's Gospel saw Pentecost as fulfilling Jesus' promise to send the Spirit who would take his place in the disciples' midst and carry on his role of advocate and protector. Historically, Acts pictured the Spirit as coming in tongues of fire and a mighty wind, both being symbols of God's irruption into human affairs. However vague the overall New Testament theology, it is clear that the Spirit sealed the union between Jesus and the disciples, raising the human spirit into communion with the living God.

We shall have more to say about this communion in the next chapter, when we meditate upon the church's symbiosis with Jesus like branches with their vine. Here, then, we are free to consider the effects the Spirit is said to work on human nature, in the light of the resurrection. For looking at things from Jesus' human side, the spirit of his resurrection exalted and perfected all the yearning, openness, and love that this extraordinary man from Nazareth had exhibited. The mind of Jesus, which was made for light, and the heart of Jesus, which was made for warmth, found exquisite, nearly unimaginable fulfillment through his Spirit-suffused resurrection and ascension. We do not have graphs of Jesus' brain waves or any memoranda he dictated to document this claim, but the later Christian theology of human nature proves that it is faith's perduring instinct. Under the symbols of resurrection and ascension, the New Testament invites believers to consider Jesus as a man completely and paradigmatically fulfilled. In his finish, God writes large the fulfillment that all who have minds and hearts may hope to receive.

Augustine pondered in this vein and, as was his wont, came up with a saying memorable for both its depth and its lapidary style: "You have made us for yourself, O Lord, and our hearts are restless till they rest in thee." Jesus, as restless during his earthly life as a hen concerned for her chicks, found in his resurrecting Father and supportive Spirit inestimable rest, inestimable peace and joy. The radiance of the Easter Christ which so many artists have depicted is the overflow of a humanity brimming with fulfillment. At the imaginative limits of Christian theology, Jesus now stands with the Father and in the Spirit as the leader of many brothers and sisters who enjoy the Trinity's eternal life. His humanity is now a full citizen of God's realm, and his followers are given the right to hope that heaven has mansions for them.

Heaven, of course, is at core nothing more than being with God definitively, as *hell* is nothing more than being without God definitively. To be with God is glory; to be without God is ruin. For when we analyze human nature with an openness to Christian faith, we find that human nature is simply God-ward being. The most specifying thing one can say of a human being is that she is a creature aware of opening onto God, pursuing God, with a yearning foretaste of God's unlimited truth and love. This is plain when one is in the grip of the Spirit, obscure when the Spirit leaves one low and dry, but intrinsic to a Christian understanding of both "God" and "man."

When the Spirit seizes us, or gentles us to quiet and joy, we perceive the world as a sacrament. Other human beings are then images of God; subhuman creation is then a parade of God's "vestiges," of footprints where God walked and saw that all he had made was very good. So the Spirit conveys grace, favor, consolation, like a pregnant woman brooding warm life, like a clean breeze smoothing away furrows. When we are without the Spirit, the world is a trial—the claims of faith seem fatuous, evil grinds us down, there is no comeliness in us or about us. Paul distinguished these two patterns, the way of spirit and the way of flesh, concretizing their different effects:

> Now the works of the flesh are plain: fornication . . . sorcery, enmity, strife, jealousy, anger, selfishness, dissension, party spirit, envy, drunkenness, carousing, and the like. . . . But the fruit of the Spirit is love, joy, peace, patience, kindness, goodness, faithfulness, gentleness, self-control. (Galatians 5:19-23)

Not only does this give us a set of experiential indices, what we might call the symptoms of the Spirit and of the Spirit's lack; the passage also can incline us to believe the supernatural existential confirmed: Clearly the spirit gives these signs everywhere, breathes inside institutional Christianity and outside, as she will.

Overall, then, the Spirit is the personification of God come into human beings' spirits. It is the downpayment or pledge *(arrabon)*, in time, of the heavenly life Jesus has opened beyond time. Loving unto death, being raised by his Father's love to the other side of death, Jesus shares in a divine breathing forth *(spiration)* which makes those who open themselves to it sharers in his victory.

Love

When we boil the signs of the Spirit down to their essential stock, we arrive at the Christian conviction that God is Love (I Jn 4:16). The best analogue we have for God, the most persuasive explanation as to why God should have created the world and saved humanity through Jesus, is the love that faith in Jesus discloses. Generative, powerful, careful, suffering, and triumphant, this love makes Jesus God's central metaphor. It is the thread through the labyrinth, the touchstone that never fails. Once again, Paul has done us the favor of describing this phenomenon, essaying to some extent the way it appears:

> Love is patient and kind; love is not jealous or boastful; it is not arrogant or rude. Love does not insist on its own way; it is not irritable or resentful; it does not rejoice at wrong, but rejoices in the right. Love bears all things, believes all things, hopes all things, endures all things. Love never ends. (I Corinthians 13:4-8a)

So the good news, the Spirit of resurrected life, the converted heart, all are a matter of love. Opening to God, who loved us first, we return that love by letting God's Spirit take over, fashion us to the measure of Christ, make us images of the Image. This love-relationship with the spirit is both like and unlike the love affairs we regard as merely human (actually there are none such); it is both immersed in and distinguishable from our romances, parentings, friendships, erotic and suffering labors. Perhaps this relationship is best seen, though, as the gift that creates a new horizon, a new outlook on all reality.[18] Gratuitously given by God, this relationship with the Spirit becomes the undertow that moves our depths, prompting us to cry out Abba, Father.

The love God bestows on us, the loving self God offers, resembles our human loves. It is a power that brings us alive, similar to our erotic response to a beautiful person or a beautiful work of art. The man transfixed by the fall of his beloved's hair, or the student mesmerized by Michelangelo's *David*, feels something godly. Their *eros* is not so different from God's *agape* that we should despise it. No, their eros, their ardent, seeking love, is afire with the sort of quickening and longing that Jesus himself felt for the good of salvation, the beauty of his Father's arms opening to all of prodigal humanity.

The same holds true for human loves that are crafting, careful, nurturing, and perhaps tamer. The person who works well in the laboratory or at the sewing machine, who loves to see order emerge and grow, reflects something of God's skillful, careful, playful work. Binding as they can become, the related instincts to conserve rather than waste, to go quietly rather than clanging, to treat gently rather than abuse, also reflect God.

To be sure, God sometimes seems spendthrift in nature, flinging stars and splitting atoms. Evolution has strewn the biosphere with dead ends and maladaptations, and history has made Shiva, the Hindu destroyer, all too plausible. But the biblical refinements of "God," the biblical juxtaposition of the small still voice to the bellowing thunderstorm, sanction a peaceful nonbureaucratic love of order. When Robert Pirsig spoke of "quality," telling us that the mechanic we want is not the one assaulted by wild music, but the one quietly lost in his work, he sketched a lovely aesthetic, fusing reason and imagination at the point of order, the point where beauty draws not just desire, but reverent respect.[19] I find such an aesthetic very Christian.

There are political variations on this theme. God is like our successes in building community, like our dispositions to create three from one and one, and like the dispositions that such a "more" itself urges on. A family circle whose members are bonded by sharing, a church bonded in service and prayer, a team successful by selflessness, a town successful by fair-sharing—each of these "political" achievements reflects the communal love of the Trinity, where Father, Son, and Spirit differ only relationally, sharing all but their (to us mysterious) places in their one circle of light and love. We cannot build community, commonality, two-in-oneness without love reflective of God. We cannot marry well, raise a family, build a church, or further a collaboration without something of God's tact, warmth, and self-spending. Through our successes in building communities, we testify to the basic community of trinitarian life. Through our failures to build community, to unite nations and reconcile foes, we testify to our distance from God, how our loves are unlike God, how they refuse to follow trinitarian patterns.

Last, the final price of community, as the final price of salvation, is a love willing to suffer. The law of the Cross takes few holidays. With the nations so disunited, only the heroes who spend themselves, usually to the point of martyrdom, keep this bottom line clear. Only the Gandhis and Martin Luther Kings remind us that, for sinful humanity, great love almost inevitably turns cruciform. As Jesus' suffering love made him a stumbling block to his own disciples, so suffering love continues to make "God" confounding today. For while it is not strictly orthodox to say that the Father, the Godhead as underived and originating, suffers in himself, it is scandalously orthodox to say that God goes out of himself to suffer in Jesus for humanity, taking "love" to depths we shall never fathom.

CHAPTER 4. *VINE AND BRANCHES*

Abiding

Although we shall never fathom God's suffering love, to abide in God, who suffers and loves, is the inmost activity of Christian social life. John states Jesus' views on this matter succinctly:

> Abide in me, and I in you. As the branch cannot bear fruit by itself, unless it abides in the vine, neither can you, unless you abide in me. I am the vine, you are the branches. He who abides in me, and I in him, he it is that bears much fruit, for apart from me you can do nothing. If a man does not abide in me, he is cast forth as a branch and withers; and the branches are gathered, thrown into the fire and burned. If you abide in me, and my words abide in you, ask whatever you will, and it shall be done for you. By this my Father is glorified, that you bear much fruit, and so prove to be my disciples. As the Father has loved me, so have I loved you; abide in my love. If you keep my commandments, you will abide in my love, just as I have kept my Father's commandments and abide in his love. These things I have spoken to you, that my joy may be in you, and that your joy may be full. This is my commandment, that you love one another as I have loved you. (15:4-12)

So when we "abide" in Jesus, letting the Spirit take us into Jesus' phylum of humanity united to God, we become part of the inmost activity of what we have come to call church life. And while this figure of the vine and its branches is my own favorite, Paul's analogy of the church being one "body" with Christ, as members to head, evokes much the same feeling. Both images disclose that there is something organic about Christian life, something of the German *Mitsein (a being-with)*. To be a Christian is to be with Jesus and his other members, to abide in the "whole Christ" the church Fathers perceived. How can we make this abiding more intelligible?

No doubt it has several levels. There is, first, the level of thinking at least somewhat as Jesus thought, of tending to put on the mind of Christ. Aside from the question of baptism, the first operative signs of Christian life would seem to be the indications that a person is beginning to conceive of the world, speak of the world, act in the world somewhat as Jesus did. For example, she begins to regard the world as God's gift, as created by a free impulse of God's generous love. She begins to regard human beings compassionately, not letting their torpor or even their malice defeat her willingness to forgive them. She has extended this compassion to herself, asking herself for generosity but realizing that God is greater than her heart, even when it condemns her. And she no longer flinches from the demands discipleship may bring. Not rushing to embrace the Cross, which would probably be precipitous, she does refuse to separate Easter joy from Good Friday suffering.

At a deeper level, the maturing Christian comes to abide with Jesus heart-to-heart. Not only Jesus' cast of mind, but Jesus and his God themselves become the center of his thought and love. So a sense of personal sharing grows. Jesus the friend, the comrade, the "pioneer of our faith" (Heb 12:2) comes into play. If the person is fortunate enough to receive good counsel, he learns how to adjust his imagination, his mind, and his will so that his whole being attends on Jesus, or the Father, or the Spirit. He learns the prayers of "quiet" and of "simple regard," as these are called by the masters of prayer.

Parallel to this deepening contemplation is a deepening action. In the zones of work and service, the person endeavors to put his body, his money, his time on the line for Christlike values, for Christ present in other human beings, especially the suffering. For these strengthening connections to Jesus and the Trinity are not at odds with closer ties to other people. Rather, they build up the relationships of marriage, friendship, collaboration, church fellowship, and political alliance.

The deepest form of abiding, which verges on mystical union, shines forth in the saints. Paul could say, "I live, now not I, but Christ lives in me." For the saints, to live was Christ, and to die was gain, because it meant more of Christ. Time was their chance to add what was wanting to the sufferings of Christ, in the sense of an opportunity to give Christ another mind and heart in which to pass over through death to saving resurrection. Christ had died and been raised once and for all, but his pattern of death/resurrection had stamped itself on all his members. If that was the genetic code of the vine, it would be the history and physiognomy of the branches.

In prayer, this meant dark nights of abandonment, so that self-reliance could be pruned for greater fruit. In ministry, it meant identification with the poor, the

sick, the oppressed—the constituency of the Beatitudes. So the most root-going mystics were potentially
the most root-going social critics. The kingdom of God
suffered violence, the violent bore it away—not with
bombs and brickbats, but with love willing to mortify
the flesh, love willing to lay down life for friends, or
even enemies.

Socialized, politicized, set before an altar or in the
midst of folding chairs, these patterns of abiding could
become the seeds of a new ecclesiology, a new
theology for the church. The church begins with our
being-together-with Christ. However that might be
translated into German, in English it means shared
discipleship, comradeship, following after. It means
the abiding of the branches together in the vine, the
union of the members together with the head. It
means that my *I* and your *I* become *we* to the *Thou* of
Jesus, the Thou of Father-Son-Spirit.

Prayer

This conception of a ground-level ecclesiology
might do much to ease the trouble that many
Christians have with prayer. Alerted by Paul's "pray
constantly" (I Th 5:17) and by the example of many
outstanding saints, serious Christians such as the
anonymous author of *The Way of a Pilgrim,* a modern
Russian Orthodox classic, have felt an almost burden-
some responsibility to attend to God constantly, day
and night.[20] In the pilgrim's case, the Orthodox
tradition of the Jesus Prayer (constantly repeating
"Lord Jesus, have mercy") came to the rescue. When
the pilgrim visited various Russian monasteries and
spiritual centers, he found this tradition as well as

other teachings from the *Philokalia,* a collection of sayings from Eastern Christian experts on the contemplative life, available to help him.

But many Christians unwilling or unable to devote their whole lives to pilgrimage also are uneasy with their obligation to pray. Indeed, the clergy themselves frequently feel ill-equipped to handle prayer, thinking that only those with special gifts or special training should attempt such "deep" affairs. And even the many Christians who seldom observe the evangelical counsels or commands to pray do wander into this area when they feel twinges of dissatisfaction, feelings that their personal absorption with God, their personal relation to Jesus, is less than it should be.

There is no painless solution to the "problem" of prayer, no lazy person's guide to Christian enlightenment, but there is theological help close at hand. As a general rule, we can expect that God does not command what he does not give us the power to fulfill. This is a subthesis of the Christian theology of grace. More precisely, God has given us, in the divine life of grace and the abiding presence of the Spirit, the basis for a solid, growing prayer life. Paul again provides the classical text: "Likewise the Spirit helps us in our weakness; for we do not know how to pray as we ought, but the Spirit himself intercedes for us with sighs too deep for words. And he who searches the hearts of men knows what is the mind of the Spirit, because the Spirit intercedes for the saints according to the will of God" (Rom 8:26-27).

First, then, the Christian can be confident of God's help at prayer: The Spirit can do what we do not know how to do, and the Spirit's prayer in our hearts is bound to be acceptable to the One "who searches the hearts of men" (an Old Testament designation for God which Christians would apply to the Father), because God cannot pray to God unsuccessfully.

Second, Christian prayer can come out of the closet and stop apologizing for itself as though it were something esoteric or a bit precious. Essentially, Christian prayer is just an expression, an actualization, of Christian life whose essence, in turn, is simply sharing in God's love life. As a practical love of one's neighbor in ordinary deeds of helpfulness, cooperation, and forgiveness is merely the expectable overflow of lively faith, so prayerful love of God is merely the expectable overflow of lively faith.

Third, this means that prayer is essentially communing with God: attention to God, petition of God's help, praise of God's beauty and bounty, simple love of God's self. It is the name we give to "the lifting of minds and hearts"—as the traditional description has it—which makes us aware of God, which focuses our consciousness in God's "direction."

An analogy to personal communication is quite easily found. You have a good friend who lives in the neighborhood. More days than not, you talk with her, sharing good things and bad. She is congenial, supportive, challenging, helpful. Slowly she becomes familiar, habitual, part of your established mental atmosphere. When she is not in the forefront of your consciousness, she abides in the background. But the good in her, the intrigue of her, the strength from her, slowly make her part of your very self. So you come to understand what the ancients meant when they described a friend as "another self" or as "half of my soul." You know that, with some steady effort, you can embark on a relationship, a love, that can extend for a lifetime, that has as much "room" in it, as much space for growth, as you are willing and able to try to fill.

The comparison with God falters, of course, because we do not see, hear, touch, share with God as we do with flesh-and-blood fellow humans. But the basis of the analogy, the reality in God which sanctions friendship as a comparison, is something far richer than human sharing. If human sharing can yearn for communion and occasionally achieve it very intimately through great friendship or sexual love, the sharing that God offers is richer and deeper, because God can be in and with us more fully than can any human.

That is the implication of the Pauline text. God, whom Augustine saw as "more intimate to me than I am to myself," has, in the Spirit and the life of grace, taken our deepest personal substance—what the mystics call the fine point of the soul—into the active processions of love that the Persons of the Trinity share, that indeed constitute the Trinity. So our prayer, our reaching out toward God, becomes part of the Spirit's return to the Father, with the touching addition that the Spirit picks up our weaknesses, our needs and intentions, making what troubles or delights us her own, and so the Father's.

Anamnesis

The Spirit's assumption of our affairs into his return to the Father occurs in Jesus, the Christ resurrected to eternal communion with the Father and the Spirit. In other words, Christian life, church life, places us with the Incarnate Son, in relation to the other members of the Trinity. We "stand" receptive toward the Father, cooperative (conspiratorial) with the Spirit, because our point of insertion into the Triune life of God is the Son. So it is Jesus' Father and Jesus' Spirit whom we reverence and enjoy, just as it is Jesus himself who is the head of the church, the firstborn of the many brothers and sisters the Father wants for his people. One of the first things Christians need to underscore on their agendas, if they would prosper and bear fruit, is the need to *remember* this definition of their situation, this outline of the way their faith tells them Christ has shaped human existence.

Anamnesis is a Greek word Christians have used for *memory,* and using it may help us to take a fresh look at remembrance. If we have read Augustine (who wrote in Latin), we know that memory fascinated him. It was such a formidable capacity that he used it to symbolize the unlimited recesses of the Father. If we ourselves can go back and back in memory, bringing to present consciousness details of our first bicycle, of the ice cream that rewarded our brave tonsilectomy, the Father can go "back" without limit, since he is the uncaused cause of everything, the unbegotten begetter of the Son and all other likenesses of creative love. So our memory is part of the way we are images of God, just as it is an essential part of our being human. Without memory we would have no language, no culture, no history. In order to speak a whole sentence, let alone write a physics exam or perform a double-bypass operation, we need the wonderous human ability to make the past present, to keep what we learned yesterday alive today.

The main Christian prayer, the Eucharist, has the shape of a liturgical anamnesis. Gathered together for Sunday worship, the people of God do the main work God has given them: They believe in the act of salvation, abide in the vine. They do this by recalling the story of salvation, the narrative of God's mighty acts on human beings' behalf. This is why Scripture is so important to the church, so intrinsic to what makes the people of God who they are. Scripture is not a dispassionate collection of episodes that eccentric scribblers happened to jot down. It is a committed, passionate recital of the nearly unthinkable drama of the God who chose to go out of herself into a human form, so that she could lead a history that would be captive to destruction free to salvation, to health, and to overflowing fulfillment. As the Protestant churches, especially, have emphasized, the proclamation of God's Word that Scripture serves brings God himself into our midst. If God has chosen to speak forth a Word, to make a revelation, it is only fitting that we make this revelation the prime source of our wisdom, the prime directive for our action.

Communal Christian prayer therefore has tended to begin and to be shaped throughout by readings and proclamations of the Word available in Scripture. The charge laid upon Christians, as it earlier was laid upon Israelites, is to *hear:* to open their hearts, stir up their faith, remember their calling. "If today you hear his voice, harden not your hearts" (Heb 3:8). So most Christians begin their worship with music and petitions that might prepare attentive spirits. Then they have listened to scriptural readings and proclamatory sermons intended to make God contemporary, present here and now.

The Catholic churches have followed this with a sort of dramaturgy further intended to make the story of salvation contemporary. Remembering Jesus' last meal with his friends, they elaborate a rich symbolism: They take nourishment, celebrate fellowship, enter further into the life of the vine, and recall again the passion, death, and resurrection that have made the world come alive with hope. The reenactment of the meal has a pivotal point in the iteration of Jesus' words when he designated the bread and wine as himself, and it comes to a climax in the reception of the bread and wine as a Communion with Jesus.

For the Orthodox tradition, the whole drama has been submitted to the Spirit, who moves over the sacramental gifts and in the hearts of the faithful so that the action occurs in God (a sort of social counterpart to the private occasion when the Spirit causes prayer to occur in God). The other sacraments, especially baptism, have entailed a similar dependence on the Spirit to transform them into dramatic agents and symbols of grace.

For all the problems this liturgical anamnesis has encountered through the centuries, all the ways it has had to struggle to bring people of different cultures into the one Christian story, it has been a remarkable pedagogy of the Spirit. The early church Fathers were impressed by God's skillful teaching of humanity, especially the buildup of both Hebrew revelation and Greek philosophy to the full burst of light in Christ. We do well to take on something of their appreciative mood. Those who remember the Christian story, who follow the liturgical cycle year after year, slowly position themselves in the midst of a marvelous meaning. Slowly their little lives become trickles of a great stream, and their little selves become free to permit the glory to belong to God.

Mission

The abiding of Christians in Christ through private prayer and communal anamnesis is far from the whole story of the church. To follow Jesus, their head,

Christians must also move out into the wider world. They must, one might say, run alongside if they are to keep up with a moving head. The early terminology that called the Christian faith the Way captured some of this more dynamic character. Alone, the image of branches inhering in the vine, good as it is, can lead to an overly static view of the church. The missionary is grounded in the fact that Jesus himself was sent to perform a work. He had a charge, a mission, and he enlisted his followers as helpers.

Thus from apostolic times the church has felt impelled to preach the gospel to new audiences, in fidelity to the charge Jesus laid upon it. Indeed, the rapid spread of the Christian community in the first century is unintelligible without this self-understanding. It is Paul's missionary activity that the New Testament best documents, but we know the other early Christian communities felt a similar need to reach out beyond themselves. When it became clear that the church would be open to Gentiles and so should not think of itself as only a refinement of Judaism in light of the Christ, the missionary impulse gained the whole ecumene, the whole inhabited world, for its stage.

The story of Christian mission is therefore an essential part of church history.[21] However, our concern here is less with church history than ecclesiology. That leads us to ask, What further coloring does mission put on the picture of Church life we have been developing? Since the main line of our treatment has been the divine life of the branches in the vine, to be consistent, we first should look to Jesus himself for the attitudes the church missionary ought to have. From the memory of Jesus provided by Scripture, and the experience of sharing life with Jesus and the Trinity provided by prayer and liturgy, how ought we to imagine the outreach of Christian faith?

Very positively, I would say. Not only is such outreach a natural ingredient, part of church life, and so something to be encouraged, but it also should take place in a positive manner with the sense of humbly offering a beautiful gift. This was Jesus' own attitude. Somewhat in contrast to John the Baptist, who preached a stern call to repentance almost as an end in itself, Jesus' call to repentance and conversion spotlighted a further dimension. One was to *turn around* in order to face in a new, much more hopeful direction. One was to hear the word of judgment on one's sins, since that was the preliminary to hearing the glad tidings of salvation, of the Kingdom come. The Kingdom, as we have indicated, was Jesus' central preoccupation, and as the angels are imagined to have sung joyously at Jesus' birth, so "joy to the world" is a good epitome of Jesus' message. The world was to hear the surpassingly joyous news that God's reign was breaking forth, that all humanity's longings were on the verge of fulfillment. Moreover, those who then suffered from the world's injustices could count themselves especially blessed: The kingdom of God was theirs in a particular way.

To be sure, Jesus' mission and person provoked opposition, leading him to counterbalance his Beatitudes with a series of woes. But the woes applied only to those who blocked their ears to the gospel, who would not be converted from self-righteousness to God's ways of grace. None of the depression to which Jesus was tempted, none of the burdens that humanity's hardheartedness forced him to carry ever eviscerated his mission's central joy. He had good news to proclaim, a splendid Abba to share. The spirit of God was upon him, that he might console, heal, and save.

At its best, the Christian church has reproduced these attitudes of Jesus in its missionary activity. At its worst, it has rather self-righteously approached the world with a punishing or imperial cast of mind. Historians can detail the particulars of this ambiguous performance; I would only point out that recent and current history should incline Christians to regain a positive outlook. As recent history has shown, when Christians approach the rest of the world with colonial, triumphalist attitudes, as though they were an immaculate elect forced to hobnob with dirty heathens, it is disastrous both politically and theologically. The job of the missionary, whether in Tierra del Fuego or the local supermart, is to graciously announce God's gracious self-offer. By word or by silent example, as the occasion warrants, Christian mission is mainly the offer, the making available, of what the missionary thinks is a wonderful gift.

But just as Jesus left people free to reject him, refusing to call down fire and brimstone, so Jesus' missionary should leave people free. Just as Jesus was large-minded enough to say that those who did not oppose him were with him, so the Christian missionary should be large-minded. Fire and brimstone, self-righteousness, manipulation, or compulsion have no more place in today's Christian mission than they had in Jesus' day. As Jesus was self-effacing, desiring to focus attention on the good Father of the kingdom rather than on himself, so Jesus' missionary should be self-effacing, focusing attention on Jesus rather than on herself.

Ministry

Like mission, church ministry also is outgoing. Primarily, it is the service that Christians offer one another and the world, on the model of Jesus, who was in the disciples' midst not as an overlord but as a servant (Lk 22:27). In fact, when Jesus girded himself with a cloth and knelt to wash their feet, he symbolized the deepest dispositions of Christian ministry. Thus the Holy Thursday liturgies which reenact this foot washing are meant to exemplify the way church leadership should comport itself throughout the whole year. Obviously, human weakness contrives to make that nearly impossible, and some church dignitaries are about as servant in their attitudes as are leading politicians (*civil* servants), but the basic ministerial charge from Jesus remains undiminished by such abuses. The Son of man came as a servant, to give his life for the ransom of many.

The forms of Christian ministry have been various. As the recent study of Roman Catholic scholar Edward Schillebeeckx asserts:

> Apart from apostleship or the "apostolate," the Christian communities did not receive any kind of church order from the hands of Jesus when he still shared our earthly history. . . . This primary, fundamental datum of the New Testament must already make us very cautious; we must not be led astray into speaking too casually about divine ordinances and particular dispositions in respect of the community and its leaders or ministry.[22]

Thus historically, church ministry has assumed forms we might call monarchical, collegial, congregational, and other styles. That is, Christians have governed by one-man rule (pope, bishop), by the rule of elders (presbyters), by a democratic polling of the entire local community, and by other mechanisms. Whatever the form of a church's "order," though, the main responsibility of its leaders has been to stay faithful to the original constitution of the church, the basic union of the branches with the vine, so that worship and mission might prosper in love.

Later we shall have occasion to reflect upon the ecumenical problems that have arisen from the different forms of church order and ministry. Here let us reflect on the view of Christian ministry suggested by our central ecclesial theme of vine and branches. First it suggests that the main concern of those chosen to lead the church should be the flourishing of church life, the prospering of the branches in the love life of the vine. Karl Rahner has proposed the analogy of a chess club: The main function of officers of the club is to see to it that the members have the opportunity to play chess well.[23] So too with the officers of the church. Their main function is to see to it that Christians can live their lives of faith well. This requires a certain healthy pragmatism, much like that of Jesus himself: By their fruits you will know them. When ministers are producing an atmosphere of freedom, love, encouragement, hope, and wisdom (which should include some sternness, as well as much clarity), they are doing their jobs well.

Second, *ministry* is one of those terms that apply, with proper adaptations, to all the members of the church. It is not just the ordained leadership that is called to serve the upbuilding of the church and the alleviation of the world's sufferings. The entire Christian membership should spend itself in worship and mission, in reconciling enemies and binding up wounds. This need not be puffed up into heroic scenarios. Much excellent ministry occurs in ordinary offices, schools, hospitals, and family kitchens, where people lay down something of their lives (their time, their money, their energy) for the sake of others. Ministry also can stem from a more or less deliberate motivation in people's choice of work. The doctor who chooses a rural practice, rather than an urban, can be exercising strong ministerial instincts. The teacher who perseveres with little appreciation, because she knows that today's children are tomorrow's society, can be exercising strong ministerial instincts. And so with other people who want to "make a difference," want to do something that "counts," and so put service to others above their own ease or bank account.

Third, none of this requires that the minister hate his or her work, carry it as a great burden. Rural medicine, grammar-school teaching, work in the Peace Corps, and other forms of public service can be stimulating and enjoyable. Jesus presumably took some pleasure and satisfaction in his ministry, even when it became difficult. But it is characteristic of ministerial work that it satisfies the worker obliquely rather than directly, because foremost, ministerial work, like art and science, is the pursuit of something objective rather than the pursuit of self-satisfaction (though at the deeper levels of maturity the two can coincide).

If art pursues order and beauty, and science pursues the logic of nature, then a Christian ministry pursues the objective service—the help, the upbuilding, the healing—of its given sector or audience. Ministry to the church itself pursues the help, upbuilding, and healing of church members, their ability to live the

Christian life well. Ministry outside the church pursues
the help, upbuilding, and healing of alcoholics on Skid
Row, teenage prostitutes, confused workers in the
defense establishment, and so on. Both say, "How can
I help?" Both think, "How would Jesus help, how
would he serve?"

CHAPTER 5. *JESUS' PROGRAM*

Restructuring Human Life

The help Jesus offered human beings in his mission and ministry can only be called radical. It went to the roots *(radices)* of the human condition. As we noted previously, Christian theology holds that Jesus is the Second Adam, as momentous for human history as the first parents who began our line of beings who can reflect. If the first Adam somehow started things off on the wrong foot, so that all subsequent descendents played a game tilted from their first breath, the Second Adam put things back on the right foot, assuring that at its deepest level, reality was not tilted and unjust.

So deeply did Jesus' death and resurrection penetrate early Christian consciousness that the Fathers who reflected on his ultimate accomplishment discovered a quite objective sense in the Pauline theme of a new creation. However mythic the language of Adam and original sin may have been originally, Christian theology came to consider sin and grace quite objective realities, quite objective "existentials," which affected the human race universally. To say that where sin had abounded, grace abounded the more was therefore to say something very provocative. The world, which once had no solid basis for hope, no solid basis for thinking evil would be defeated, now did have such a basis. So Jesus resurrected was a great victor, a champion who liberated all history.

With the demise of Christian culture, many of these theological notions have lost their persuasiveness. Thus modern Christians have had to probe the experiences of grace assiduously, so as to be able to point to specific times and places where grace and liberation have occurred. This trend continues today. For instance, one finds a convert describing her experiences of grace as an ongoing process, a strand which began unobtrusively enough but gradually came to determine the very design of her tapestry.[24] Cradle Christians, too, have been offering faith-filled interpretations of moments when they sensed God's directive presence, moments when they felt so called to change, grow, and surrender that ever after, their lives were different.[25]

Commonly in such processes and such moments, there is a sense that God, the original reality behind and beyond the world, the world's Mystery, is now calling and sustaining. Both admit that grace can be life-changing. So an uneasiness with the church of one's birth can grow to the point where one must make a change, where one is peaceful only when worshiping and believing in new patterns that one feels are more adequate. Or one can become so disillusioned with a school that pays lip service to teaching, but actually wants only prestigious publication, that one must quit one's job; so upset with a country that speaks in high moral tones, but supports dictatorships around the globe, that one must take to the picket lines. God gives one no peace until these changes are made. God forces one to grow.

But to pursue God in such a way, or to let God pursue oneself in such a way, is quite literally to restructure human life. Those who conceive reality to be fraught with God's solicitations, who feel a challenge to distinguish God's ways from the ways of the world, confident that Jesus' Spirit offers to stand with them, move through a different system of meaning, a different interpretation of "life," than do those who do not think in this way.

Recently I came across a good illustration of this thesis in Maxine Hong Kingston's book, *The Woman Warrior*.[26] Kingston is the daughter of Chinese immigrant parents who shaped her childhood in terms of their old-country ways. One of the earliest stories she remembers is about her aunt, her father's sister, who had no name in the family circle, who was never mentioned. That aunt had disgraced the family by becoming pregnant while her husband was away. Kingston's mother so vividly narrated the story of the aunt's punishment by the irate villagers—their masked entry into the house and the destruction of all the family's possessions—that as a little girl, Kingston's greatest fear was that she would bring some dishonor upon her people. The aunt herself was so stricken by shame that she threw herself and her newborn baby into the family well, where both drowned.

The rationale of this entire disturbing episode, the explanation for such an oppressive sense of family honor and shame, lies deep in the traditions of folk and Confucian China. To dishonor one's line was to set up a destructive wave that would ripple through all of reality, including the realms of the ghosts and departed ancestors. Beyond the factors a sociological analysis might disclose, such as the village need for unanimity in mores, with all families pulling together against life's many hostile forces, one senses a bondage to Paul's "principalities" of this world (Rom 8:38). The ancient Hellenistic world in which the disciples first preached the gospel suffered a sense of oppression similar to that of pre-Communist China. Fate and necessity took most of the joy from Greek and Roman hearts. Thus it was indeed a restructuring of human life when a person embraced Jesus, because it was a complete reassembling of that person's hope. Even today it remains true that our belief about what we may hope speaks volumes about who we are, about how we conceive reality.

The Dynamics of Conversion

Jesus' program for restructuring human life depends upon hope-filled conversion. It is when one turns away from the principalities and powers of "this world" because of a more hopeful news that one is pointed in a new direction, that one's personality and world change substantially. But what is it that the Christian convert may hope? We have dealt with this question, at least indirectly, in several of the previous sections, but the demand of our contemporaries for fresh experiential descriptions suggests that it is fitting to attempt to answer the question directly.

Some Christian conversions amount to a *turning away* from guilt, in hope of peace and confident surrender. Often the guilt stems from a malformation of conscience in which a Christian church has played a part, but whatever the source of the guilt, the conversion experience is liberating. In the phrase of the British convert C. S. Lewis, it leaves the new believer "surprised by joy." Catholic adolescents entrapped by their church's rigorous sexual morality, which in the past defined every act of masturbation as a mortal sin, could be surprised by joy, set on the path of conversion, when they realized in a retreat or a college theology course that God was concerned about their hearts much more than their genitals. Secular, previously unreligious people, burdened by guilt from a failed marriage or an intense conflict with their parents, can be surprised by joy when they realize that God's parenthood can emancipate them from depression or the remnants of an Oedipal complex.

More generally, conversion offers to all who have bad feelings about themselves, to all who think they are worthless, the welcome of a loving God who is much greater than their judgmental superegos. God calls them lovable. God sees the good they want to do, the generous people they want to be. And God says, "That is enough. I can work with that. Just lean on it a bit more, just open it a bit wider. You are very dear to me, smudges and all." And that gives great hope that one day all guilt's roarings will diminish.

Other Christian conversions employ a motif of meaning. The *turning,* in such cases, is from a sense of aimlessness, or even absurdity, to a realization that the world has a basic order, a basic sanity. With God as Source and Goal, Creator and Judge, the chaos of human history and natural evolution can be stayed, a cosmos (ordered whole) can emerge. Much of this basic order and sanity remains mysterious, since the whole is clear only from God's overarching view, but snatches of it appear frequently enough so that the Christian ethos becomes credible.[27]

For example, the convert tests the proposition that

the basic need of human beings is honesty and love. He or she tries it out with the kids, the people at the plant, the other pillars of the League of Women Voters. The proposition gains some refinement: Human beings sometimes resist their basic needs. The scope of the experiment widens: It takes some perseverance, some hanging in, to become a credible proponent of honesty and love. The unexpected revelation occurs: The resistance of people to honesty and love increases the credibility of the Christian teachings on sin. One must battle cynicism—for instance, about the American electorate—but there are enough successes with the kids, enough good feelings and higher levels of job satisfaction at the plant to make the proposition, and so the convert's new vision, seem verified. Living in Christ's patterns, following Jesus' way of honesty and love, seems experientially valid. It seems to work—not in the sense of gaining one a new Cadillac, but in the sense of organizing one's experience more meaningfully, gathering one's lifetime into patterns that allow one to hope for an even more joyous future.

A third set of Christian conversions plays in the key of friendship and community. *Turning around* brings one into contact with a new set of people who prove congenial at more than a superficial level. Fully possessed of human foibles, they ring true in matters that count. Basically, they are goodhearted, honest, and generous. Basically, being with them draws out one's better self. Whatever their particular politics, they make the local community work, they are solid citizens. Whatever their particular jobs, they strive for competence and compassion. So the convert feels less lonely in her ideals, more encouraged, because she is now in a circle of like-minded people. This circle challenges her to grow to a deeper and richer life of faith, but it also offers her the solace of knowing that others suffer setbacks and struggles like her own.

In themselves, few of these sorts of conversions are limited to Christian faith. One can escape certain types of guilt through humanistic psychology, gain certain types of meaning through Marxism or Buddhism, find a congenial group at Weight Watchers or Alcoholics Anonymous. The distinctive theme that runs through a Christian conversion is the reference of freedom from guilt, the sense of new meaningfulness, or the enjoyment of a new community to Jesus' teaching and person. The hopes for justification (freedom from guilt), meaningfulness, and community that Jesus inspires have the distinct impress of an Abba of love, a conquest of sin and death, of branches rooted in a very strong vine. These and the other things we yearn to find, we hope to have happen, are pledged in the impressive coin of Jesus' own body and blood. The "cloud of witnesses" (Heb 12:1) from the Christian past is very helpful, but it is the Jesus at the center of the New Testament, the Jesus at the center of the Christian liturgy, who is the final foundation of all Christian hopes. The Christian convert finally *turns around* because Jesus is so compelling.

The New Center

Thus far we have interpreted Jesus' program, his plan for the flourishing of human beings, as a restructuring of human life through conversion to the good news, the brilliant hopes of the Father's kingdom. Another way to understand Jesus' program is to reflect again on the center that Jesus himself enjoyed, on his radical orientation to the Father. Continuing the prophetic critiques of the Hebrew Bible, Jesus' preaching implied the death knell for all false gods, all idols. The good news of the kingdom meant that only the true God, only the God of Light, Life, and Love, was to command human hearts. The people who previously had sat in darkness, eccentric to actual reality, now had the chance to see a great light. The people whose previous relations toward nature, society, their selves, and ultimate Mystery had been warped now had the chance to become concentric with the creative love that made all things. To reinterpret Deuteronomy's words, "Behold, I set before you this day two ways, of death and of life. Therefore choose life, choose to center your being in God."

Turning around, changing over to this new center, was an exciting experience for the first Christians, especially for those who had been Gentiles, adrift in the polytheism of the Hellenistic world. When they descended and rose with Christ in baptism, they felt they had plumbed the waters of spiritual death and escaped. For while the Hellenistic religions, like the religions of pre-Communist China, had their measures of wisdom, their traces of the true God, they were replete with fears and taboos. Centering in the new God whom Jesus preached, the old God of Abraham, Isaac, and Jacob now showing himself a gentle Abba, the early Christian converts felt emptied of many fears and taboos, felt fresh and clean.

Through the centuries following those first conversions, Christians did not always retain the wholly positive, fresh and clean sense that Jesus' new center offered them. The blazing icons of Eastern Christianity struck fear in many hearts. The barbarian invasions and bubonic plagues that ravaged the West helped to paint God's picture angry. Some fresh air returned with the Lutheran Reformation, but the severity of many of the Protestants who followed also put a frown on God. From their stripped worship and dour ethics, Puritanism was a logical outcome.

The result was more than a little clouding of the sun of justice, the Father of love. Jonathan Edwards, the brilliant eighteenth-century New England preacher, put this trend in indelible form when he wrote his sermon about sinners in the hands of an angry God. To unkind critics, the sermon brought back the worst stereotype of Old Testament religion, in which people's backs were bent from groveling before God's bad temper.

More recently, the trend called secularism is the main force that has diverted Christians and many others from the new center that Jesus offers. *Secularism* is not a precise term, but its general drift is the this-worldliness, the lack of transcendence, that has followed on the West's (highly successful) preoccupation with natural science and technology. For many modern intellectuals, the great discoveries of Newton and Einstein, Darwin and Freud had desacralized the cosmos. No longer was there any need for the "hypothesis" of God. The proper concern of human beings was human affairs, matters of space and time. In French philosopher Auguste Comte's schema of human history, religion stood as a matter for childhood, something adults had long ago outgrown.

We are heir to all this history. The fall of Rome, the medieval crusades, the religious wars following the Reformation, the colonializations following the sixteenth-century explorations—all have shaped the way we receive "Christianity." Ironically enough, however, few of these historical memories and few of the more recent movements into which they have folded mount a significant challenge to Jesus' God. That Christians have misunderstood or abused Jesus' teaching makes Jesus' God "impossible" only to the weak-minded or faint-hearted. The strong-minded and good-hearted can see that humanity without Jesus would be, if anything, worse.

The agnostic or atheist who impresses the fair-minded person by his intelligence and goodness, his light and love, is much more an argument for than against Jesus' God (the fontal light and love that all human goodness evokes). And the political regimes built on fierce atheism have put the evils of Christendom in the shade. One need not accept all of Alexsandr Solzhenitsyn's politics to find his work *The Gulag Archipelago* a shaking demonstration that when God is ripped from people's souls, diabolical evils rush in.[28]

Cognate analyses which trace the fate of other people whose center is not the real God, but money, power, pleasure, status, or some other variant of false self-love, reveal a similar if usually less diabolically evil result. Negatively, by contrast, one comes to see that the new center of a God truly divine, a God beyond the world yet holding the world in love, reveals that all such false centers, all such idols, lead to mental disease. From the vulgarity of most American entertainment to the lunacy of much American politics, many of our people are revealed to be distorted, spastic, in soul, because they have closed themselves to the ultimate Source of light and life. Like the psalmist's fool, they have said in their hearts that there is no God, no reality to living Mystery. Like the psalmist's fool, their atheism has made their lives wobble in absurdity.

Neighbor as Self

Jesus' program, then, rests on a radical monotheism. The one God he called Father is the sole treasure on which Jesus' followers are to set their hearts. But the one Father would be parent to a vast family of brothers and sisters. As we can see from the fact that his sun rises, his rain falls on just and unjust alike (Mt 5:45), even evildoers receive God's bounty. So reflecting on how God has loved us, the early Christians concluded that we ought to try to love one another in the same way. God has gone out of himself for our sakes, giving us his only begotten Son. He has made our cause, our plight, his own. We should try to treat one another in the same way. We should try to love our neighbors as ourselves. Narrowing the distance between mine and thine, making a community from shared sorrows and shared joys, we would be imitating Jesus' God. That is one way to view the link between Jesus' two great commandments: When we love our neighbors as ourselves, we love as God, the most prodigal lover, first loved us.

It is not hard to see that this second plank in Jesus' platform is as challenging, as far-reaching as the first. If a radical, root-going monotheism clears the world of idols, then a radical Christian charity, loving neighbor as self, would overturn most of the antagonisms by which human beings seem to define themselves and do business. For example, ancient societies distinguished sharply between members of the tribe and outsiders—so much so that frequently they considered outsiders less than human. Thus both the Chinese and the Greeks called foreigners barbarians. Many ancient peoples pictured their own land as the center of the world, the navel of creation. So small a

nation as Japan figures in that country's chronicles as
the place where Creation occurred. Even Jewish
thought around the time of Jesus bore traces of
xenophobia. If the Bible entreated Jews to be good to
the stranger and to be assured that God had a role for
the Gentiles too, it yet provided a basis for thinking
that Jews were God's elect, God's chosen people,
while Gentiles rode second class. In Jesus' own day the
enmity between Jews and Samaritans focused these
feelings sharply. For Jesus to illustrate his teachings
about neighborly love with a Samaritan hero (Lk
10:30ff.) was a pointed attack on Jewish ethnocentrism.

The time between ancient civilizations and those of
today has not lessened the explosive charge in Jesus'
teaching. As nation has raged against nation, the
neighbor usually has been more an enemy than
another self. Sad to say, this judgment holds for
"Christian" nations almost as much as for heathen.
One could write the story of modern Europe as a
demonstration of the thesis that Christians normally
treat one another as foes. One could write the stories
of the Christian sects in the same way. We are far from
having evolved to the point where we allow the other,
the person or nation different from ourselves, to be as
human as we, much less to the point where we love
her, him, or it the way we love ourselves. Jesus is far
ahead of us in this matter, almost out of sight. Indeed,
a dispassionate judge might say that most of us have
little desire to catch up with Jesus. He is a super-
marathoner, and we dislike even working up a sweat.

And yet, as in so many other cases, the easy
condemnation suggested by the big picture is not the
whole story. People do still yearn for a world
community, as even the battered United Nations

organization shows. They do still yearn for a unified Christian body, as even the weak World Council of Churches suggests. Imperfect as they are, these ventures never would have been launched, had there not been an echo of the call to neighborly love sounded by Jesus' preaching. A kindly observer could say the same for the American way of marrying and mating. High divorce statistics and much domestic squalor not withstanding, generation after generation leaves father and mother for the hope of at least once loving a neighbor as a self. The symbol of two persons trying to become one flesh is both ordinary, because applicable to so many, and extraordinary, because so pregnant with possibilities. Thus Pauline theology (Eph 5) likens Jesus' followers to a bride, Jesus to a bridegroom, and the life of the branches in the vine to a marriage.

Social insights, seeds of a conversion, are therefore as nearby as even casual sex. On the other hand, if sex stays casual, it shrouds the possibility of loving another as oneself. For the one way we do not love ourselves is casually, accidentally, intermittently. Except for the rare case of pathological self-hatred, human beings love themselves from dawn to dark.

How perceptive and exact of Jesus then to tell us, so apparently simply, that the rule for good social life is to love other people as we love ourselves. What an incision through the flab and gristle of the ethicians and the lawyers. Do you want consideration, understanding, sympathy, steady help? Then show them to your neighbor. Do you want fair dealing, reliability, a chance to be a person rather than a number? Ditto. Again and again, ditto and ditto, Jesus' genius blazes forth. Treat others as you want them to treat you. Do not do to another what you would not want her to do to you. Make sure that you walk in the other person's moccasins, that you bear the other person's burdens, before you judge. Good social life is as simple, as utopian, as that.

Ecumenical Implications

Since the question of the present state of the Christian churches was important to the conception of this book, from time to time I shall turn the discussion to ecumenical implications. As we conclude Part One, let us reflect on the effect Jesus' program might have on the separated churches. Waiting to see the morning star, the churches' reunion, let us heed Revelation 2:29: "He who has an ear, let him hear what the Spirit says to the churches."

First, suppose the churches were to love one another as God has loved them. Suppose they were to treat their neighboring Christian communions as they treat themselves. What changes might such a fidelity to Jesus' program produce? At the least, it might open some space for fresh maneuvers. At the most, it might restore the sense of organic sharing, of symbiosis, that is at the center of the Johannine and Pauline ecclesiologies.

Minimally, the people of church Alpha, in Uppah Montclair, might reflect that God also makes his rain to fall, his sun to shine on the people of church Omega, in Lower Smearsville. The same heaven overarches both churches. The same Lord calls both to account. Neither church would want to find itself like the Pharisee, rejected by God because it is sure of its virtue. Both churches would identify with the publican, who beat his breast and confessed his sin. So on substantial matters, the two churches would come out dead even. All have sinned and fallen short of God's glory. All have been washed by the blood of the lamb. Only the shallow members of either congregation would let differences of diction or dress obscure such basic equalities. True believers in both camps would blush to remain unreconciled.

Maximally, Alpha and Omega might bend around to make a full circle, a whole alphabet. Considering their superficial differences of diction and dress as gifts to be shared rather than as causes for division, they might entertain one another and rap. If a catholic taste in music can span from Mozart to Scott Joplin, so a catholic Christianity can span from Anglican diction to Mennonite dress. In the space cleared by God, the new center, all sorts of dances can be sacred: the stately procession of the Episcopal churches, the miters bobbing and the trains upheld; the rollicking patter of little Pentecostal feet, conjuring the joy of slavery lost. Neither music nor ballet is rigid in Christianity. Neither suffers an inhibiting canon. Any music of talent and faith can take us to God. Any dance of penance and joy can serve us well. "For freedom Christ has set us free" (Gal 5:1), including our liturgies. If we choose not to worship together, that is our judgment, not a hindrance from the Spirit. To the clean, all things are clean. To the prayerful, all forms of prayer are useful.

Second, if they exploited this freedom, the churches would be in a position to hear a harsher statement. If Jesus' prayer in John 17 be believed, Christian unity is Jesus' ardent desire. Indeed, it is the sign by which the world should know that the Father sent Jesus and that he loves human beings as he loves Jesus. So church unity is no innocuous nonessential; it is the heart, the guts of church mission outside. If Jesus has been the great metaphor, the primal sacrament of God's love in human time, Jesus' followers, his branches, are to be the continuance of the metaphor. The way they stand together in the world, their posture of affection and service, is the very basis by which outsiders will judge "Christianity." "See how they love one another," the early Christians provoked. Admiring such charity, many pagans rushed to join. "See how they stand off from one another," today's pagans might well say. "Look how they perpetuate their divisions." Each such judgment slashes at Jesus' credibility, as foreign missionaries, especially, have found. What are they to say to the Asian or African who asks why there are so many different churches? How can they deny that the prior task is to bring about order at home?

And it does not really ease the shame to point out that other traditions, too, have split and split again. That Shiite Muslims may hate Sunnis, Reform Jews castigate Orthodox, Mahayanan Buddhists spurn Theravadins does little for the Christian cause. The ignominies of 1054, when West and East separated, and 1517, when West separated again, remain stuck in our craw. No, the church scores no points because the rest of religious humanity is likewise fissiparous. Only peace and concord are arguments that the Kingdom has come. Sensing the heart of the Christian matter, Augustine could say, "Love and do what you will." Seeing what Christians have willed, a latter-day Augustine might delay his conversion, waiting for a time when Christians again will love.

We will be judged by our love, all orthodox Christian moralists agree. The very stuff of Jesus' program is love. The first ecumenical implication of Jesus' program might therefore be the need to step back and look once again at the big picture. In a world of 4.5 billion, we 1.0 billion Christians will carry clout only if we are truly members of one another in Christ.

2/LOVING GOD

The three major families of Christian churches overlap and share considerably in their ways of loving God, but it is useful to reflect upon some of the distinctive emphases or gifts that each offers the full Christian body.

Protestant Christianity, for instance, has laid special stress on God's sovereignty. Coupled with the Reformers' return to Scripture as the paramount church authority, this has led to a rather prophetic stance with an influence on Protestant worship and social practice that remains active today.

Roman Catholic Christianity has perhaps best preserved the sapiential portions of scriptural revelation. Insisting that Scripture correlates with tradition and that reason correlates with faith, Catholic theologians have been effective proponents of a Christian balance, a manifold both/and.

Eastern Orthodox Christianity has been especially mystical. For its entire membership, not just its elite, Orthodoxy has stressed that the Spirit of God has been given in grace to make us sharers in the divine nature. Orthodox worship continues to inculcate this mysticism today.

If one were to organize these three traditions'

strengths and weaknesses, asking what they make of human history as a whole, a provocative vision might emerge. For all that God has chosen to act in history, history finally occurs in God.

To distill these reflections and point them toward practice, I conclude by stressing how love of God occurs in radical contemplation. Christians who love God open their hearts utterly to God precisely as God, as Mystery drawn near.

CHAPTER 6. *PROTESTANT PROPHECY*

The Protestant Principle

Paul Tillich, one of the most influential Protestant theologians of the past generation, attempted to cut to the bone of his tradition by spotlighting what he called the Protestant principle. One of the discussions in his masterwork, *Systematic Theology,* formulates this principle succinctly: "The Protestant principle is the restatement of the prophetic principle as an attack against a self-absolutizing and, consequently, demonically distorted church. Both prophets and reformers announced the radical implications of exclusive monotheism."[1]

We suggested some of the power this principle can carry when we focused on Jesus' God as a new center for human existence. But the principle or idea bears further reflection when one attempts to determine how Jesus' first command might best be obeyed today. The prophets and the Reformers, Tillich says, derived their message from an exclusive monotheism. For them the God to be loved with whole mind, heart, soul, and strength was emphatically as Israel had said in the *Shema:* "Hear, O Israel, the Lord our God is one

Lord." Emphasize that "one," lean hard on the exclusivity it can connote, and you build a highway to the object of Jesus' passion. There was none like the Abba who ruled Jesus' heart. Nothing in nature or in nations' experience emerged as a worthy competitor. For Jesus it went almost without saying that the earth is this Lord's, and the fullness thereof. For Jesus, the nations followed the one God and obeyed his behest, whether they realized it or not.

We begin our probing of the love of God, therefore, with a stern call to remember that God is unique, far removed from the creatures we know familiarly. If we are to know God familiarly, it must be by God's initiative and condescension. The Word that God speaks and the Spirit that God breathes forth are completely gratuitous benefactions. That God should be a Father is itself astounding, for one can feel the chill his sovereignty might emit. As the depths of the universe, the most distant planets, show far more ice than fire, so God the one Lord might well, on the basis of natural analogues, be utterly cold in his brilliant perfection.

Jesus and the prophets, however, say that this is not so. The otherness of God, they say, is the perfection of the divine love. The divine love is so powerful, so pure, so creative that we must never allow anything human to attempt to obscure it. If the sin of the angels is epitomized in Lucifer's "I will not serve," the sin of the church is epitomized in its self-absolutizing, its tendency to direct attention from God to itself. When it should be wholly subordinate to the vine, wholly instrumental to the ongoing Incarnation, the church is tempted to look out for itself, to preach its own law and institutional advantage.

"Disgusting church," we are tempted to say, until

contemporary ecclesiology pulls us up short. Like Pogo, reflective Christians now meet the enemy and find it is themselves. Like David when he accepted Nathan's indicting story, the Christian of prophetic and reforming faith is soon brought to mutter, "I am the man." For all its historical ties to the sixteenth-century Reformers' critique of Roman Christianity, the Protestant principle would thin to mere polemics, were it not applicable all around. We the people of God, we the human race, are ever prone to self-absolutization. The idols we most frequently erect are but foci for an ever imminent self-worship.

Stepping back from his usual emphasis on the individual life cycle, psychologist Erik Erikson (who, like Tillich, has interesting bonds with Martin Luther) spoke of the regular tendency of human groups to fall into "pseudo-speciation."[2] This is a more horizontal and so perhaps more easily discernible form of self-absolutization. Looking at the world, people after people has distinguished itself from the rest of the human family. "We are a distinct, special species," they said. So Greeks and Chinese, as we mentioned earlier, considered all foreigners barbaric. So whites considered blacks subhuman and Nazis tried to kill all Jews. The biological criterion of a species, the ability of its members to mate successfully, has gone by the boards. The theological criterion, the ability of its members to image God by mind and heart, has passed outside the pale.

Focusing on self-satisfactions, on the will to inflate or the will to empower, tribe after tribe has fashioned fortuitous criteria, such as the color of people's skin or the line of their blood. Psychologically, most peoples are unwilling or unable to bear a nonspecial status. Being just part of a huge extended family flies through their psyches like a loose rod through an engine. Theologically, they are not able to bear the oneness of God, which makes all God's children brothers and sisters. Theologically, the purity of God's love blinds their eyes and sears their hearts. Like the workers who came early to the hiring place and grumbled at the master's generosity to latecomers (Mt 20:1-16), even Christians grumbled when they heard that God could be generous outside the Mediterranean basin. So, for instance, they have felt it necessary to denigrate Buddha, Confucius, and Muhammad. To exalt their prophet, their incarnate God, they often think it necessary to blacken other peoples' gods. More often than not, they only exalt themselves.

The Prophetic Word

As they abased themselves, seeking to exalt only the one true God, the prophets of biblical religion experienced God's self-disclosure as amazing grace. Though they seldom stepped back coolly to measure the speculative possibility that God is able to be aloof from history, their passionate conviction that God is involved in history did not lead them to take God's revelations for granted. Rather, the prophets of biblical religion received God's Word as an event fraught with divine freedom and power. Seizing the prophet's mind and heart, God's Word became an almost crushing imperative. So Isaiah felt the need to cleanse his lips with a burning coal, and Jeremiah asked to be released from such an exhausting mission. So Jesus was brought to pray that his bitter chalice be removed, and many Christian prophets have suffered for their preachings. Once having crashed into a person's life, once having restructured a person's sense of history, the prophetic Word from God dominates all that follows. Judaism, Christianity, and Islam share this conviction, and so they share a great deal of "theo-logy." For instance, Muhammad, the *rasul*, the seal of the prophets, felt he had no choice but to recite what God had given him. Today his Qur'an *(Recital)* mediates a prophetic Word to almost 600 million believers.

Interesting as it would be to follow up on this comparative prophecy, our concern here is Protestant Christian prophecy and love of God. Certainly a main effect of that prophecy in recent times has been the stressing of God's priority over human initiative as it responds to the biblical and Christic Word. Karl Barth virtually begot such so-called neo-orthodox theology with the second edition of his commentary on Romans (1919). And despite all the later refinements of Barth's position and neo-orthodox theology, a strong appreciation of the priority of God's address to human beings over human beings' approaches to God has remained a distinctively Protestant gift to the church.

For example, Eberhard Jüngel, who has been one of the recent stars of the Protestant theological faculty at Tübingen, continues the Barthian prophetic tradition.

> [Jüngel] sees himself primarily as a theologian of revelation, thinking from a faith which can occur authentically only in response to the address of God's word to humanity. In this sense Jüngel's version of neo-orthodoxy is first and foremost a theology of the Word, or, as he most often prefers to say, an "evangelical theology." It is evangelical, as was Barth's, because it centers on God, stressing God's address to humanity rather than humanity's search for God or purported discovery of God.

Evangelical theology's object, source, and norm is
the God of whom the Gospel speaks.[3]

Let us develop this line of description. The prophetic
Word, in Jesus' wake, is an evangel, *glad tidings*. It
announces (for Jüngel, especially in Jesus' cross) God's
judgment and God's love—the judgment that is God's
love. If God has given such a Word, such a loving
judgment on the human condition, the first responsibility, the first opportunity of human beings is to respond.
This is the basis for neo-orthodoxy's aversion to
so-called natural theology, in which human beings
attempt to reason their way to God, apart from
revelation. Putting aside for the moment the counter-
case that natural theology can make, which reposes on
the rights and graces of all the peoples who have not
received the biblical revelation directly, we should make
an effort to grasp the power of the neo-orthodox
position. Refusing to let us view God as just another
being, insisting that God be truly GOD, neo-orthodoxy
plumps for our wholesale conversion.

For it is indeed a conversion, a turning around, to
move from anthropocentrism to theocentrism. It is
indeed a journey to a new existential treasure. Very
few personalities consistently try to take a God's-eye
view of things, and still fewer succeed in the attempt.
The prophetic position, in fact, is at the antipodes from
the self-righteousness or dogmatism of those who
think that evangelical theology, a God's-eye view,
proliferates human certitudes. The biblical Word,
genuinely received, shatters all human certitudes. It
comes and goes as God alone decides. It announces a
plague, as well as a blessing, on the houses of all its
hearers. It is not a prediction about the future. It is not

a canonization of the covenanted past. Again and again, it is a call to set present times under the holy love of the one God. Again and again, it has no wisdom but Christ crucified. So despite the prophets' human failures that can lead to a contrary stereotype, the prophetic Word inculcates a profound humility. As with the Baptist before Jesus, it moves the prophet to say, "He must increase, I must decrease."

Evangelical theology in this prophetic sense is therefore the decrease of self-sufficiency, the increase of God's sufficiency. God has made a revelation, spoken a Word, worked a salvation sufficient for humankind. He has showered down grace sufficient to arrest our restless hearts. It is a nice index of our folly that we so often ignore this sufficiency, so often prefer human works to divine grace. So, speaking of Christians, we too often must say, "They have not known the things for their peace." When God's Word has invited them to take Jesus' yoke upon them, they have preferred such yokes as those of Kant and Marx. When God's Word has offered them the sternest yet meekest adventure, the journey of love, they have preferred Promethian independence. "Forgive them," Jesus continues to pray. "They know not what they do."

Mercy, Rather Than Sacrifice

Another concern of biblical prophecy revived by the Reformers concerned the dangers of ritual. Against the Israelite tendency to make religion a matter of sacrifice and external observance, the biblical prophets called for a faith that would produce justice and mercy in society. Thus Amos condemned the injustices of his day as false religion. It was incompatible with the genuine worship of the one God that the rich gouge the poor, the comfortable neglect the orphan and the widow. God did not need the blood and fat of sacrificial animals. Yahweh desired rather that human beings show one another mercy, that they deal with one another as they would like Yahweh to deal with them. In their best hopes, the Israelites pictured a God who was slow to anger and quick to forgive. The prophets drew on these hopes when they condemned social injustices and cruelties. "It is discordant with the covenant," they might have said, "for us to treat one another harshly. It defaces our imaging of the Lord."

The sixteenth-century Reformers drew on this biblical tradition when they attacked the ceremonial religion of Roman Christianity. To their mind, the key to the various abuses in morals and church discipline was forgetfulness of the church's true center. It was not by human works, such as showy Masses, that grace and salvation would occur. It was by God's free gift of grace, welcomed into a heart wide open in faith. Insofar as the conception of the Mass as a repetition of Christ's sacrifice had gained wide currency, and other species of "works righteousness" such as indulgences had cropped up, the core of the gospel was in peril. God wanted the liturgical sacrifices then abounding as little as he had wanted the sacrifices the biblical prophets had condemned. It was mercy that God wanted in the forefront, the mercy of the gracious salvation available in Jesus the Christ.

This retrieval of at least part of the biblical prophecy has proved momentous in western religious history subsequent to the Reformation. Despite the demurs of Roman Catholics to some of the Protestant formulations at the Council of Trent, the reforms initiated there were at least a tacit agreement that the Protestant attacks had considerable merit. My impression is that neither the Reformers nor their Roman counterparts paid as much attention to the biblical prophets' call for social justice and mercy as they might have, but I am no expert in sixteenth- and seventeenth-century theology.

More interesting to me have been the pros and cons of the two traditions' somewhat different understandings of the tension between sin and grace, although the differences should not be exaggerated. It seems to me, for instance, that Protestant theologian Reinhold Niebuhr's definition of sin should raise few Catholic hackles.[4] But I have observed both assets and liabilities in the instinctive outlooks that the two traditions have given their adherents, and here I would like to muse about the Protestant case. (In the next chapter I shall muse about the Catholic case.)

The real issue is how one spontaneously views human nature, what one spontaneously expects from one's neighbor (and from oneself). A certain understanding of the Protestant depiction of human sinfulness, which *The Oxford Dictionary of the Christian Church* says led, in Luther's case, to an affirmation of "the total depravity of mankind and the uselessness of human reason," can produce considerable lightheartedness: We are wretched but God is good, so through God we are happy and free.[5] Another understanding can take the view that there is no health in human beings and so can lead one to expect only twisted motivations. The first understanding seems to me quite admirable, and quite akin to that manifested by the great saints. Having come very close to God, they know that they have no merits before the divine purity, that everything is God's mercy and grace. I can even imagine them saying, with a certain almost bawdy realism, "Sin bravely" *(Pecca fortiter)*, as Luther is reported to have said. Human living is not a clear black-and-white affair. It is murky and compromised from the beginning. But we must plunge into it bravely, doing our best, making our mistakes and confessing our sins, for God does not want a legalistic purity, but an ardent, full-bodied love.

The second understanding gives me long pause, for I have seen it ruin cooperation and community again and again. Expecting nothing good from the human heart, indulging a deep pessimism, colleagues in several schools have played politics and promoted themselves with an amazing lack of mercy, an amazing gift for destructiveness. They have made what could have been circles of mutual support into sharply angled squares of suspicion and division. It seems to me a caricature of the Protestant theology of sin, grace, and human nature to justify such actions by an appeal to "human depravity," but I have heard some make more than half-hearted attempts to do just that. Worst of all, I have seen them sicken in neurosis, for they have thought themselves, too, only offal and dung. So, perversely enough, a wrongful understanding of mercy, of our human need for God's grace, can lead to a vicious pessimism. It will not, though, unless one loses the classical Protestant stress on God's priority and becomes blindly anthropocentric.

Holy Worldliness

The biblical prophets, and also the Protestant Reformers, manifested a certain healthy worldliness. Their prophetic word, their concern for mercy rather than sacrifice, occurred not in some private space, not in rules for a world-denying commune, but out in the public area, as a matter for the common good. It was contrary to the biblical sense of creation to conceive religion as something purely spiritual. The prophetic experience made no disjunctions such as the Hindu disjunction between the lesser reality of the material world and the greater reality of the mental world, which in rigorously logical Hindu schools—for instance, Shankara's Advaita Vedanta—led to the conclusion that the material world was deeply unreal. True enough, the prophetic thinkers called attention to the times when God's Word and Spirit lifted a person into Yahweh's orbit of power, when the reality of God became almost overwhelming, but their basic instinct was to keep matter and spirit, sense and mind, together. Jesus and Paul felt the same way.

The sixteenth-century Reformers therefore attacked the notion contemporary to them that truly generous Christian faith induced one to leave the world, opt for a spiritual as contrasted with a material vocation. Specifically, they rejected the celibacy of the Roman clergy and the exaltation of monastic life, which they believed embodied views at odds with the Bible. Roman Catholics, of course, had their own biblical texts and themes to fall back on, including Jesus' apparent celibacy and the rather early-church approval of a style that later evolved into a full-scale monastic or "religious" life. Nowadays there seems fairly good ecumenical consensus that on this, as well as on many other topics, both sides scored valid points; thus one can see Protestant, or at least Anglican and Lutheran forms of monastic life, and Roman Catholic efforts to upgrade the lay vocation.

But the Reformers' instinct that biblical faith means

one should keep one's balance in the world, work for the common society, and transmit another generation of human life played a strong role in the rise of modern and postmodern worldliness (which is itself ambiguous). For both weal and woe, both estimable service and questionable drivenness, the Protestant ethic has flowed into modern technology, banking, literacy, democracy, and now cultural pluralism.

The Lutheran church historian and ecumenist Martin Marty recently has shown some of the public-spiritedness to which Protestant holy worldliness can lead. In *The Public Church,* he analyzes the fractionalized public consciousness we Americans now suffer, and he urges the three main groups of American Christians—mainline Protestant, Evangelical, and Catholic—to labor together for a public Christianity that might better serve our times.[6] For Marty, the prophetic vocation finally anneals a spirit that can hold firm in the midst of complexities, can resist the impulse to opt simplemindedly for *the one* way, and can speak up for critical, reasoned choices. Compassionate toward the protean psyche of the modern Westerner, who is overloaded with choices in every part of life, Marty's prophet sees the only solution a mature faith can approve—we must learn to live with a measure of confusion. Negatively, this means that we recall the many ways the Bible denies its heroes and exemplars—its Abrahams and Jesuses—an easy, obvious set of solutions and successes. Positively, it means that we help one another confess a faith that is on pilgrimage, that feels confident God will give it bread today but knows it will have to ask again tomorrow.

The holiness possible through such worldliness may not be apparent to today's Christian who is more confused than challenged by our cultural pluralism. It seems fairly apparent to people like me, who are looking for signs of God's present mercy. The charities we support through our taxes, the pains we endure through our mistakes (which in our complex culture are probably more numerous than in simpler cultures), the assaults on our meaning and coherence—these may more than match the ascetic intensity and intellectual certainty other generations could offer to God.

We know more about the universe, more about history, and more about many aspects of human behavior than did past generations. This can give cause for great wonder at God's power and subtlety, but also for much depression. The great voids in the stellar universe can whisper that creation is cold and uncaring. The gross patterns of history which feature wars and brutal dominations can shout that human beings are worse than wolves. The knowledge we gain about human behavior can show layer upon layer of impure motivation. To live with these knowledges, to bear the many negativities they suggest, demands no small courage and self-denial. Indeed, the crowds who cannot bear such demands, who flee to our many parlors of distraction, testify to a quiet heroism, a modest saintliness, in those who stay and keep trying.

Ecumenical Implications

Protestant holy worldliness finally depends on the prophetic instinct that all of creation reposes in God's hand. God therefore can call a person to labor in any part of creation. Such a call *(vocation)* is further backed by Christ, who freed all of creation. Though human beings are sinful, indeed to the point of tempting us to pessimism about human nature, they can clothe themselves in Christ's virtues through faith. Casting themselves upon Jesus as the Old Testament prophets cast themselves upon Yahweh, Christians can say prayerfully, "The Lord is my rock and my salvation; whom shall I fear?" They can temper their anxieties in a world full of spiritual dangers with a confidence that if God calls them to labor in that world he will supply all that they and their work require.

This means that the prophetic strain of biblical faith, which Protestant Christianity, especially, has appreciated, colors the love of God in hues of freedom. Beholden only to the Creator and Lord, the Christian stands free of all human tyrannies. So the exclusive monotheism of which Tillich speaks does indeed have "radical implications." As Peter and the apostles told the high priest in Jerusalem, "We must obey God rather than men" (Acts 5:29). The roots of Christian faith lie in the conviction that only God has full sovereignty over human hearts. Exclusive monotheism means that only God is GOD. As a result, Christian citizenship in any temporal society is limited to that which coincides with God's will. If temporal leaders should command something contrary to God's will, Christians are duty-bound to resist.

This tension in a Christian's political allegiance has caused much concern through the past two thousand years. Both temporal sovereigns and church leaders have struggled to clarify a workable compromise. Before Constantine freed Christians from Roman suspicion early in the fourth century, the Empire doubted that Christians could be good citizens. Roman allegiance entailed a religious, as well as a political fidelity, and Christians felt they could not call

Caesar "Lord" in the worshipful tone he demanded. On the other hand, as early as Paul's reflections in Romans 13, Christians had argued that they were excellent citizens because their faith looked on temporal authority as being established by God. By their faith, they were required to obey the emperor and his lawful subordinates in all that was commanded, save sin. The key issue, therefore, became *sin:* What was a moral command, and what was an immoral? History suggests that the church and the state never mastered this issue.

Since the sixteenth-century Reformers' prophetic challenges to authority, one tends to think of Protestantism in terms of the troubled individual conscience standing up to overweening or dubious authorities, especially to the ecclesiastical authorities of Rome. All the medieval struggles between crozier and crown had not clarified the relations between church and state definitively, so the Reformation did not face an opposition neatly divided into religious and secular authorities. Indeed, the successful Reformers themselves became powerful temporal forces —for example, in Zurich and Geneva. Partly as a result, those who later objected to either church or state authority in the Protestant realms felt entitled or obliged, on Protestant principles, to dissent and separate farther.

Looking at the results of this process, Protestant ecumenist Robert McAfee Brown spoke of authority as the "Achilles heel of Protestantism."[7] According to Brown, if the core of the Protestant spirit is "constant renewal at the hands of God," the blight is an often intractable attitude toward authority. From the conviction that human beings need constantly to renew their obedience to God comes the profound Protestant dictum *ecclesia semper reformanda (the church is ever in need of reform)*. This can produce a spirit of constant striving, an earnestness always to do better. On the other hand, it can produce an intolerance of compromise and a certain overresistance to authority. The precisely ecumenical consequences emerge in the Protestant tradition's tendency to split into more and more churches, as well as in certain Protestants' almost paranoid aversion to Rome.

The grounds Rome gives for such aversion will come up for review in the next chapter, as will some of the pros and cons of the Catholic spirit. Here the sadness I wish to elucidate, in view of an ecclesiology of vine and branches and Jesus' prayer in John 17, results from the separationist tendency to prefer life in the part rather than in the whole. Although the ecclesiological and missionary consequences of this attitude should make its disastrousness obvious, many Christians (in all three traditions) cheerfully exalt the conventicle over the full Body. Since they do not see that, because of the Incarnation, Christian prophetic faith must endure human weakness as well as laud exclusive monotheism, they have come to call stiff-neckedness a virtue.

CHAPTER 7. *CATHOLIC WISDOM*

Scripture and Tradition

If the Protestant gift often presents itself as a prophetic urgency toward reform, the Catholic gift presents itself as a seasoned balance, a wise ability to grant complex realities their due. So stated, this Catholic gift reminds us that many Christians in Protestant churches consider much of their faith "catholic" (in the sense of *intending to be a whole, to reach out to the whole world*), and many Catholics realize that their faith ought frequently to be "protestant" (in the sense of *speaking out against evils in society and in the church*). As Aquinas, the most influential Catholic mentor, long ago observed, the wise person does not care overmuch about names. It is the substance of a matter, not the term we use for it that really counts.

Nonetheless, Aquinas observed also that it is the property of the wise person to give order to the unruly jumble of human experience. Therefore our task here is to distinguish the Protestant, Catholic, and Orthodox gifts, so as to clarify somewhat the way Christian faith has taken shape in each of its three major families.

We can unite the two statements of Aquinas by bearing in mind that many people who bend their knees in Catholic pews manifest distinctively Protestant reflexes on some points, while on other points, people who sit on Protestant benches manifest distinctively Catholic opinions.

For example, there now are professional theologians of Roman Catholic loyalties who reverence Scripture with an ardor that, two generations ago, would have been limited almost exclusively to Protestant hearts. Parallelwise, there now are many professional theologians of Protestant loyalties who plump for the importance of Christian tradition with an ardor that, two generations ago, would have blazed only in Roman Catholic minds. Ecumenical contacts have worked many changes, many enlargements, in theologians' minds. We should recall these changes when the slow pace of progress toward the actual reunion of the churches threatens to turn us glum. As part of the effort here to extend such progress beyond the academic ghetto, let us reflect briefly on the wisdom that the Catholic emphasis on tradition can enclose.

In many of the sixteenth-century debates between Protestants and Catholics, scriptural and traditional emphases were made to seem opposed. Today, from a distance of more than four hundred fifty years, such reputed opposition melts away. For first, we now realize that Scripture itself is very traditional. If we consider only the New Testament, we know that the memories of Jesus which flowed into the New Testament were handed down for several generations and that many of the forms in which we now have those memories were shaped by individual churches' peculiar liturgies, missionary experiences, inner-church conflicts, and the like. The New Testament did not leap from the brow of Jesus' Abba like Athena from the head of Zeus. The Spirit's inspiration of the New Testament took the form of helping communities and individual authors to discern what had been passed down to them. Such passing down or handing on is precisely what we mean by *tradition*.

Second, we now also realize that the New Testament, for all its centrality in Christian life, is not the only locus of the Spirit. Just as the Constitution of the United States would be rather impotent law without ongoing interpretation, so the New Testament would be rather impotent "law" for the church without ongoing interpretation in the Spirit. The organic figures of the Johannine and Pauline ecclesiologies imply that the church is something alive, something growing. It is therefore something subject to change, for change rules all things alive and growing.

Third, it is but putting a finer point on this observation to note that the church acted with this understanding—approved change—from the beginning. It felt entitled to develop more detailed theologies, forms of ministry, spiritualities, and the like. The Pauline theology which opened the young church to the Gentiles was a development over and above the Christianized Judaism the apostles originally seem to have envisioned. Ignatius, Polycarp, and other church leaders who lived into the second century colored the original faith to match the new conditions of likely martyrdom. When the heresies that arose in the third and fourth centuries were countered, further theological interest was paid on the original New Testament deposit. In the fifth century, the Council of Chalcedon explained Jesus in language never conceived by the New Testament. And so on through the rest of the centuries, right down to the present.

Thus while the nineteenth-century Cardinal John Henry Newman may have tried to counter Protestant positions by stressing the *development* of Christian doctrine, he also exposed a bare fact, something that simply had occurred.[8] Protestants rightly can ask for criteria to distinguish true development from false, rightly can exalt Scripture as a norm for tradition, a mirror in which development must judge whether it is still the apostles' faith; but Protestantism's own history offers volumes of testimony on behalf of the fundamental Catholic conviction that the Spirit is always moving the church, always involved in its adaptation and change.

Faith and Reason

To be sure, Catholic church authorities, especially in the century prior to the Second Vatican Council (1962–1965), did not always appreciate the "development" proposed by Newman and others when they attempted to explain Catholic faith to modernity. For example, Cardinal Ottaviani, the watchdog for Catholic orthodoxy through the middle years of the twentieth century, had his coat of arms emblazoned with the motto *semper idem,* always the same. Still, it seems to me that the more lively, creative, and genuinely traditional spokespeople for Catholic Christianity have been sensitive to the tension between sameness and newness, the rights of the past and the rights of the future. Because of this, the Catholic love for God has implied a love for the world, a submission to God's historical providence, an acceptance of the ambiguities that the Incarnation of divinity into humanity entails.

The Catholic Church's own history is replete with testimony in favor of this incarnationalism. One need only walk through St. Peter's basilica in Rome to sense that the popes wanted a full imperium, a rule that would bring the best of contemporary art into the places of divine worship. From Michelangelo's "Pieta" and Bernini's baldachino, it is evident that genius was more than welcome at the center of Renaissance Catholic faith. It took some time for the new learning sparked by the Renaissance in other fields to become welcome, but the Catholic Church's quarrels with modern science and historical criticism actually ran afoul of its own better tradition. Many of the medieval discoveries which paved the way for the modern scientific advances were the work of monks, and Catholic clergy made significant contributions in astronomy and biology. Indeed, the father of modern genetics, Gregor Mendel, was an Austrian monk.

So the thesis that struggled for emergence in the Catholic church's battles with modernity was really a reformulation of the balance between faith and reason that had been struck by Aquinas. Accepting Aristotle as his master in philosophy, Aquinas had given the thirteenth century a remarkable system of thought which allowed reason full sway, yet took it up to the higher viewpoints of revelation. For Aquinas, grace perfected nature, faith fulfilled reason. Christianity brought challenges to nature and reason, grace and faith demanded conversion from sin, but what had happened in Jesus did not call into question the essential goodness of creation. Human beings were ordered toward God by the drives that most made them human. Their hungers to know and to love were God's calls implanted in the human heart. Sin did darken the mind and roil the heart, but through grace, a person's natural faculties were cleansed. Thus the first portion of the spiritual journey, the "purgative way," was an asceticism that restored the person to sanity, much as Plato's famous parable of the cave in the *Republic* pictured the beginnings of the philosophic life, the love affair with wisdom, as a turning away from shadows, an emergence into light.

Catholic historian Stanley Jaki's study of the rise of modern science suggests the extent to which the marriage of faith and reason might have prospered in recent centuries, had the church been able to get its teaching across to such giants as Newton and Descartes.[9] But the church failed, so recent centuries have thought it necessary to pit philosophy and science against Christian faith. The Catholic instinct still is to argue that this is a mistake, a piece of foolishness; and what many call postmodern thought seems to be vindicating the Catholic instinct. For postmodern science has shown us the *mystery* of the universe, all the wonders we cannot understand. In astronomy, nuclear physics, genetics, and other areas, nature is showing itself to be much more subtle and complicated than the mechanists of the nineteenth century realized. Similarly, postmodern philosophy, concentrating on language and hermeneutics (*interpretation*, especially of literary texts), has recalled the traditional Catholic doctrine of analogy. To make our way through the many pluralisms of today's global culture, we need to calibrate the likenesses and differences among people so that dialogues, rather than conflicts, will result.[10]

Licensing this sort of calibration, urging it on, the Catholic instinct grounds the whole dialogue in the analogy of being, the likeness/difference that runs through all creatures' manifestations of their Creator.

God is like the positive qualities of creation. He is more alive than dead, more intelligent than unintelligent, more loving than indifferent, more good than evil. Nonetheless, God is different in "life," "intelligence," "love," and "goodness" from us. God is consistently "other." So our tool for groping after God is very delicate. We have but a pencil of light to shine into an immense darkness, into the total fullness of God's light which we can never grasp.

Most current Catholic theologians probably would accept a chastening of this traditional theory of analogy, in view of Protestantism's case for the primacy of God's revealed Word. They probably would agree that Jesus, not physical creation, is our best metaphor or analogy for God and that Jesus discloses depths of evil in human history and depths of compassion in God that natural reason has never fathomed.[11] Still, current Catholic theologians would be likely also to point out that we must use our minds skillfully to advance such a splendid faith—that the love of God continues to require that we persuade faith and reason to be partners, rather than foes. Thus they would be likely to continue to demand more sophistication than appears in such Reformation statements as Luther's "reason is a whore" and Calvin's "the mind is a factory of idols."

Religious and Lay

If a generous reading of the Catholic instinct regarding faith and reason and Scripture and tradition judges it to have aimed at an admirable balance, so does a generous reading of the tension between religious and lay vocations. *Religious* in this case refers to the vocation of those who have turned their backs on worldly life and sought God through vows of poverty, chastity, and obedience. This vocation began early, and by the third century it was a notable Christian phenomenon. When Christianity gained a measure of respectability in the Roman Empire, numerous hardy souls went out to the desert in search of a more austere religious regime. Eventually their way of life led to the monastic rules of Basil in the East and Benedict in the West, whose aim was to provide order and direction for communities of monks and nuns.

Insofar as this monastic tradition greatly influenced the Christian clergy, and indeed the spirituality or piety of the whole church, it made a far deeper impression than the scant number of monks and nuns might lead one to suspect. Later refinements on the Benedictine model in the West, such as those of Francis of Assisi and Dominic in medieval times and Ignatius Loyola in Counter-Reformation times, retained the basic form of the vows. To this day the religious orders provide Roman Catholicism with many of its most influential saints, theologians, apologists, and servants of the church.

Martin Luther had been a monk, so he knew sixteenth-century religious life from the inside. Basically, he came to consider it an aberration from the gospel. The Catholic arguments that poverty and celibacy were New Testament counsels did not persuade Luther, and he found the second-class citizenship of the laity in the sixteenth-century church abhorrent on biblical grounds. The *laity* actually should have been the basic people of God, a democratic corps of "saints," as the New Testament suggests. If everyone baptized into Christ, everyone living the divine life given by the Spirit, is a "new creation," then the ranks and distinctions contrived by the Roman church were at best an irritating diversion, at worst a blasphemy. Instead of helping to ease the common person's burden, the clergy of Luther's time seemed to him like the Pharisees whom Jesus had so bitterly castigated—more concerned about money than about saving souls.

The merit in Luther's charges and in the similar charges made by other Reformers caused the Council of Trent (1545–1563) to undertake the reform of the Catholic clergy. Such merit did not, however, persuade Rome that the religious life itself was an aberration. Indeed, only at the Second Vatican Council did the feeling strongly impress itself that married and single Christians in the world hold much in common with clergy and nuns. Prior to that time, the religious vocation had continued to be considered the acme of Catholic faith. In the pontificate of Pius XII (1939–1958), for example, Catholics were still taught that virginity is a higher vocation than marriage.

Today, however, Catholicism seems to have accepted much of the critique that Protestantism has long leveled. Most current Catholic theologians would blush to be caught advocating the "higher" existential status of the priesthood or religious life, because modern biblical studies have taught them the clear supremacy or decisiveness of love. It is not where one stands in the church, but how one loves that is the best criterion of one's Christian "status." Roman Catholicism still demands celibacy of its clergy (against the wishes of a considerable number of its own members), as it still demands maleness. Perhaps consideration of the pros and cons of this traditional position will illumine the broader question of the alignment of religious and lay vocations in Catholic Christianity.

The pros of celibacy (and religious life) include its testimony to God's transcendence and its freeing of ministers for mobile service. By sacrificing the goods of sexual love and family life, the celibate testifies that God goes beyond the world, has a reality and love beside which worldly goods can pale. Normally, celibates need a strong prayer life and a supportive community to make this witness effective, but when they are especially free and charitable, they present to the world a challenging sign, stating that pleasure, money, and independence are not necessarily the highest goods. In the same way, when celibates, male or female, distinguish themselves by generous service as teachers, nurses, missionaries, social workers, and the like, they show the world that Christ continues to possess a love that is willing to lay down life for friends. Thus Mother Teresa of Calcutta challenges the whole world to reconsider its attitudes toward society's untouchables.

The cons of celibacy (and religious life) include the lack of realism and the arrogation of personal power it can induce in church leaders. For example, even sympathetic observers often find themselves linking Roman Catholic leaders' barrages on abortion, and their special concern with most other sexual topics, to their lack of personal experience in these matters. On contraception, even the Catholic laity opposes the leaders' teaching, and by a substantial majority. Most discussions of pastoral care among married Catholics go on for only about five minutes before someone points out that priests know very little about correlating two sexually different personalities, raising children, working in the competitive marketplace, and the like. In many ways, then, the complementarity the religious and lay vocations might offer one another seldom comes to fruition. If the Catholic ideal is a laity that would make faith worldly and a clergy or religious corps that would make faith otherworldly, the lack of parity between the two vocations, the fact that they are by no means equal in their access to church power and influence, vitiates the ideal. The direct charge that the Catholic clergy unduly arrogate all sorts of powers to themselves rings with ecumenical overtones that we shall consider shortly, but perhaps the strongest complaint within the Catholic camp itself now comes from Catholic feminists, who see the reservation of the priesthood to males (and so most church power) as sexism pure and simple.

Prayer and Work

So far, we have been describing a Catholic love of God that strives to give complexity its due. The sanctioning of religious, married, and single vocations, for example, allows people to follow the Spirit's leading with some freedom. Implicit in such allowance is the notion that the Spirit does breathe where she will. For all its formalism and hierarchical rigidity, therefore, the church of Rome has not ignored the charismatic dimension. The "consent of the faithful," which John Henry Newman reemphasized as a way to admit the charismata of the laity to greater church influence, seldom has been as strong a governing principle as Rome's direction of church affairs from the top; but since Vatican II, it has elbowed its way into such channels of influence as parish advisory boards, diocesan consultations, groups of lay people advisory to national commissions of bishops, and even lay boards available to international synods of bishops.

Glancing back at the history of Catholic Christianity, one might expect that the recent upgrading of the layperson's vocation would have produced a new Catholic theology of work. That has yet to appear, but when it does it will be well advised to consider some tantalizing dicta available from the Catholic past. For any expectation one might have that the religious vocation was geared wholly toward prayer and that the lay vocation was geared wholly toward work quickly proves to be simplistic. Overall, little attention was paid to the development of a profound prayer life among the laity, although from time to time exceptions occurred. On the other hand, from the beginning, monastic life delved deeply into the problem of ways to consecrate work. Beneath the motto *laborare est orare, (to work is to pray)*, lay an ideal of the consecration of all one's time and energy to God. In the sixteenth century, Ignatius Loyola, founder of the Jesuits, specified that the goal of his activist religious priests and brothers was to find God in all things. Jesuit spirituality was one of the most potent forces in the rise of modern Catholicism, greatly influencing most of the orders that arose after Ignatius, and a further saying of the Jesuit tradition invites us to muse a little more about the relation between prayer and work.

Challenging the assumption that work is our human business and that prayer turns us over to God, Ignatius wrote, "Pray as if everything depended on you, and work as if everything depended on God."[12] If we remind ourselves that this is the utterance of a mystic, we may realize that here is at least the outskirts of a program for finding God in all things.

The person who works as if everything depends on

God counters the labor theory of the unbeliever.
Where the unbeliever rightly sees many evidences that
success depends on personal responsibility and sweat,
the believer senses something more—the support and
lure of God. Moreover, the believer who develops this
sense realizes that only God can judge whether a given
work is successful. Even the possibility that Christ's
standards may not be the same as those of the world
leads us to a potentially explosive reconsideration of
work.

So the dictum certainly calls for faith that it is God
who finally judges the upshot of our work. Ignatius'
own hard labor and that of many of his followers shows
that working as if everything depends on God need not
lead to sloth. It should, rather, lead to peace, to a
rightful sort of carelessness. Somewhat as the Bhagavad-
Gita counsels Hindus to work without attachment to
the fruits of their work, so the Ignatian dictum, and
also such evangelical dicta as Jesus' "consider the lilies
of the fields, how they grow," say that we should keep
the worker's ego rather small, not let the worker's
worries overly intrude. The result will be a more
graceful work, in several senses: a work more
beautiful, less harried, more open to God. Paul
approved this attitude when he said, "I planted,
Apollos watered, but God gave the growth" (I Cor 3:6).
Those who really desire God's growth will hear at least
an echo of the Catholic wisdom that Ignatius was trying
to convey.

But what about praying as if everything depends on
oneself? To Ignatius, for whom God's reality was
incontestable and omnipresent, this cannot mean the
sort of secular shift the twentieth-century Protestant
martyr Dietrich Bonhoeffer had in mind when he
urged us to live "as if God were not given."

Bonhoeffer's urging has many merits, but he and Ignatius would have to hammer out some disagreement on fundamentals (largely occasioned by their having lived in two very different epochs) before their dialogue could get very far. The impulse behind Ignatius' view of prayer seems rather to be his profound sense of creaturehood and sinfulness, as revealed in the first "week" of his *Spiritual Exercises.*[13]

Were a person to come before God conscious of his true state, of his nothingness and need for forgiveness, he would pray ardently, full of need and gratitude. Both petition for God's help and praise of God's mercy would rush to his lips, would control his heart. He would have the example of Christ's prayer to console him and the hopes of the Spirit as his support, but there would be no irreverent taking God for granted, no forgetting that however much God sanctions intimacy, God is always GOD. For Ignatius, prayer is the most testing Christian activity because it is where the true proportions of faith are best clarified. Only by receiving from God the sense that he is accepted and loved can a person leave prayer able to work as if everything depends on God. Therefore today Ignatius would be likely to rearrange the Catholic tradition to say, "Pray with more sense of urgency, and work with less sense of anxiety."

Ecumenical Implications

As with Protestant prophecy, let us now consider some of the implications of Catholic wisdom for ecumenical theology. Positively, the balance that Catholicism has tried to inculcate is especially useful for complicated times. Against the recent tendency of so many special-interest groups to make their single cause the touchstone by which they judge their politicians, theologians, teachers, and others who must deal with reality in the round, the "Cat-holic" tradition urges wholeness *(kata holos)*. Sometimes Catholic right-to-lifers forget this hallmark of their own tradition, but usually it pushes most of the Catholic Church in the direction of moderation. Were all the Christian churches to open themselves to this Catholic instinct, try to reach out to the whole Christ and the whole of God's creation, half the stumbling blocks to their reunion would fall by the wayside. If they looked less to their own private interests and more to the common Christian good, they would be in a better position to love the integrity of the vine more than the blossoms of the branches.

Second, the Catholic sense of balance offers ecumenical theology both the analogical mentality we have described and a strong sacramental emphasis we have not much described. The two go together, inasmuch as sacraments are active analogies, metaphors embodied in bread and wine, water and oil. The ultimate basis of a sacramental Christian faith is the conviction that Jesus' flesh really did bear the reality of God. We shall see more of this conviction in the next chapter when we deal with Eastern Orthodox incarnationalism, but it is worth noting here. To manifest its balanced attitude toward the world, Catholicism has used some of the world's most primal elements for the worship of God. Above all, it has taught its people that Jesus is the very food of their spiritual lives.

Third, there are, of course, problems with the Catholic spirit when we place it in ecumenical perspective. We have mentioned some of these problems in connection with Protestantism's historical split from Catholicism. However, most of the frictions between Protestants and Catholics, and also between Orthodox and Catholics, no longer are doctrinal. Most are now organizational. With a little tolerance for the different styles and stresses each has developed over the centuries, the three traditions probably could agree on the requirements of loving God with whole mind, heart, soul, and strength. It is in the area of church order and ministry that they cannot seem to agree, to reconcile themselves. The major Roman Catholic contributions to the problem stem from the prerogatives claimed by the popes. These culminate in the papal claim to infallibility, but infallibility is actually invoked so rarely that it is the daily papal style, more than the occasional papal declaration, that most disturbs the ecumenical waters.

Historians seem now to agree that the Bishop of Rome was indeed foremost among the patriarchs of the early church. Because of the tradition that Peter had gone to Rome, because of Rome's centrality in the social world of the early church, and because of the Roman church's reputation for doctrinal purity, the Bishop of Rome had influence far beyond his own boundaries. However, the patriarchs of Constantinople, Alexandria, Antioch, and Jerusalem also were highly esteemed, for the early church was not a monolith but a diverse organization with several regional centers, each having its own quirks in theology, liturgy, and law. Unfortunately, the church has proved unequal to the collegial style that such origins have demanded. Byzantine politics kept the East in constant turmoil, the medieval papacy became a very princely power, and the Protestant churches burst off from one another like a row of firecrackers. Everywhere there was far too much concern for local and personal prerogatives, far too little concern for the peace of the ecclesiastical whole.

Today it is useful to specify Catholicism's continuing failures in collegiality in terms of "Romanita." The papacy and Roman curia have become an entity unto themselves, obscuring more than a little the servant character Jesus required of his ministers. Thus a recent study of Catholic missionary activity concludes that Roman-centrism cripples the abilities of missionaries to meet the real needs of non-European peoples.[14] In ecumenical matters, the recent popes have been rather affable toward counterparts such as the Eastern Orthodox patriarchs and the Archbishop of Canterbury, and they have countenanced considerable de facto cooperation between Catholic agencies and the commissions of the World Council of Churches. But they have shown little willingness to put off their tiaras, roll up their sleeves, and speak straightforwardly with Orthodox and Protestant churches about what they are willing to sacrifice, what powers they are willing to trim, for the sake of Christian unity.

All this leads me to conclude, perhaps ironically, that the Catholic ecumenical sin is essentially the same as the Protestant. The stiff-neckedness that has caused Protestants to split and resplit is a species of pride. The imperial tone and retention of power that have been Catholic fuel for the fires of division are but further species of pride. "We must be as we have been in our grandest self-conceptions," Catholic leaders tempt the observer to impute. "We must not decrease, even that Christ might increase."

CHAPTER 8.
EASTERN ORTHODOX WORSHIP

Liturgy

The Eastern Christian churches have had their own problems with an imperial style, and they too have shown more than a little fractiousness. But they have tried mightily to impress on their members the grandeur of God, that it is fitting that God should increase and humans decrease. This is clear from the Orthodox liturgy, which rises to the Lord of the universe through choral music and incense, prostrations and gorgeous accoutrements. John Meyendorff, a leading Orthodox theologian, has explained some of the rationale for such a liturgy:

> This is not a question of mere ritualism, but an appreciation of the corporate significance of the Gospel message combined with the realization that the new life in Christ is indeed manifested by and communicated in the sacramental nature of Christian worship. That is why the Orthodox layman pays particular attention to the form and manner in which the liturgy is celebrated. He never regards it, as does his brother in the West who is accustomed to a liturgy celebrated in a language which he does not understand, as an act involving only the priest,

> but feels responsible himself for all that is done in
> the house of God.[15]

At the core of Orthodox liturgy, then, is the "new life
in Christ," the sharing in the divine nature that comes
through Christian grace. (One could note, parentheti-
cally, that Meyendorff was writing at a time when the
Roman liturgy was still in Latin and that his instinct to
think of the West as Roman Catholic Christianity, with
little attention to Protestant Christianity, is somewhat
typical of Orthodoxy. Rome was the great counter-
player through most of East's history, so to the East, the
"West" is first and foremost *Rome*.) The East has
pondered this conception of grace more deeply than
the West, I think, and thereby has rooted its liturgy
more profoundly. While the West has stressed the
celebration of Christ's sacrifice to God for sin and the
community gathered in fellowship, the East has
developed a "mystagogy," an ongoing initiation into
the wonders of the divine life.

To be sure, the celebrating of Christ's sacrifice to
God for sin and the gathering of the community for
mutual support are good ends for liturgy to pursue.
These ends are not opposed to mystagogy, and any
mystagogy completely lacking them would tend to
become vague, a sort of religious aestheticism. But
with a proper concern for these and other matters,
especially social action, mystagogy can claim pride of
place at the center of Christian worship. Christians'
main activity, according to an ecclesiology expressed
in terms of the vine and the branches, is to abide in
their God. Their first reliance for this work is the Spirit
poured forth in their hearts by their Lord's resurrection, so it is fitting to place the climax of the eucharistic

liturgy, as Orthodoxy has done, at the epiclesis, the moment when the Spirit is invoked to move above the gifts of bread and wine and transform them into Christ's personal substance. Like the incense that spreads through a small Orthodox church, perfuming even the farthest corners, the Spirit moves in the hearts of the faithful and over their gifts (which stand for themselves), to knead the faithful into one dough, bake them into one high shiny loaf.

Liturgy means *work of the people,* so what is done at the Sunday mysteries, on the day that is especially the Lord's, is axial for the life of the church. To worship is to love God with whole mind, heart, soul, and strength, and so to fulfill Christ's first command. True, private prayer also fulfills Christ's first command, but liturgy better expresses the corporate and sacral character of Christian life. It is an act of a local church replete with the sense of the universal Church. Indeed, liturgy even suspects that its praise is taken up into the worship of the heavenly Church, the Church Triumphant, which, with the angels, sings to God unceasingly.

The Eastern church has maintained a strong sense of the angels, the heavenly corps of saints, and the instinct of all creation to sing the praises of its Creator. It has maintained the sense that its communal prayer is what one of its great theologians, Maximus the Confessor, called a cosmic liturgy. This relates to the Eastern understanding of Christ as the Pantokrator, the Lord of all, which we shall discuss below. It also relates to the scenes in the book of Revelation where the "saints," the members of Christ's Body, bow before the celestial throne and pay joyous homage to "the lamb that was slain," the Son who so loved the Father and the world that he gave his earthly life as a sacrifice.

Thus the Eastern liturgy invokes the Seraphim and the Cherubim, the angels and archangels. Its mood is somewhat like the awestruck emotion that courses through Jewish *merkabah* mysticism, which has focused the mystery of the Godhead on the chariot that was seen by Ezekiel (Ezek 1). God is so glorious that he strikes the creature nearly dumb with fear and magnetic attraction.

The difference in emotion between Eastern Christian mystagogy and a mysticism such as that of the chariot is the confidence that Christ offers the Christian believer. The grace of God, God's acceptance of the creature (to the point of sharing the divine life), should still the terrors the divine holiness can provoke. Joy, not fear, is the hallmark of Christian grace: God is so good he chooses to be merciful, loving, re-creative in all the exercises of his power. Even his judgment is a form of his love, an overflow of his goodness. "Therefore," Eastern Christianity, especially, says, "Praise him!"

Jesus Mysticism

In medieval times, when the Western church stressed Jesus' transcendent divinity as the Logos (partly in reaction to Arianism, which had denied Christ's divinity), Francis of Assisi and others promoted devotion to the Infant Jesus, who was nearer and less threatening than the exalted Logos. In somewhat the same way, Eastern Christianity has set, in counterpoint to its beautiful but somewhat formal liturgy, a warm, close devotion to Jesus that frequently has developed into a profound mysticism. The preferred form for this devotion has been the Jesus prayer, which we mentioned earlier. Constantly reciting the words "Lord Jesus, have mercy" or some close variant, the Orthodox devotee gradually develops a "Jesus consciousness." At advanced stages, he or she never loses a sense of connection to Jesus, of identification with Jesus.

Mother Alexandra, abbess of a small Orthodox monastery in Pennsylvania, shows how vigorously this tradition has continued to flourish today, how strongly the Jesus prayer gives one a sense of connection to other prayerful souls, and how deeply Jesus consciousness can penetrate the devout person's awareness:

> I had a most striking proof of uninterrupted communion with all those who pray when I lately underwent surgery. I lay long under anesthesia. "Jesus" had been my last conscious thought—and the first word on my lips as I awoke. It was marvelous beyond words to find that although I knew nothing of what was happening to my body I never lost cognizance of being prayed for and of praying myself. After such an experience one no longer wonders that there are great souls who devote their lives exclusively to prayer.[16]

This sort of mysticism has analogues in other religious traditions. Devotional Buddhism, for example, has developed the nembutsu, an invocation of Amida Buddha meant to aid one's rebirth in the Pure Land. The basic structure of human consciousness seems similar everywhere, so the practice developed by the mystics, yogins, or shamans of one tradition often have analogues elsewhere. In its understanding of Jesus mysticism, however, Christianity finally draws on its peculiar theological conviction that believer and

Lord share a single life. The practice of the Jesus prayer but exercises a presence, an awareness, that lies latent by grace in the hearts of all believers. Putting aside the practical question—How is the devotee to function in the workaday world while he or she is learning to concentrate on Jesus constantly?—we can imagine Mother Alexandra's achievement as a marvelous "translation" of Paul's "It is no longer I who live, but Christ who lives in me" (Gal 2:20). She now has with Jesus a coincidence of mind, heart, and will. As all those adept in the Jesus prayer report, increasing union with Christ brings deep peace and joy (though they also report difficult times when the prayer is very trying).

It is no accident, of course, that Eastern Christianity should have developed its Jesus mysticism in the context of a vigorous monastic life. Both Greek and Russian Orthodoxy have prized the solitary and communal forms of monastic life, to the point of making the bishopric and other high church offices open only to monks. (This law, plus the further restrictions on married clergy and on women, suggest that Eastern monasticism, like its Western counterpart, has given the church a somewhat frightened attitude toward sex.) Monastic life offers the freedom to concentrate on Jesus almost full-time, as it offers the freedom to celebrate the entire daily liturgy, the various "hours" that pace the church through the day.

Eastern monasticism tends to be conservative about relations with the non-Orthodox, but its Jesus mysticism easily could reach out to both separated Christians and serious religionists of the non-Christian traditions. For example, the Jesus consciousness that the *Philokalia* and other Orthodox classics wish to inculcate through the Jesus prayer bears affinities to Ignatius Loyola's "finding God in all things." Centered in the Christian God, both the Orthodox monk and the Jesuit adept feel the world to be a unity. Concentric with the divine "heart," the divine love that makes everything be, their hearts can repose in God anywhere.

Second, the Orthodox Jesus mystics might reach out to Protestants, especially Evangelicals, for whom an intense personal relationship with Jesus as Lord and Savior is the crux of Christian religion. My impression is that the Jesus consciousness of Evangelicals usually does not have the full resonance of that of the Orthodox, because Evangelicalism has neither a millennium of experience behind it nor a monastic environment around it, but there is sufficient similarity in their focal points to make these two movements potential partners to a fruitful dialogue.

Third, outside Christianity, serious practitioners in several traditions approach Ultimate Reality, or God, in ways cognate to Orthodox Jesus mysticism. Hindus who use a mantra (a *power-laden word* such as *om*), repeating it constantly, employ psychodynamics akin to those of the Jesus mystics. Hindus whose passion is identification with Krishna are comparable to those Orthodox whose passion is identification with Jesus. Muslim Sufis who use words such as those of the bismillah ("in the name of God") mystically, letting them echo deep in their consciousness, visually, as a mandala *(a power-laden object of sight),* are other non-Christians whom the Orthodox might consider cousins. Jesus mysticism, then, could knock on many doors, if the Orthodox chose to set it in a generous ecumenical perspective.

Icons

We shall take up such a generous perspective in the next chapter, when we meditate on the way all human history reposes in the one God. Here our topic is the artistic imagination through which Eastern Christianity has filtered much of its love for God. As all who have wandered through Orthodox churches know, the icons of Jesus, Mary, and the saints are among the most striking expressions of Eastern faith. Perhaps the best tie between our preceding reflection on Jesus mysticism and this present reflection on Orthodox iconography is the monastic atmosphere that has nurtured them both. In the silence at the center of Orthodox monasticism, where solitaries conceived their intense love of Jesus the merciful, artists conceived their striking expressions of Jesus the Lord.[17]

The importance of iconographic representations of Jesus, Mary, and the saints became almost exaggerated in Eastern Christian history, because of the fierce controversies that divided the East in the eighth and ninth centuries. Emperor Leo III, who had served as a military administrator in Asia Minor (an area long cool to representational religious art), began the campaign of the iconoclasts *(icon smashers)* in 726. With fluctuations due to imperial shifts (now an emperor against images, now an emperor in favor of them), the battle raged until 843, when the Regent Theodora ordered that the holy images be solemnly reestablished. At issue throughout was the way the Incarnation should be understood. With influence from Jewish and Muslim opposition to representational religious art (in the name of strict monotheism), the iconoclasts argued that Christ's humanity had been deified and so, like divinity in general, should not be represented. The iconodules *(icon reverencers)* argued that Jesus' humanity was not in competition with the divine Word but rather served as divinity's supreme form of self-expression (divinity's own artwork, one might say).

Since the time of Chalcedon (451), authentic Christian faith had been held to the proposition that in Christ there is one divine person, but two natures— one human and one divine. Each of these natures is complete and true; neither lacks anything owed to "divinity" or "humanity." Thus the divinization of Jesus' flesh, through the "hypostatic" union of his humanity with his divinity, could not mean that Jesus' humanity had been suppressed. God's assumption of a human nature must mean the perfection of that nature, not its enfeeblement or contraction. The light that glowed from the flesh of the resurrected Jesus was humanity at its fullest, its most fulfilled. The risen Lord was not a denigration of ordinary humanity but a mysterious pledge of the fulfillment that all flesh filled with the Spirit might hope to gain.

Further, since it was natural and fitting for matter-based human nature to express itself through images, it was natural and fitting to represent Jesus the God-man through images. Christian incarnationalism, sacramentalism, imagination—all conspired to argue so. God had pitched his tent among us, the prologue of John's Gospel said. God had made Jesus' flesh his image, his icon. Those who held to this Christian center could never deny the rights of the faithful to worship God through material representations, for that would be denying the final reality of the Incarnation.

The same arguments applied to Mary and the saints,

with even stronger force. If God had chosen to use them as (lesser) manifestations of divine power, it certainly was proper to represent them for the edification of the faithful. Mary, indeed, was, above all, the God-bearer (Theotokos). The one to whom she had given birth, the one who had assumed flesh from her, was God's very Word. Mary's icons therefore were holy in a participatory way, as were the icons of the saints and of Jesus, for an icon shared in the reality it represented. To the Platonic mind of the Eastern theologian, the participation of the below in the above was taken for granted. As all the beings of creation participated in, drew their reality from, the divine Being, so an icon of Christ participated in the holiness of Christ himself.

This did not mean that the icon itself was worshiped. The iconodules never argued that Christ and his icons were identical. But they did argue that the iconoclasts were heavy-handed in their charges of idolatry. Not knowing the difference between reverence and worship, and ignoring the religious needs of the common faithful, the iconoclasts fell into what we today might call a puritanical excess. If the iconodules had not won the day, the full humanity of Christ might have been lost to Eastern faith.

But the iconodules did win the day (though at the price of many martyrs), and so Eastern Christianity has continued to enrich the whole Body of Christ with wonderful imagery. The stern, sacral faces of Mary and Jesus are a moving rendition of the solemnity of the Madonna and Child. The mother, the holy Virgin, is the bearer of the Christian's God, and the Child, small as he may seem, is the Pantokrator. If the Eastern Roman emperor had been a magnificent figure, formal and powerful, how much more so must the Pantokrator be. That he raises his tiny hand in blessing, that he assumes the pose of a saving teacher, is a great expression of the divine grace, the divine condescension. One ought not to take it lightly. Rather one should bow low, humble one's flesh and one's spirit, and take the goodness of God to heart. Orthodox icons, finally, are eloquent witnesses to the goodness of God.

The Pantokrator

The goodness of God, the love of God poured forth into the world (which is the lure of our loving response), found one of its most profound conceptualizations in the Eastern notion of the Pantokrator. By his Incarnation and resurrection, Jesus was the Lord-of-All. Texts such as Colossians 1:15-20 gave this conceptualization a firm scriptural basis:

> He is the image of the invisible God, the first-born of all creation; for in him all things were created in heaven and on earth, visible and invisible, whether thrones or dominions or principalities or authorities —all things were created through him and for him. He is before all things, and in him all things hold together. He is the head of the body, the church; he is the beginning, the first-born from the dead, that in everything he might be pre-eminent. For in him all the fulness of God was pleased to dwell, and through him to reconcile to himself all things, whether on earth or in heaven, making peace by the blood of his cross.

The notion of the Pantokrator undertook to gather up that long string of "alls."

The link between this notion and Orthodox iconography frequently was very close. When the iconographers sought to picture the power and full meaning
of God's entry into creation, the notion of the
Pantokrator led them toward an imperial, lordly
depiction. Of course the political atmosphere of the
Eastern empire led them in this direction too, but it was
Eastern theology more than Eastern politics through
which Jesus became the King of creation. Sensitive to
the ontological intent of the scriptural images, to the
reality a passage such as Colossians 1:15-20 was
striving to imagine, the iconographers drew a divinized humanity that might credibly command the stars
and the seas, might fittingly receive the dramatic
worship of the Eastern liturgy. If Christ was truly all in
all, it was necessary for the iconographers to portray
him as the ruler of all.

It seems likely that Pantokratorship also played a
part in the East's tendency to unite church and state,
even to risk sacralizing the state. From the time of the
historian Eusebius (c. 260–340), who rejoiced in the
church's access to power through Constantine's favor,
the emperor was more than a simple secular function-
ary. Rather, he was a sacral figure, not too different
from the ancient Near Eastern kings who had mediated
cosmic order to the state. Participating in the cosmic
power of Christ, the Christian emperor commanded
with a holy authority. For Eusebius and others of his
cast of mind, Paul's accreditation of the state's power
in Romans 13 was a minimal assumption. Maximally,
the holy emperor was the equivalent of a thirteenth
apostle.

Thus the emperor did not lose all the religious
stature he had carried in the pagan empire. Between a
strong Christian monotheism, which could not bend

its knee to Caesar or call him Lord, and a sense that Caesar mediated God's ruling power, some accommodation occurred. Whether it should have or not, the notion of the Pantokrator probably eased this accommodation. The emperor participated in Christ's universal lordship, was an image of the heavenly King. Thus through most of its history, the Eastern church has not felt the empire to be a secular domain, a realm empty of numinous forces.[18] The imperial powers, whether Greek or Russian, usually have worn semi-sacramental garb.

Perhaps the main service the Pantokrator doctrine could render today is that of giving impetus to a more satisfactory Christian theology of nature and politics.[19] If Jesus really rules the eons and galaxies, really is head of all creation's levels of being and stages of evolution, then physical nature is not something we can treat with irreverence, let alone with disdain. It is part of the Lord's realm, instinct with at least a trace of the intelligibility and goodness of the Logos. In a secondary way, it images the divine reality. Thus beyond a praiseworthy reverence for all life, Christian theology urges a reverence for all being. Rocks and waters are valuable, dignified, because they "hold together" in Christ. We suspect this when we are held rapt by a lofty mountain or beguiled by a changing sea. Could we raise our suspicions to full consciousness, we could confess that all things offer us grace.

Portents of ecological disaster therefore could lead to a more worldly Christianity. So also could portents of political disaster, of economic and spiritual collapse. What might such a worldly Christianity do? It might sharpen the balance that a sane ecology or politics entails. From the sense that God's love offers us the strength (through the theological "virtues" of faith, hope, and charity) to love the world in its transcendent source, a worldly Christianity might help agriculture, technology, economics, and politics seem very important (seem participants in God's importance), but not idolatrous. In other words, it might show that the Pantokrator gives dignity to all human activities, but assures that none of them swell out of proportion to claim the whole stage, the whole of human love. Because he rules nature and the states, the lordly Christ can bring sanity to our natural and political relations.

Ecumenical Implications

Orthodox Christianity has participated rather intensely in the ecumenical exchanges of the twentieth century, but many of its representatives now seem less than sanguine about the prospects for full reunion. Thus Robert Stephanopoulos has recently judged that "there appears to be no consensus in the essentials of the faith, no coherent synthesis of a universal orthodoxy, no actual communion in the sacramental structure of the body of Christ." A few sentences later, however, one sees the basis for his negative assessment: "I belong to a tradition that maintains that, while the true composition of the church is known only to the Lord of that church, still it must be only one and visible and it is found precisely in the historic Orthodox communion."[20]

So, like the intransigence of Rome, the intransigence of the Orthodox makes serious ecumenical negotiations more than difficult. It also throws cold water on even low-level ecumenical exchanges. For example, the Archimandrite Aimilianos, head of the

Greek monastery of Meteora, told the visiting Western monk Basil Pennington that "the East, Orthodoxy, has nothing to learn from the West."[21]

Pennington prefaces this report with the observation that Aimilianos was not in the least bit offensive, and the rest of the narrative shows that the two monks, Eastern and Western, had much to share. I admire Pennington's charity, but I find his ecumenical theology Pollyannaish. What Christian can pronounce his own tradition perfect without giving offense? The attitude that we have nothing to learn from Christians of other churches, or from non-Christians, is precisely what has gotten the Church universal into such a shabby state. Confusing the cosmic outreach of the Pantokrator with Christ's presence to their local church, Christians again and again have acted with complete self-sufficiency. In superficially good conscience, they have prated about the church as a "perfect society" and about the need for other human beings, whether dissident Christians or benighted pagans, to join *their* particular conventicle. The result has been an astounding innoculation against repentance, an astounding encouragement of division.

If there is one conviction necessary for church reunion, and necessary as well for good ministry, it is that all of us have a great deal to learn. We all have sinned and fallen short of God's glory. We all are unprofitable servants, more stupid and lackluster than most of us imagine. Were we to come to our senses, regain a hold on reality and humility, we might begin to see the ravages our self-sufficiency has worked. The Church now stands in the world as almost a mockery of Jesus' prayer for unity. On every street corner of the West, a different gathering thinks of itself as the center of salvation-history. The Orthodox church, which

Stephanopoulos claims stresses oneness and visibility, is itself a basket case of squabbles over jurisdiction. Like Rome and many of the Protestant churches, it has arrived at ecumenical gatherings with a long list of nonnegotiables; nowadays the nonordination of women stands high. No wonder "there is no consensus in the essentials of the faith." For consensus, one first must understand the meaning of *essential.*

It is not my point to make Orthodoxy a special whipping boy. We have already pinned the tail of pride on Protestantism and Catholicism, so this is simply an evenhanded reference to Orthodox asininity. None of the historic communions seems willing to conceive the essentials of faith deeply enough for its simplicity to emerge. None seems willing to believe that Christ is a new creation, in whom membership dissolves all bases for division. If Paul could say that there is neither Jew nor Greek, neither slave nor free, neither male nor female in Christ (Gal 3:28), we should be able to say that there is neither Catholic nor Orthodox, neither Protestant nor Evangelical. In Christ there are only unprofitable servants, commissioned to love God with their whole minds, hearts, souls, and strengths, and to love their neighbors as themselves. There are only ministers charged to build up the Body, to reconcile the world by the power of their love.

Orthodox rigidity, Orthodox insistence on past forms, blocks such an essentialist view, as do Catholic and Protestant equivalents. Still, Orthodox worship might be just the dynamite we need to blast such rigidity away. Focusing the believer ardently on the Pantokrator, Orthodox worship possesses the potential to cast all worldly concerns in the shade. Its God is in his heaven, so all might be right with the world were we to obey that God by showing one another mercy, by circumcising our hearts. Then, opening this worship to all who confess Jesus to be their Lord and Savior, Orthodoxy might lead a march toward sacramental communion, toward the food a unifying spirit most needs. Let fuss about jurisdictions and forms fall away for the moment; let the Spirit for once have center stage; and then discussions about making the historically divergent bodies complementary could occur in proper perspective. Then the past might neither devour the present nor abort the future. God is the only one to whom the angels sing the Trisagion. God alone is holy, holy, holy. Right praise *(ortho-doxy)* has always blessed the Church catholic by protesting for such an exclusive monotheism. Would that it did so with full ecumenical entailment today.

CHAPTER 9. *HISTORY IN GOD*

Order in History

When one worships God, one implicitly places all of one's life under God's sway. Indeed, one implicitly places all of history under God's sway. For if worship is to avoid neurosis, to become more than a fantasy projected from uncontrolled human needs, it must intend, must bore toward, something real, some One real. For Christians this One is the Creator, as real as the primordial question "Why is there something and not nothing?" For Christians, this One is Jesus' Abba, drawn near because of his own goodness, to offer his own love. If these designations are only whistlings in the dark, Christians are, of all people, the most to be pitied. If there is no Creator or Abba, we should all eat, drink, and be merry—as merry as absurdity will allow us to be. On the other hand, if creation is a genuine mystery, which no caused being ever can remove, then human beings have not spent the past fifty millennia worshiping in vain. If Jesus was a trustworthy prophet, then the Creator is offering us a full measure of joy, pressed down and overflowing.

Aware of these questions, these options, and

genuinely erudite about intellectual history, the contemporary philosopher (political scientist, historian) Eric Voegelin has devoted a long career to the search for the order that time under God may offer, for the intelligibility of human history.[22] In the first three volumes of his *Order and History,* Voegelin acted on the methodological axiom that the order of history emerges from the history of order.[23] If he could uncover how past societies had organized themselves, had come to terms with reality, he would be able to track the basic meanings, the key intelligibility lines, of human time.

Between volumes three and four, Voegelin paused for seventeen years, largely because he first suspected and then confirmed that this methodological axiom was liable to imaginative bias and distortion. Subtly, it could insinuate an image of history as linear progress, straightforward development, ever-increasing differentiation. But the facts, or the empirical data, of his historical studies called this image seriously into doubt. Contrary to Karl Jaspers and others of the linearist inclination, Voegelin could find no "axial time" around which human history as a whole configured itself. For example, the various axial thinkers—Confucius, the Buddha, the Hebrew prophets—did not know of one another. They were divergent sparks, rather than a consecutive flame.

So the mature Voegelin has come to stress the mystery of human history. What order we can descry still is rooted in the different societies' efforts to situate themselves in reality, but it is an order we cannot place tidily on a time line. All we can say is that societies everywhere seek to order themselves in the world, some choosing more compact symbolizations, and

some more differentiated. The compact symbolizations stress the truth of the cosmos—the reality that
human life is part of a natural and biological whole.
The more differentiated symbolizations stress the
truths of the human spirit—the reality of "leaps in
being" like those of the Greek philosophers and the
Hebrew prophets. Such leaps finally lead to the
conviction of classical philosophy that human existence is an in-between *(metaxy)* bounded by the
unseen God above and the chaotic forces of matter
below. They also lead to the biblical conviction that
God must move the human heart if it is to arrive at right
order, justice, and love. So the twin sources of
Western culture—Greek philosophy and Israelite
revelation—both situate human existence, individual
and social, as a quest, a responsive search, for God the
unseen measure. We best conceive existence as a
movement *(zetesis)* from the human side, in response
to a drawing *(helkein)* from the divine side. Its primary
imperative is an open soul, a soul desirous of moving
ever more deeply into the mystery disclosed by
honesty and love.

The order of human history, revised, is therefore the
story of human efforts all over the world to live forward
into divine mystery. The plot line contains overtones
of greater or less differentiation, but nothing is rigid.
One can find this essentially human quest in Egypt of
the third millennium and in Upanishadic India. It
advances wonderfully with the Buddha and Lao Tzu. If
Plato and Paul are special heroes, no human being, no
human society lacks the essential reality which Plato
and Paul so greatly clarified.

So there is a certain equivalence among the
symbolizations that all societies, Western and Eastern,
Christian and pagan, have thrown up. Like the

Christian churches, they all have sinned and fallen short of God's glory. They all have felt the gentle solicitation of God's grace. The capital human task, both psychological and political, is to give their just due to the complex forces of a human world that is moving forward into divine mystery; it is to find a balance between human materiality and spirituality, human individuality and sociability, all the while searching for God (who may respond dramatically). The order of human history, its most desirable pattern, is therefore quite like T. S. Eliot's dance, his graceful movement forward from the still point.[24] History, above all, is the story of human beings' joyous quest for God, for the sovereign fullness of meaning with which time, at its best, is pregnant.

Providence

Time at its worst is so disordered that the joyous quest for God turns into an agony. When a society closes itself to divine mystery, deflecting its people away from the source of true order by bad symbolizations, the body politic suffers as though a limb were out of joint. Instead of joy, the controlled excitement of the quest for a known unknown, there is widespread anxiety—the *angoisse* and *angst* that existential philosophy has spotlighted. Nonetheless, even when the times are out of joint, human existence enjoys the essentials necessary for wisdom. Even in suffering and disorder, the vocation to order continues to echo. Indeed, as we learn important things about health only when we fall ill, so we learn important things about personal and social order only through sin and injustice. This is not to say that sin and injustice are good or inevitable. It is to say that when they occur, they do not render existence futile. By the "it should not be" they carry, they further specify the goal of our human search. For those who follow this line of reflection, the Christian doctrine of providence will pack considerable firepower.

Langdon Gilkey recently has reworked the Christian doctrine of providence from a semi-Whiteheadean point of view.[25] Like many other contemporary treatments of history, Gilkey's is sympathetic to the demand (of those who insist on human maturity) that human time must really count for something, must not be just a play with an outcome that God has determined from the beginning. This seems to dovetail with the second of the Whiteheadean God's two natures. By his "consequent" nature, the White-headean God interacts with the world as a limited being: He does not control the world's fortunes and he suffers from the world's follies. One might say, then, that the Whiteheadean God is in history, is involved and bound as are other historical entities. The proviso would be that this God must also have a "primordial" nature, outside history, and that his limitations be self-chosen, in the service of his will to be-with his creation.

The whole Creator-creation relation, of course, is finally mysterious, and Gilkey has on his side the biblical insistence that God cares for human beings, labors on our behalf, and even has gone out of himself, assuming a human nature, so as to live and suffer with us. I wonder, though, whether other lines of biblical thought, especially those elaborated by the Orthodox and Roman Catholic traditions, do not force some counterbalance.

First, how solidly founded is the distinction between

God's consequent and primordial natures? Does it have what the scholastics (who would have denied it) called a *fundamentum in re,* a basis in God's own reality, or is it a sort of *distinctio ex machina,* a construction meant to get the theologian out of a tight spot more than to offer a radical solution? Second, if one thinks hard about the Godness of God, the deathlessness and limitlessness that stand the Creator over against the creature, then it appears more likely that history occurs in God than that God occurs in history. "All things hold together in Him," the Logos, because he, God's eternal self-expression, is the comprehensive pattern within which any participation of the divine being and intelligibility must occur. Creation therefore is in the divine being of the Logos, and it is less than the divine being of the Logos. He is more and it is less, just as eternity (the total simultaneity proper to God) is more, and time (the consecutive duration proper to material creatures) is less. To be sure, all words such as these we stutter about God are only symbolic or analogical, extrapolations from the experiences of the ordering quest which is moved by God. Still, I think that most of the glimpses the Christian tradition has gleaned tend to exalt God rather than human history. He is first and it is second, not vice versa.

This is not to deny the merits of a view of theological imagination such as Julian Hartt's, which stresses the historical and the verbal.[26] Historical and verbal concerns have been staples of recent Protestant theology, and Hartt has rendered them well. It is rather to remind Hartt, and others who draw little on the Orthodox and Roman Catholic speculative traditions, that Christianity, from its biblical faith, has also spotlighted eternity and silence. For the ecumenical doctrine of providence I would like to see emerge, these latter deserve equal time. We will not have a fully Christian view of history, and so of human endeavor, until we take into account the divine drawing that is correlative to the human striving. We will not have the faith-filled view we presumably want until the divine *helkein* assumes a priority over the human *zetesis*, for until then, we will have forgotten the prevenience of grace. Faith, hope, and love are gifts of the Spirit, not human attainments. We love God and one another only because God loved us first. Indeed, we exist only because God loved us first, called us into creation.

Providence, then, means that God's view is always first. However quickly we must rush to deny that human beings can mount to God's view, in our sketches of the scheme of things, God's view—God's oversight, care, and pledge of success—must come first. As Jesus said that God numbers all the hairs of our heads (Lk 12:7), and as Christian faith has long said that God will wipe every tear from our eyes (Rev 21:4), so a contemporary Christian view of God's providence should say that the outcome of history is not in doubt, that Christ has shown history to be held in God's love.[27]

Suffering in God

Thus far, we have spoken of history as being most basically a human quest for God (in response to the divine initiative), and of God's provision for this process—God's priority in the process' foundation, direction, and ultimate context. Both these considerations offer a solid basis for speaking of God's involvement in human history, but the Incarnation offers a still more solid basis. If one believes in the Incarnation (assumes it to be a realistic statement about Jesus' identity), then one can say that God took a form through which he could become patient with history. The divine Son so identified with the humanity given by Mary that Mary became the Theotokos, the God-bearer, allowing an eternal reality to take up a career in time. Through its notion of the *communicatio idiomatum,* the exchange of properties between Jesus' humanity and his divinity, Christian theology sanctioned such speech.[28] Indeed, it even sanctioned the statement "God (the Logos) died on the cross." Thus with a different "concretizing," one might reinstate the Whiteheadean notion of suffering in God.

But why should we care to associate God with suffering? For the Greeks this was impossible, and the Greeks had a lot to do with the structuring of Christian theology because they had a lot to do with the discovery of the way the human mind and the ontological order are structured (reciprocally). This had both negative and positive results. As a stumbling block to faith, the Greek attribution to God of impassibility *(nonsuffering)* made the notion of Christ's cross scandalous to many. As a support of faith seeking understanding, however, the Greek attribution of impassibility to God located the "divine" suffering in the humanity joined to the Logos. That the Father should suffer, or that the inner Trinitarian life should have some defect, was impossible, and so heterodox. As we saw when considering the controversy over icons, some Christians (not those eventually proclaimed orthodox) considered Jesus' glorified flesh to be beyond humanity and thus unrepresentable. The logic of their position might well have led them to consider Jesus' glorified flesh also beyond suffering, and then questions should have arisen as to the moment at which his flesh became "glorified," since from the inception of the Incarnation (as Johannine theology suggests) it was uniquely united to God. At that point it would have been but a short step to the early heresies (e.g., Docetism) that denied Jesus' sufferings, because they denied his ordinary humanity. Thus in questioning the proclivity of Hellenistic thought to dissociate divinity from suffering, contemporary theologians may be doing the preservation of faith in the Incarnation a great service.

However, although we accept the reality of Jesus' humanity, the consequent reality of his sufferings, and the accommodated sense in which, through the hypostatic union of Jesus' humanity with the Logos we may say that God has found a form through which to be in history and to suffer, we have yet to show the value of such suffering. Its value lies in the association we humans must make between suffering and love. We must make this association because for us, suffering is an essential ingredient of existence, at least in the sense that we all undergo more of our life than we create, and often in the sense that we undergo pain, whether physical or emotional. To love God passionately (note the word play) we must come to terms with these conditions of human existence, this essential ingredient of our situation.

God finally is the author of our lives, our condition, so our yes to God, our responding love, must embrace such negativities or causes of suffering as death, disease, and human sin. Somehow we must rise to a higher viewpoint or descend to a deeper humility that will allow us to circumvent the protest, even the defiance that such negativities rightly raise in our hearts. We should protest evils, including the evil of physical suffering. We should say and pray, "It ought not to be." After this, however, we should proceed in our imitation of Jesus and surrender to our Father's will, commending our spirit (our fate, our meaning) into our Father's hands, as Jesus did.

That is what a lively doctrine of providence would solicit. It is what the "abandonment" of a de Caussade entails.[29] But the doctrine gains its greatest force when we place suffering humanity in union with the vine, so that human travail becomes an affair of the organic union, the mystical Body, between Christ and his followers (conscious and unconscious). In the covenant, God and human beings share all things of historical moment. God therefore shares the sufferings of humankind. The Father chooses to have a stake in human welfare, the Son chooses to be head of a suffering Body, and the Spirit chooses to groan with us in our depths. All these sufferings take place in God. We have the Word of biblical revelation (e.g., Hosea) that God's love in these matters is such that he is as though wounded by our pains, pierced by our infidelities.

More practical than such speculations, however, are the conclusions that simple believers long have drawn: God stands with us in our sufferings, God fights with us against evil and death. At bottom, Christian faith holds that God has defeated suffering, death, and evil. It holds that the light shines in the darkness and that the darkness has never overcome it. By suffering evil, Christ conquered evil—so took evil into the divine embrace that he crushed its spine. This (the doctrine of the Pantokrator) hardly is credible, as a matter of empirical observation, on the map of human history. It is quite credible, as a matter of spiritual intuition, on the map of what becomes "possible" when one feels the divine lure.

Universal Grace

When one feels the divine lure, it also becomes credible that all human history so reposes in God that Christ's grace reaches out universally. I find this proposition enhanced by current reflections on the interconnectedness of the religious traditions' histories such as those of Wilfred Cantwell Smith.[30] Smith says that as a matter of empirical observation, Buddhism and Christianity, Judaism and Islam, interconnect, impinge on one another at dozens of points in their time lines. For instance, the Buddhist story of Gautama's renunciation of the princely life influenced centuries of Christians in the transposed form of the story of Jehoshaphat. The Buddha, one could even say, mediated Christian grace to a thinker such as Leo Tolstoy, whom the Jehoshaphat conversion story sparked to a change of life. If we take human history seriously, giving its myriad such examples their due, we find that God's offer of love, God's lure in terms of honesty and goodness, is a concrete universal. Empirically as well as notionally, God has been active in all times and places with a will to save.[31]

No doubt many Christians still object to this proposition, either on speculative or practical grounds. Speculatively, many do not know how to square God's continued activity with Christ's unique mediatorship of saving grace. Practically, many think it downplays the importance of Christian conversion, church membership, and missionary activity. Both objections have some merit, but neither proves cogent in the final analysis; an attempt to explain this may shed more light on Christ's relation to a God-held human history.

Speculatively, there seems no reason not to see the

Logos shining in the light of a Buddha or a Confucius, and no reason that Jesus' life, death, and resurrection cannot be the point where the meaning of the one unified human history is decisively disclosed. The Logos reached by Christian theology, Christian faith in Jesus seeking understanding of the inner life of Jesus' God, is the comprehensive expression of the divine light. It is therefore the true light, which enlightens every person who comes into the world. When a Gautama comes to enlightenment, he participates in the luminous Logos in a special way. His participation is limited, since he is a finite personality embedded in a finite culture, so his expression of the Logos is limited. Nonetheless, it may be profound enough, adequate enough, to spark a movement that enlightens millions through subsequent centuries. Indeed, his movement may finally have such depth and breadth that a Christian and a Zen Buddhist can describe one another in terms of "anonymous Christian" and "anonymous Zen Buddhist."[32]

Being human, Jesus also does not exhaust the light of the Logos. For Christians, his union with the Logos is unique—so much so that the Logos gives him his very personhood—but historically, his genuine humanity assured that he would be limited in his language, his range of behavior, his store of examples, and the like. There is room, then, for other revealers of the Logos. It is fitting that non-Jewish cultures should have received God's light through non-Jewish prophets. Still, the one Logos, in whom all creation holds together, is the source of all prophets' light. The one God, whom Jesus called his Abba, is the source of all peoples' grace. Choosing to become intimate, "personal," with the world, God has used myriad teachers to draw all human beings upward toward the divine life of light and love. All the joyous quests of human beings have moved by virtue of the prevenient divine *helkein*.

However, human history actually is composed of specific people and cultures which intersect, and on this level there may occur one breakthrough more decisive or definitive for the intersected whole than any other. Christians see Jesus' life, death, and resurrection as that unique event. By the singular act of resurrecting Jesus, the one God of all history has placed in history an almost unthinkable meaning that is applicable to the lives of all people. He has conquered sin and death—not merely metaphorically but physically, literally. Thus Christians traditionally have believed, and thus excellent exegesis continues to prompt them to believe today.

On one level, this may indeed amount to a "scandal of particularity," for it is not clear why God should have chosen one rather obscure man in whom to manifest the universal divine offer. On another level, it would have been *necessary* for a truly historical revelation of this magnitude to deal with only one person, at a discrete time and place. So while it will remain strange that God should have chosen to raise only Jesus, and this raising will remain the best basis for the Christian claim that Jesus is the Son of God in a way no other religious genius ever has been, Jesus' victory can still apply to—illumine, be the exemplary cause of—all other human beings' situations. If one goes deeply enough into a single instance of the human condition, one reaches factors that apply to all men and women.

This explains why, practically, Christians should not be overly worried that universal grace will diminish the importance of conversion, church membership, or Christian mission. They should, rather, emphasize what God has done, how universal grace amplifies the good news, and then reconceive themselves and their ministry in more joyous and exemplary terms. This could lead them to see that they are to come into lands, into hearts where God has preceded them, to *offer* (not to force or to bestow) the best clarification they can of what it means to be human and saved—to offer the light of Christ. They are to plant, water, and let God give the amount of increase, the number of overtly Christian conversions and church memberships, that he will. Their best missionary tactic, they should recall, will be their love for one another, their sacramental unity. Only when their conviction of Christ's importance has inspired a rich church unity will they have grounds for complaining to God that he has not made their historical importance sufficiently clear.

Kataphatic Theology

Such a reconception of explicit Christian faith and mission is indeed more humble than many self-conceptions of the past have been, but it better equates to the demographic fact that today fewer people than one in four are Christian. Today (as in the past) God is at work in many more places than the church is at work, and the church should be more eager to demonstrate how explicit Christian faith can benefit human prosperity than to lecture non-Christians on the superiority of Christ's wisdom. But the importance of God's presence to worldwide human history should have a chastening effect on all Christian pride, and so it is not only ecclesiology that would do well to lower its voice. All discourse about the mysterious God who holds human time in his hands should speak more softly, using by preference those expressions of praise that give the divine prevenience its due.

A theology would not be Christian, however, if it had nothing at all to proclaim. Purely negative theology stands in conflict with the Incarnation, for the Christian God has made Jesus a truthful metaphor of the divine nature and intent, and while Jesus is ever a mystery, his wisdom and bearing are not obscure. Jesus tells us that the quest for God, the response to God's attraction, is light enough for history. He says that the attempt to love God as he did is an "answer" adequate to the puzzles of time. Of course, it is a peculiar answer, not as much a statement as a process, a way of life. As the famous paradox of Zeno was solved by walking, so the puzzle of the miasmic flats of human history is solved by traversing it.

One starts from "here" (this time, this place, this personality) and takes a step in the direction which one's best present wisdom points toward. One responds in terms of the way one thinks one should work, play, pray, bring up the kids, today. Sufficient unto this day is the "evil," the burden, of trying out one's sense of what is wise, what is loving. Then tonight, one can take stock. In traditional terms, one can examine one's conscience. If one does this over a period of several months, one will find that certain patterns emerge. For instance, it might turn out that one works best when one sets an agenda the night before. Or one might realize that there is no pleasing a fourteen-year-old, no matter what one does, and so back off from giving advice. The constant problems of work or child-raising are always changing, but slowly one can become more adept at moving with their flow.

For faith, we can bring all such problems to God.

Examination of conscience therefore is really a colloquial prayer. And for faith, all our problems come into clearest focus when God brings them to a higher viewpoint, a bigger perspective. In that bigger perspective, they are all more mysterious than they were before. Who, for instance, can program the quirks of creativity? Who can say why Tuesday was a black day and Thursday solved all problems? So too with bringing up children. Each chip shows how little the old block knows. Each mind has graces and needs all its own. Reflecting on such things day by day, one comes to see Christian faith as a sort of Ariadne's thread. Far from being a prepacked set of answers, there is only direction enough, food enough, to get one through today.

Kataphatic theology is a speaking theology, a theology that describes God affirmatively. God is, affirmatively, present enough, sufficiently illumined by Jesus the Christ to give history its salvation. There is enough of God's presence to direct history day by day. In all times and places, the divine drawing leads the docile soul from shadows and pitfalls toward the fullness of ineffable warmth and light. As Jesus suggests so evocatively, God's grace does not remove suffering, depression, and defeat. It does not gut history of its cancers. But it does stand ready to catch those who fall back from prideful perspectives, and it does give mystery its due, allowing us to stroll through time as a trust-walk. Job said, "Though he slay me, yet will I trust in him." "History reposes in God," to reinterpret Jesus' words, "in such wise that two sparrows are not sold for a farthing without God's knowing about it, God's taking it into account." How much more when we buy and sell, make and unmake our souls?

We can say this of God, can affirm this splendid minimum, and find it to be enough. We can concentrate on how Jesus spoke, what Jesus loved, and possess our souls in patience. We need not know the days and the hours the Father has appointed for the things we think great. This day, God may require our souls, or she may give us thirty more years. We need only be clear that if today we hear her voice, we must not harden our hearts. If today the light shines in our darkness, we must try our best to comprehend it.

That is what God seems to say, what God's kataphatic theology of wise living seems to boil down to. Do what you can today. Learn today from what you did yesterday and from what you did not do. Calculate the height of the tower you would build, have some prudence about tomorrow, but do not let tomorrow become more real than today. You can only love God, only find God today. God is here, in the human condition Jesus spotlighted, only moment by moment, now after now. Even when God is the absolute future, the horizon luring all nows, he must reach down into today. Even when God is the jewel of the past, we must recall him into today. Loving the lovable Mystery today is all that we can do. The good news is that it is enough, because history reposes in God.

CHAPTER 10.
RADICAL CONTEMPLATION

Apophatic Theology

Polar to kataphatic theology is apophatic theology—faith seeking to understand that God's mystery is always greater than we can conceive. This proposition is not limited to Christian theology. When the Upanishads say "neti, neti," they deny that God is really like any item of our human experience. The nirguna Brahman is ineffable, beyond anything the human tongue can utter. True, there is a Hindu kataphatic theology focused on the saguna Brahman. But the immensity of the Hindu ultimate overshadows the best Hindu theology, as it also overshadows the best Christian theology. When it does not, Christian theology has lost its contemplative soul.

Contemplation is one of two basic human activities through which I am venturing to summarize an actualization of Jesus' program. By *contemplation*, basically, I mean *attention to God as God*. We shall deal with prayer and religious study, two species of contemplation, momentarily. Here I want to stress the negative, apophatic dimension which all attention to God as God should bring to the fore. Our American culture is not good at contemplation, partly because it seldom lets the mind or spirit remain still. However, the mind or spirit must be still if we are to appreciate God's no-thing-ness, the full Mystery that is reality of an order different from things. We Americans tend to stuff our minds as we stuff our stomachs and our family rooms. We sense that a lean and hungry look can be murderous, but we fail to notice the appearance of most Olympic runners.

Apophatic theology is lean religion for those in shape. It can develop in good times or bad, but bad times seem more likely to bring forth its wisdoms. The splendid moment in the sailboat, the time when a child falls asleep—these whisper of God's "more," but we seem more heedful of the whisper when it comes to us through suffering. So the steady drumbeat of Greek tragedy insisted that wisdom results from suffering. So apparently it was necessary for God to mount a cross in order to get his message through. The message has roots in the prophets: As the heavens are above the earth, so are God's ways above our ways. It took form in Christian wisdom literature: No one has ever seen God. It is the leitmotif of all history, biblical or supposedly profane: We do not grasp the big picture, cannot declare how the great patterns run.

This is the primordial reality about us. We are the beings cast into Being. Mystery is our milieu. We do not understand the universe—its origin, breadth, or destiny. We do not understand the atom—whence comes its explosive power. We do not understand life, which is much more than replication. We do not understand death, which practically defines our personal condition. And, perhaps even more puzzlingly, we usually avert ourselves from this so-central

nescience, fleeing the unknown whose acknowledgment would make us wise (like Socrates). In a culture
expert at distraction, we conspire to make our
knowledge, our libraries and computer printouts,
disguise this great embarrassment. Our conspiracy, of
course, is child's play. One cannot disguise the soul.
Now and then, even the most distracted of us, the
richest in busyness, call a halt to the overload. Now
and then even the most bovine of us stumble into a
moment of reflection.

It is our moments of reflection that give us our
specific difference. We are the animals who can
reflect. And latent in our reflection is a "universe," a
sense of "God," an uplift toward the whole. The
joyous quest begins when two acts of reflection link in
search of self-understanding. The divine drawing is the
peace, the gentle rightness that such linkage insin-
uates. Without neurosis, with stabilizing peace, the
quest-drawing opens our very center. The difference
between human health and human disease, Bergson
implied, is whether or not we let our centers open,
whether or not we let mystery be real.

God is not a thing. That is the baseline of apophatic
theology, the foundation of the deepest contemplation. For us, God must be no-thing-ness. "Things" are
definite and comprehensible, but God for us is
indefinite, mysterious. He or she or it cannot be
definite and really be God. A nonmysterious God is a
contradiction in terms.

A nonmysterious God is also a frustration in souls.
We are not made, finally, for things. We have a
foundation in matter, an at-homeness with things, but
at our core is the light, the openness, the hunger that
reaches out for more. The mysterious God is the More
we sense to be an All. He is the surplus, the totality that

we catch obliquely when we quiet our minds, still our imaginations, hush our wills, and simply abide. A touch of yoga, one lesson in mental discipline, and all our concepts, all our images, all our projects lose their unquestioned primacy. Deeper, more foundational, is the awareness, the pure consciousness, of the human being as spiritual.

God is the objective Other who draws the human being as spiritual. From the shadows and images of purely sensate life, as Plato pictured it, we must turn around toward the heavenly light. God is the great converter, the great turner-around. He supports our courage to say no to "things," to aspire after love. So God is the great master of apophatic theology. So no-thing-ness turns sweet only in the Spirit.

The Cloud of Unknowing

The Spirit has made apophatic, or negative, theology sweet for Eastern Christianity since the time of Dionysius (about 500). Through Dionysius' mystical theology, God's no-thing-ness became a staple of Eastern contemplation. His "On the Divine Names" influenced Thomas Aquinas in the thirteenth century: Aquinas' theology contains a strong conviction that we can never know what God is. And the sixteenth-century Spanish mystic John of the Cross taught a similarly negative version of God's otherness, which the devout soul learns through "dark nights" of the senses and the spirit.

Protestant theology has tended to distrust this Eastern Catholic tradition, since its uncritical use could devalue the biblical Word; Morton Kelsey speaks for a countervailing school of Christian prayer when he stresses the value of imagining God, of not letting the incarnational God or the senses-tied human personality dwell in darkness alone.[33] The imaginative depictions of Christ in Ignatius Loyola's *Spiritual Exercises* run to the same point, as do the simple gospel scenes that Christian piety has employed from the beginning. Negative contemplation therefore is far from the whole story when it comes to Christian prayer. Nonetheless, it is an important part of the story and perhaps the most challenging for today's uncontemplative American spirit.

One of the best examples of apophatic contemplation is the anonymous fourteenth-century English classic, *The Cloud of Unknowing*.[34] East and West, it has received great praise for its simplicity and depth. Moreover, its central image, the cloud, is a very helpful representation of the way God's no-thing-ness asserts itself, while its correlative stress on naked human love (as the best response to the cloud) is a nearly perfect translation of the Johannine *abiding*.

When theologians discuss God's presence, the reality of grace, the union between Christ and his members, and the like, they often get up a head of steam that takes them far away from the experience of lay people. "Where can I find all these marvelous realities?" the layperson often wants to ask. Well, we can find this marvelous reality of the union between Christ and his members in a Christian church any Sunday morning, for the bond the members have, the "reality" that gives meaning to their songs and prayers, is Christ, their leader. And you can find God present to your awareness, "there" in your head and your heart, as the no-thing that frames all the things you think about, all the things you love. To be sure, you must exercise some faith to find this no-thing and consider it significant, just as you must exercise some faith to identify the assembly of Christians at the corner church on Sunday morning with the grand union of the branches in the vine. Still, with faith, God's no-thingness can become suggestive, plausible, even helpful, as can the doctrine of the Mystical Body.

Faith, of course, is not limited to theological endeavors such as negative contemplation. The biology student who looks through a microscope to study paramecia first takes it on faith (from her instructor) that what initially is just a blur, and then (with the right focus) becomes a moving glob with funny parts, is significant. It is the same with a student who takes up the study of Chinese or a sinker who begins elementary swimming. We all start new activities—new explorations of meaning or new combinations of bodily motions—with an act of faith. The only difference with negative contemplation is that here we are asked to believe that what we do *not* see or hear or touch is real and significant. From Dionysius to the author of *The Cloud,* an esteemed line of teachers tell us that "*un*knowing," saying "*not* this" and "*not* that," can be an expressway to God.

For those with decent morals (those who have no grave problems with the ethical requirements of Christian life), a little mental discipline, and a taste for quiet rumination, God may well choose to appear as a clouding of the mind, a sort of blanketing or even stupifying of the reason, which calls our "normal" effort to focus sharply into question. This normal effort is analytic: We focus on parts, trying to break things down, because we have found that a good way to deal with material things or problems. Analysis, though, has limits, especially with persons. There are perceptions, wisdoms, that we grasp only when we correlate analysis with synthesis: efforts to let the whole, all of Sue or Tom, be a whole.

The analogy applies especially to God, because God is not a material thing or problem. God is rather a simple, partless, spiritual whole. When God impresses the divine reality upon us experientially, then, it is "more" than we can handle. Certainly we cannot handle it analytically, because to analyze is to shift attention from simple wholes to discrete parts. But we cannot even handle it synthetically, because the whole in this case is infinite, more than a normal gestalt. So God's real presence to us, the reality attributed to God by both the ontology of creation and the theology of grace, can be like a cloud that overshadows our minds, blocking out the sun, and so blocking out the clear light in which we "normally" see things. Thus dealing with God can be like flying through a series of clouds at thirty thousand feet. Initially, we tend to lose our orientation, our sense of up and down, left and right. The clouds are a wraparound reality, and so is God. Seamless, simple, surrounding, God confuses the analytic mind, upsets our mental business-as-usual. "The superficial mind will not do the job," the Spirit soon seems to whisper. "You must go beneath the mind, forget about images and ideas, accept my invitation to abide heart to heart, to concern yourself simply with loving."

Loving the Real God

The main obstacle that most people of contemplative inclination experience is distraction, being drawn away from loving God simply, opaquely, heart-to-heart. Our imaginations and intellects tend to sport on their own, seducing us away from a core concentration. To counter this tendency, The Cloud proposes a sort of Christian mantra. Slowly repeating a simple word that summarizes her own deepest affections, a

word such as *love* or *Christ* or *mercy*, the person drawn
to the cloud anchors her spirit in God. Sometimes it
helps to correlate the mantra with the intake and
outflow of one's breathing. At other times one can ride
it upward toward God, as though it were a tiny chariot.
The key is that one should become convinced that
simply loving, simply abiding, is worthwhile. *The
Cloud* goes out of its way to assure the reader that it is
much more than worthwhile. The anonymous author
thinks that it is the best thing one can do, both for
one's own sanctity and for the wellbeing of others.[35]

How can this be so? It can be so because of the
Spirit's operation in the believer's depths. When Paul
speaks of the Spirit's movement in our prayer with
sighs too deep for words (Rom 8:26), he tips us off to
the core integrity which the Spirit wants to reform.
When John of the Cross and other mystics discuss the
ultimate significance of "infused contemplation"
(mysticism strictly so-called, through which the person
experiences God's touch or speech), they speak of a
transformation of the deepest personality. The dark
nights entailed by deeper prayer are the shifts
necessary for a thoroughgoing conversion, similar to
the prophet's prayer that God remove his heart of
stone and replace it with a heart of flesh. God would
transform us through the Spirit's action so that her
grace, her presence, her love became truly real for us.
She would have the Spirit burn away our inclination to
disorder and aberrant sensuality by recentering us in
the divine Mystery. The most direct way to accomplish
these variants of conversion, or reconstitution, the
apophatic contemplatives say, is to open one's heart to
the spirit, to abide docilely in the cloud.

Moreover, abiding in the cloud, with or without the
use of a Christian mantra, is significant socially, if the

doctrine of the vine and the branches is true. By another of the paradoxes that stamp the deepest spiritual life, closer union with God does not diminish our relations with other people, but enhances them. We move closer to our neighbors, friends, and spouses when our relations with them are rooted more profoundly in God. When we have more of the mind of Christ, our prayer, including our petition on behalf of others, can be more effective. When we have more of the love of Christ, our service can be more effective. We receive the mind of Christ and the love of Christ most directly when we open ourselves to God's present mystery, God's self-offer in grace. Perhaps we can best understand apophatic contemplation as simply this opening, this abiding with empty hands. It is like the moment in romantic love when words would distract from the lovers' bond. The lovers' bond is the union of their hearts, their whole selves. They feel united *cor ad cor*. To rise from this depth to the more superficial level of the mind and the word would be to thin the sharing.

Another analogy for the sort of loving that is the core of Christian contemplative prayer is sexual intercourse. When two people make love, they communicate in a wraparound, holistic way. Their words are only part of the complete self-gift they offer and receive. The comprehensive "word" of their sexual self-donation is simpler, more integral, than that created by speech, however poetic or truthful. This is not to say that human love does not need verbal communication. It is merely to say that the attunement, understanding, and union of sexual love can be deeper and more comprehensive than verbal communication.

So too with God's romancing of our hearts. We can use words and thoughts. At times we must use words and thoughts. But there is a "rounder," deeper, simpler, more inclusive kind of loving for which the soul seems increasingly to hunger. There is a being-with, a sharing, akin to the embraces and losses of self that occur in sexual love. Now and then contemplative prayer may be orgasmic, moving the contemplative to utter fulfillment, but its more usual achievement, for the majority who are not at the level of infused contemplation, is a quiet nurturing, a humble pacification and enjoyment. The psalmist speaks of thirsting for God as the deer thirsts for water. Contemplative prayer slakes this soul-thirst. In it, the Spirit nourishes the human spirit, offering that for which our hearts, our core selves, have been yearning. In Johannine terms, the soul drinks of Christ's living water.

None of this makes complete sense, of course, to one who has not experienced it. Only those who give contemplation a try will have the basis for evaluating it. But for those who have not given it a try or who are little inclined to give it a try, let me propose a few other analogies. For example, aesthetic and naturalist experiences also can be close to religious contemplation. The person rapt in admiration of a great painting or piece of sculpture loses himself, is one in spirit with the piece of art, in a way akin to the religious contemplative's loss and union. It is the same with the person lost in a natural scene, a view of the sea, the mountains, or the desert. The spring winds that blow the green Kansas grasses can stir the soul, bringing a rush of joy, a call to drop one's worries and simply participate, simply abide with the beauty of it all. A good preacher would lean a little on these analogies to show the similarity to the spiritual dynamics of religious contemplation, and so clarify its "naturalness."

The Study of God

Contemplative prayer spotlights the heart, trafficking in exchanges of love. Are there cognates for study, contemplative convictions and methods to spotlight the mind? It seems to me there are and that their gist is the value of reflective understanding, of meditative study and rumination. For, complementary to research and direct understanding *(formulating hypotheses to organize the data of the research),* there is a return of the student to himself that points toward an intellectualist contemplation.

Most of the wisdom-regimes of the world's great traditions have fostered this sort of study. Buddhist meditation and Taoist "fasting of the spirit" conjure it, as do the more affective sections of the Talmud (for example, the *Pirke Avoth*). In each case, the accent is not informational or quantitative, but qualitative. In each case, one senses that the purpose of the student is not so much to master the matter as to be mastered by it. So, for instance, students used to turn to the Greek classics, the tragedians and philosophers, in order to be drawn to the depth of an Aeschylus, taken to the heights of a Plato. A "classic" was a text never out of date, because it was always more humane than the callow student who encountered it for the first (or maybe even the tenth) time.

Christians often have read their Scriptures and master theologians in this way—as classics. Thus the *lectio divina* of the medievals was a slow, reflective use of esteemed texts, in which the stress was not on information, but savor. The reader ruminated *(chewed over)* the text, letting it feed her whole spirit—intellect and will, imagination and emotion. She considered it cleansing nourishment, new eyes to see with, new ears with which to hear. In contrast to the distanced relationship of a "scientific" approach, the religious reader dealt with the text intersubjectively as the voice of an authority, inviting dialogue. In contrast to the "hermeneutic of suspicion" recently in vogue, the religious reader offered the text a willing spirit, a favorable prejudice.

Consider, for instance, a classic such as *The Imitation of Christ,* which reflects the dour mentality of the early fifteenth century when the bubonic plagues were never far away. It strikes a modern as unbearably grim. But suppose we grant it a certain suspension of disbelief. In the maneuvering space of that grant, something of Thomas a Kempis' depth, his appreciation of the tragic side of Christian life, can begin to impress itself. Easy as it might be to mock such sentiments as "seldom have I left my cell without coming back less a man," we can find ourselves taking another look at distraction, making another estimate of the many vanities to which we all are prone. We may even go so far as to ask ourselves the question that is really important: How might death make *me* more serious and "efficient"?

No doubt, reading in this way, studying with this accent on personal implications, nourishment, and savor has its dangers. The great edifice of recent "critical" research rises up to argue for at least a complementary side. A full study of anything, including documents about God, should provide for exact analysis, rigorous logic, and wide information. But in the great religious traditions' final view of things, information, analysis, and logic are still preliminary, still only *propaedeutica.* They are but half of study. To pass on to the wisdom portion of study, one needs to reflect on the self that studies—its prejudices and needs—as well as on the human spirit that undergirds all study, the human capacity to know. Finally, one also should estimate the "universe" that ripples out from a judgment about any part of our manifestly inter-related, processive reality, about the whole that the human spirit anticipates. And as one undertakes this second part of the student's task, one finds that the depths of the mind are not far from the depths of contemplative prayer. For the depths of the mind, too, inculcate silence before the mystery of being.

Erik Erikson has discussed the "virtues" needed by the human personality at different stages in the life cycle, and the virtue, or strength, which he finds requisite for the last stage, is wisdom.[36] Eriksonian wisdom is the ability to love life in face of death. Christian wisdom could be much the same. In virtue of Christ's cross (Paul's candidate for Christian wisdom), the believer studies a life that is headed for the grave without blanching. In pursuit of the Christian God, he has nourished his soul on texts such as Paul's to the point that death has become bearable and life lovely.

Such a study will not be all wine and roses. Before long, the serious student of God will find that the best texts study the student, estimate his stature. Indeed, they find him wanting, and so they demand that he change, that he be converted to a deeper level of honesty. That is part of the "pruning" that John's Gospel says the branches are sure to need. It is a Christian version of the classical insight that wisdom comes through suffering. If the student cooperates, however, he can come to a knowledge of God far beyond that furnished by the exegesis of texts and the analysis of doctrines. Through a study of God that is directed by God, a study in which the Spirit is teacher and master, the student can come to know mystery intimately.

So theology, the study of God, has more levels and possibilities than most academic beginners realize. The greatest Christian theologians, the church Fathers and doctors, have combined erudition with hard-won personal wisdom. They have grown balanced, judicious, and prudent; a few have won a sense of humor; but they all have ended by offering their deeper mind, their reflective intellect, to God, the great Mystery. They all have opened to a love that fulfilled reason by grace.

Ecumenical Implications

What might radical contemplation in deep prayer and study offer the ecumenical theology of love of God? Has it significant implications for the sharing of Protestant prophecy, Catholic wisdom, and Orthodox worship? You will not be surprised to learn that I think it has. In my view, radical contemplation could induce all the churches to be more obedient to Christ's first command. It could enhance all their efforts, alone or together, to love God with whole mind, heart, soul, and strength.

This is so because radical contemplation but summarizes our deepest efforts to attend to God as God. It but summarizes our deepest responses to the central Christian proposition that God is in our midst as a good Father, a saving Son, a teaching Spirit. None of the traditions is so prosperous at present that it need not review its attention to God as God. Neither Protestant, Catholic, nor Orthodox is so distinguished for depth, for absorption with the true mysterious God that it can ignore a contemplative call to conversion.

For example, the sovereignty of God that bulked so large in Calvinist theology, furnishing Protestant prophecy an almost awesome backdrop, awaits persuasive translations for our day. The acids of modernity have eaten away much of the splendor that the Word of God used to bear, as they have eaten away much of the allure of the Kingdom. We are not likely to neutralize the acids of modernity, however, unless we undercut the superficial mind that makes analytic, or functional, reason supreme. We will make persuasive translations of the master concepts of biblical faith only if we view them as words addressed to the ground of the human soul. For it is only at the ground of the soul that we may hope to find a reality credibly associated with God that we might proclaim sovereign for our time. It is only a word cutting to such joint and marrow that could bear the Kingdom to our contemporaries. In my view, radical contemplation is the best path to the ground of the soul, the human joint and marrow. It is the best path that the voice from the whirlwind and the small still voice could create in our day, too—a *kairos,* a time of special opportunity.

Protestants, then, would do well to supplement their praiseworthy immersion in the new hermeneutical disciplines with a retrieval of the contemplative outlooks used by Origen and Augustine. They would do well to remind themselves that Luther and Calvin, Wesley and Williams, ruminated on God's Word. They would also do well to consider the Catholic experiences with *lectio divina* and infused contemplation, the Orthodox experiences with mystagogy and negative theology. Assuming that these other traditions have received God's grace and that today's unifying world demands a unifying church, Protestants could use Catholic and Orthodox species of contemplation to round out their particular genius, finally protesting any love of God less whole than the whole Christ says it might be.

Catholics are under similar imperatives. As they move into a contemporary, modern, or postmodern intellectual horizon, Catholics must remember not to lose their holistic wisdoms of the past. They have been the people of both/and, but they need to renovate their balances today in the face of demands for a message of both greater interiority and greater social justice. This renovation does not require the launching of new movements as much it as requires the encouraging of the spiritual and liberation theologies now beginning to catch fire. Greater contact with Orthodox sources would offer more fuel for Catholic spirituality, and greater contact with Protestant sources would advance a biblically based theology of liberation.

Moreover, Orthodoxy still needs to remind Roman Catholicism that the church is much more a matter of the Spirit than of human laws, and Protestantism still should remind Roman Catholicism that the work of lay people is often the leading edge of church prophecy, the place where the action (rather than just the talk) is often occurring most dramatically, sundering structures that are resistant to God and attempting to build a city of peace.

Orthodoxy, rich in contemplative worship, needs better scholarship and greater industry. It has yet to come to grips with modern secularity, and it will waste a lot of energy if it ignores the recent Protestant and Catholic experiences and insists on reinventing the wheel. Both Protestantism and Roman Catholicism now offer Orthodoxy a more evolutionary view of Christian *tradition,* and the effort of both to draw resources from Orthodox spirituality for a radical Christian contemplation in the twenty-first century would be very instructive. Further dialogue—how to read Scripture, how to find God in all things, how to coordinate the kataphatic and apophatic theologies—would force all the traditions to face the *simplicity* that radical contemplation now urges upon the Church ecumenic.

That is the final burden of my preachment. Radical contemplation urges the Church ecumenic to dig deeper, so as to better render the one thing necessary, the pearl of great price. In terms of the first commandment, the one thing necessary (for our peace) is passionate openness to God. The pearl of great price is a populace with open souls, a populace in joyous quest for God's Word, God's wisdom, God's praise. We have reasons on all sides to believe that God's drawing, God's prevenience of our joyous quest, is available. Christ is with us all days, even unto the consummation of the world. Were the churches to attend to Christ radically, and to his Father and Spirit, they would find their center of unity, the really significant rung in the "hierarchy of truths."[37] Putting other things aside, they could act on this de facto unity and make the church one again. So radical contemplation, profound love of God, asks us to be deep enough, simple enough to find the ways we already are one.

# 3/ LOVING NEIGHBOR

We make the transition from loving God to loving our neighbor by studying the notion of community. Just as deep contemplation might induce the Christian churches to discover the de facto unity they have in the divine life, so a deep "politics" is most likely to emerge if, from the outset, we appreciate the theological dynamics of human communication.

In the view of Christian faith, the people most problematic in current human communication are the marginal, those whom the predominate patterns (of business, education, worship, and the like) shunt to the wayside. Liberation theology has done the church the service of recalling how central to Jesus' God the politically marginal are, and our study of this aspect of a Christian social theory is largely an elaboration of liberationist views.

Today, however, we must place the marginal and all the other problems of a Christian ecumenical theology in a global perspective. Increasingly, the 4.5 billion of us human beings share a single small planet. Increasingly, even the most remote "they" turn out to be much the same as "we." Few events bring this home more powerfully than the current ecological crisis, which we shall either solve as a united race or repent from a common grave.

In the same way, the global future calls our race to a unified economy, and this call is especially bound to challenge us of the affluent West. Future love of neighbor therefore is likely to entail considerable financial sacrifice, but only the naïve can believe that the Christian churches are now preparing their people to accept this sacrifice well.

So parallel to the call for conversion that sounds in any serious study of radical contemplation is the call to conversion that howls in any deep reflection on human sociability. A generous, obedient response to Christ's second command therefore emerges as a very radical politics, a very far-reaching effort to treat our neighbors as ourselves.

CHAPTER 11. *COMMUNITY*

Significant Others

The love of neighbor as self is a radical, root-seeking enterprise. When Jesus illustrated it through the parable of the good Samaritan (Lk 10:30-37), he assaulted the assumptions of his Jewish contemporaries. Mercy toward any human being in dire straits was to mean more than did the sacrifices of formal religion. When the Son of man returned to pass judgment, he would render his verdicts in terms of how we had treated the hungry, the thirsty, the naked, the stranger, the sick, the imprisoned (Mt 25:31-46).

Needy humanity therefore was a principal object of Jesus' love, a principal target of Jesus' religion. His program of love for God and love for neighbor undercut such superficial distinctions as race or religion and went to the heart of our human situation. By sharing creaturehood and suffering, all human beings were more alike than unlike. They were more to be pitied, helped, and ministered to than feared, scorned, or left on their own.

Obviously there are countless implications—political, economic, educational—panting to break out of Jesus' not-so-simple parable. We shall examine some of these implications in due course. To begin, though, we do well to ask about the psychology that Jesus seems to assume. What does his teaching propose that we should have in our heads and hearts when we look at the rest of humanity, at our neighbors both near and far? In the jargon of recent social psychology, Jesus' teaching seems to propose that we consider all other human beings as at least potential "significant others." Any person who wears skin like ours, has blood and bones like ours is at least latently a friend, a comrade, one who can make a claim on us.

That is the obvious message of the good Samaritan. Disregarding the fact that the man who had fallen among thieves was not one of his Samaritan kin, the good journeyman considered only the victim's needs. He was moved to compassion, sharing the victim's pain and plight. He was moved to action, converting his tender emotions into deeds. Finally, he was moved to generosity, spending his resources on the victim without guarantee of recompense. Brotherhood, solidarity, co-humanity weighed more than worldly calculations. The act of compassion was primordial, justified by its own doing more than by inference to a deeper principle. The Samaritan sensed that he, a fellow traveler, was equally vulnerable to thieves, and he knew what he would want a passerby to do for him, should he ever fall victim. So he treated the battered unfortunate as he would have wanted some one else to treat him. Without a lot of fuss, he loved the victim as he loved himself.

Our society now is such that we have Good Samaritan laws guarding our spontaneity against charges of culpability and neighborly malpractice. No doubt these laws have merit, but it is hard not to see in them a reflection of a deep soul-sickness. After two thousand years, we have not penetrated the humanity hidden in Jesus' brief parable. All our churches and all our scholars have not gotten Jesus' message across. So we do not do unto others as we would have them do unto us. So we let the Golden Rule mottle and tarnish. Again and again we hear that charity begins at home, that we must look out for number one. Again and again our children go on the sour sauce, hearing that few others are significant.

For years I have been both amused and alienated by ethicians and moral theologians who also seem unable to grasp Jesus' simple rules for social prosperity. Of course they are right to impress upon us the complexity of modern life, the many ramifications of our choices in medical issues, economic issues, and national defense, national security. They are even right to build up the muscles of our minds by exercising us in deontology, teleology, axiology, and their other rare Hellenes. But they are wrong to have helped us to encounter so much experience and miss so much meaning. They are wrong to have so complicated the heart of the Christian matter. By not contemplating to complement their analytic reason, they have missed the deep direction offered by Jesus' "as yourself." By not acting to complete their weighty prescriptions, they have missed the good effects "as yourself" inevitably bring. I know that "as yourself" begs further analysis and precision. I know that one person's "inevitable" is another person's "possible." Yet I remain amused and alienated.

We are limited creatures. Our stores of energy, money, feeling, and knowledge are not great. It is not practical for us to succor every hobo. We would go blind were we to shed tears at every tragedy. But the conclusion to be drawn from these realistic statements is neither a politics of nonentitlement nor a theology of lowered expectations. The conclusion to be drawn is a politics of well-structured, well-institutionalized compassion and a theology of radical human equality, of profound love for one another in God, our center. As always, our ignorance and sin cause us to miss these high watermarks. Even the Christian churches do not love one another. But that must not obscure Jesus' plain message. For Jesus, every man and woman was a very significant other.

Sharing Symbols

Cultural anthropologists who probe the qualities that hold communities together recently have had a field day with religious symbols. Clifford Geertz, for example, has come to see religious symbols as the primary way a society speaks to itself about its situation in the world, and in his tour de force on the Balinese cockfight, Geertz shows how thick and matted such religious symbols can become.[1] Traditional societies developed immensely complicated symbol systems through which they communicated great subtlety and nuance. Only as a result of the study of such societies are we beginning to realize the complexity of our own (supposedly nontraditional) society's symbol systems. Thus our understanding today of the many civil functions of religion gives the lie to any *simpliste* notion that we Americans do our civic business as a purely secular affair (because our Constitution provides for the separation of church and state).

Be this as it may, the current interest in symbols for

Christian reflection on community could be significant. Alerted by the anthropologists, we might now ask, What vehicles carry the common meaning necessary to knit a body of Christian believers together? What myths, rites, images, and notions would best symbolize the common creed of Jesus' disciples tomorrow? The logical answer, in terms of the ecumenical theology we are developing here, is found in the cluster of symbols compacted into the Incarnation. At least on the first level, the Christian carriers of meaning should be symbols that spotlight the humanity of God. For it is but tradition and orthodoxy that insist that the divine Word took flesh in Jesus of Nazareth, that insist that his human name is the one through which we are saved.

The first extension of such an incarnational theology might look to Jesus' cross. When historians of religion write their books comparing the world's great traditions, they frequently represent each tradition by one of its self-chosen symbols. Thus they may represent Buddhism by a wheel or a lotus, Judaism by a star of David or a scroll of Torah. More often than not, their symbol for Christianity is a cross. Perhaps due to the influence of Constantine, who is supposed to have seen a vision of a cross accompanied by the words "in this sign you will conquer," the cross has come to stand for (the irony at the center of) a Christianity expanded to the ends of the earth.

So the consummate failure of Jesus the man, his rejection by his own people and his ignominious end, now parades forth brazenly (because of the resurrection). The crucifix, which can be abhorrent to refined pagan taste, symbolizes the distance of God's ways from even refined paganism (and suggests the malice that refined paganism may carry, almost unaware).

With arms outstretched, making the universal appeal of a great mandala, Jesus speaks from the cross of God's suffering love. At the least, this is a peculiar symbol around which to structure a human communication and community.

At the most, the cross is a scandal, an affront to the way most of us spontaneously do our clustering. For spontaneously, most of us run toward pride and pelf, might and money. It is the beautiful people whom we spontaneously put in the captain's chair—the winners and charismatics. As a matter of history, though, these symbols seem to have welded few communities permanently. Certainly they have been the major ways we have represented success, life at the top, but so few of our societies have burned very long or shed a very noble light that our predilection for money and power is more the condemnation of money and power than their recommendation.[2] So, certainly relatedly, the presidential ball, the papal coronation, and most of our other installation ceremonies stand rebuffed by Jesus' cross. "It is what you do about human suffering," Jesus says, "that is the index of your social accomplishment. It is how you understand neighborliness—above all, its moments of pain."

Once again, therefore, Jesus' program cuts more deeply than most of us like. By the cross, it spotlights the other's right to be treated like a self. The gathering symbol of a community that calls itself Christian must be human flesh, bruised like that of Christ on the cross. It cannot be the secular good life, the weekends made for Michelob. By this criterion, most of us turn out to be heretics, unwilling to confess Jesus' flesh. In practice, we do not believe that human existence, spirit in the world, is the nodal point of divine revelation. When orthodoxy says that Jesus reveals both divinity and a godlike humanity, we look in other directions. "The Word only seemed to take flesh in Jesus," we half-say to our half-selves and half-neighbors. "God can't expect us to take the cross seriously."

So we do not cluster especially well, and we do not have a sign with which we are conquering. We do not generate world-winning compassion, and we do not stop the ongoing crucifixion by war. Yet in almost any Christian meeting place, a cross or crucifix hangs near the center. In almost any Christian creed, crucifixion follows Jesus' suffering under Pilate. So we share a great symbol of mercy and reconciliation, but not very well. So we are one in the central symbolic matter, but not very well.

War

In any short narrative of human history, war emerges as a major form of crucifixion. Across the plains of the oldest civilizations, the advance and repulse of the conqueror has been a major preoccupation. Nor have we outgrown this preoccupation today. On the contrary, new courses such as that embarked upon by the United States in November of 1980 have proposed that military matters top the list of our national agendas. That the money for such shifts in priorities would come largely from programs directed toward the poor suggests their contra-Christian import. It would not be hard to symbolize the new motif as beating our food stamps into swords.

For the human community at large, war is the constant threat that cripples communication and unification. As long as might still threatens to make right, no nation can rest secure. The recent record of the Christian churches seems to me admirable on this point, perhaps the area where they deserve greatest praise. Despite the jingoism of some civil religionists and the valid criticism that many of the churches could do more, it is important that church leaders across the spectrum of Protestantism, Catholicism, and Orthodoxy have spoken eloquently against war. Recognizing the profound threat of nuclear devastation, they have clarified the proposition that a just war is hard to find. Apart from the case of a Hitler or a Pol Pot, negotiation is obviously the better option. Lately I find myself musing about some elementary consequences that might spin off from the current Christian opposition to war.

First, there is a seemingly abstruse, but actually quite practical question from the theology of grace. How are we to regard our neighbors, our fellow-citizens in the world community? Are we to consider them only a step removed from the jungle, driven by evil passions of which they quickly lose control? Or are we to consider them generally benevolent—generally eager, rather than reluctant, to do what is right? Related, of course, is the question, How are we to regard ourselves? Are we, the selves whom we usually love rather dearly, attracted more by darkness, or by light? These questions are somewhat knotted historically and speculatively, with Protestants and Catholics (to speak only of the Western tangle) tending to take different sides. My interest here is more practical than speculative, however, so I see little point in rehashing past polemics. Let me rather use my space to argue for a hopeful, rather than a hopeless view of human nature.

In my sense of human psychology, people are attracted only by something they consider good. They may be mistaken in their consideration, but rarely if ever do they pursue negativity or evil as such. So a man steals money from his employer—not for the sake of being a criminal, but for the sake of paying his bills, or living more luxuriously, or redressing some real or supposed injury. It is the same with nations that go to war. They seldom desire the carnage of war for itself. Normally, it is the desire for more land, or more power, or restored honor that starts their military engines. The wellsprings of human action, then, incline most of us to conceive our lifetime as a series of opportunities to pursue things or projects that attract us by their goodness. In principle, by basic disposition, we usually are open to an appeal cast in terms of the pursuit of (a better, or deeper, or more handsome) good.

Were we to use this simple but significant psychology to guide our education, politics, and diplomacy, we might be able to display some of the wisdom with which a balanced Christian view of human nature (affected by sin but more affected by grace) should be filled. For such a view could make our first word, our initial posture, positive, inviting, and eager to persuade. Plato told us long ago that we would obtain decent political life, good community in the polis, only if we became powerful in *peitho,* persuasion. It seems to me that history and daily experience have proved Plato completely right. Fear, compulsion, and riding roughshod have built little lasting community. Cooperation that is grudging slips away when first it can. But by treating others as equal to ourselves (with some awareness of the massive changes this could entail), we might remove politics and diplomacy from the shadows of missiles and tanks, and into the light of plain speech and fair-dealing.

I do not consider this a utopian proposal. I consider it an alternative to the present pattern among nations, which seems to me dysfunctional, and their present (theological) anthropology, which seems to me graceless. Perhaps it will help to illustrate the realism I think the proposal could carry if I further suggest that the United States does need a strong military defense, because there are objective evils lurking on the horizon; and that the best way to obtain a strong military defense with which good Christians could live would be to work toward a nationwide draft.

The notion behind this suggestion is that if national defense were to become the business of all of us, a matter of our entire national community, its purpose might become more hopeful, more rooted in common sense. My draft would include women, for biology and history have conspired to make them the consummate peacemakers. It would include young and old, in the hope that they would play complementary parts. Rich people would have no more right to exemption than the poor. Peoples of color would not find themselves the only cannon fodder. War and defense, holocaust and peace, would touch all of us directly. There would be no dictatorship by a corps of specialists whose humane training, philosophical assumptions, and sense of the common good were open to serious doubt. With such a broadly based militia, our country would have many more resources for its defense, and so perhaps a more trustworthy national security.

The Art of the Possible

Many people who read the foregoing approach to questions of war and peace will be tempted to ask, Is national security possible on such a hopeful basis? In my view of Christian grace and ground-level politics, the more cogent question is whether national security is possible on any basis not so hopeful. Hope, after all, is the virtue that orients us toward the future. It is the strength to expect good things from the times to come. For Christian tradition, hope is a theological virtue, like faith and charity. Because of Jesus, the Christian considers future time a friend rather than an enemy. When people communicate on such a basis, believing that the future really can prove to be better than the past, they cast out lines of mutual invitation. "Come, let us reason together," their invitations read. With a little favoring wind, such invitations soon can become lines of mutual support. That is how communities start to build—from cells of mutual support.

One of the many social problems in our world today results from our frequent failure to develop cells of mutual support. At the elementary levels of social dealing, many of the world's citizens lack an effective community. The West has seen an evolution from the extended to the nuclear family, and then the explosion of many nuclear families—through divorce, generation gaps, and the pursuit of aloneness. The flight to urban and suburban centers has placed many people in circumstances in which they feel anonymous. The person who belongs to an effective neighborhood or church circle is fortunate indeed.

All the more significant, then, is the rise in Latin America of *comunidades de base*—grass-roots ecclesial communities.[3] In the midst of their growing consciousness of faith's political implications, many Latin Americans have begun to come together in small groups to celebrate the Eucharist, discuss their faith, support one another in a common struggle, and share their individual resources.

What is the art that makes a basic Christian community possible? Mainly, it seems to be the evocation of a common hope. In the Latin American case, the hope is that solidarity in faith can prove stronger than the violence of so many countries' military juntas. People "disappear" (in staggering numbers) when they oppose such juntas, and only a profound hope leads their families and friends to believe they have not disappeared in vain. Some basic communities develop to the point where faith seems to demand political or even military action. Thus Ernesto Cardenal's circle of *campesinos* at Solentiname would furnish recruits to the Sandinistas, especially after Somoza, the Nicaraguan dictator, had destroyed the little church, the dispensary, library, and other facilities the *campesinos* had built. Such treatment of the poor embarrassed the government, as did the community's straightforward reading of the gospel.[4]

So military opposition is one action that becomes possible when a group gathers around the Christian proclamation. If the dominant power structures are evil, the gospel will raise opposition to them. Even when the dominant power structures are not evil to the Latin American degree, the gospel still tends to be countercultural. Thus North Americans united in effective church circles where they come to know others who are repulsed by their nation's foreign policies find themselves voting, writing, and speaking out against the prevailing tides. In this way many North American Christians have protested United States' policies toward El Salvador, Guatemala, and other troubled spots. "Business and the military have conspired there," many of these critics say, "to stain our hands with blood."[5] Stanley Rother was a quiet peaceable man, brought to such prophecy by what he saw day after day in Guatemala.

It is possible, then, that grass-roots communities will spawn grass-roots oppositions. It is possible that people who come together under the sign of the cross will stand for the hope of the gospel, stand against the hope of mammon. The art of this possibility is awesome. Only the Spirit is skillful enough to make martyrs of people who do not have a martyr complex. Only a humble confession of faith, a humble opening to God, can lead to a humble struggle against the ungodly. Such a struggle is possible only if the Spirit roots people in something deeper than themselves, something quiet and immovable. When Alexsandr Solzhenitsyn received the Nobel Prize for literature, he spoke of such a something. "One word of truth shall outweigh the whole world," he said.[6] The peasant faith of old Russia, couched in wonderful proverbs, had ingrained this Johannine theology.

The light (of truth) has shone in our world, and the darkness of our world has never conquered it. All those who love truth come to the light, while all those who do evil avoid the light. The art of gathering basic Christian communities to celebrate God's powers and to oppose the powers of darkness is a function of light-loving, of truth-telling. It is a function of proclaiming God's Word of hope and freedom, which opposes the world's misanthropy, slavery, and mammon. God's Word tells us that it is not money, not power, not might, but divine light that rules creation—not joyless calculation, but hope. In Christ, as orthodox art portrays him, all things are possible. In Christ, all things are new.

The One and the Many

Community, we might say, is the new thing where the many of us who are limping after the light find fellowship. It is where our disparate forms of the joyous quest overlap, becoming cords that freely bind. In a genuine community, individuals become more themselves, not less. The sacrifices they make for the sake of common weal return to them tenfold. Why do we hope this could be so? Why should our desire to participate, cooperate, be part of a greater whole, pulse so strongly? A variety of answers spring to mind.

First, I suppose, there is something biological. Our physical life comes to us only as a participation in the much larger story of the entire human race—indeed, of the entire creation. The matter now in us belonged to others very recently. We participate in the genetic endowment of our parents, and they in turn are but the most recent representatives of a long bloodline. The seventeenth-century Christian missionaries who struggled to understand Chinese ancestor worship often came to grief at this point, because they missed the Chinese reverence for blood-lineage and history. In China, "clan" was a notion with sacral overtones, because human life resided in the midst of a sacral cosmos. The head of the imperial clan mediated the virtue *(te)* of the "way" *(tao)* that ran through everything. In miniature, the head of the local clan mediated *te* similarly. The Chinese realized that none of us exists, biologically, except as a clan member. We are each but a new bud of an ancestral trunk or branch. In our very matter, therefore, there are imprints of our participation. All our stuff suggests that we always have needed to belong.

Second, there are the psychological and sociological

variants on this theme. Whether or not there is such a thing as a collective unconscious, our dreams and our art demonstrate that our modern psyches run in (mythic) tracks as old as paleolithic hunting. Since before that time, each of us has become a human being only by participating in a given culture, and it was likely that human maturation would have misfired completely apart from the shared world of the tribe. Without language and tradition, none of us would even be able to say "I" now.

So participation is the constant presupposition of our psychic and social, as well as of our biological lives. To be is to be part of, participant in. This holds for our work and our love (Freud's two requisites for psychic health); it holds for our prayer and our politics (Carmody's two additions to Freud). Most of us work in an institution, or an office, or a factory. Those who do not—for example, the writer scribbling away at home— still usually participate in an extensive loop of the economy. Thus the solitary writer takes calls from or sends mail to agents, editors, and marketing people, who in turn deal with lawyers, printers, booksellers, and others (on her behalf). Somewhere a few hermits may still exist, all alone with only the All, but they are a rare, if not an endangered species.

Our loves and prayers and politics repeat the same message. Human love is relational. "Lover" is an other to whom we are bound romantically. "Child" is an other to whom we are bound parentally. We pray our love to God as part of a religious tradition and community, even when we man the prie-dieu alone. Our contemplation of "simple regard" never obviates our need to petition God's blessing on the President and the pope, the miscreant and the aunt still ailing.

Politics is an even easier instance. We need to be

polite to one another because we inhabit the same city-state. We need to be civil because we are all citizens. The tenant in the apartment complex needs to get along with the manager, or else his drain will stay clogged. The manager needs to get along with the tenants, or else his units will become empty. Even professional politicians participate in the ebbs and flows of public opinion. Distant as they may seem from their constituents, they are but an election away from potential unconstitution.

So we, though many, are one public body. Though living on many streets, we make one neighborhood. Though living in many neighborhoods, we make one city. And on and on, through the levels of the one state, geographic region, nation, continent, the one earth. We, though many, *are* one—one this, one that, one something else. Our being is being-with, our personal existence is communal.

As the Greek fathers said, though, we need to become what we are. In their case, we needed to become the immortal beings that God's grace had made us. In the several other cases we have noted, we need to become co-workers, conjugal lovers, "conspirators," associated citizens. In each instance the one struggling for faith is a blessed babe, a prince of peace. It is what Teilhard de Chardin called the hyperpersonal, a social reality that advances evolution to its highest stage.

For the Christian theology that sparked Teilhard's vision, such an omega point already exists in cosmic history. The commonality of cosmic history is such that the omega is also the alpha. The Body of Christ, in which the fullness of the Godhead dwells corporeally, is already the ideal unity that lures all plurality. It is already the basal one where the very many can find a common rest. That rest is not inert or ashen, as our senses perceive the grave—it is alert, coruscant, as apocalyptic faith perceives the saints before God's throne. There human togetherness is the ultimate reflection of God's triunity, of community par excellence.

CHAPTER 12. *THE MARGINAL*

Poverty

Among the most dismal reminders of our distance from God's perfect community is the great disparity in human wealth. Some people have incomes a hundred times those of other people. Some people want for nothing, while other people starve. We, though many, are one in having a body that needs food and clothing, a mind that needs education and employment. But chance and sin, both original and personal, have conspired to obscure this elemental equality. So it is now traditional that great disparities in wealth obtain among nations and among any one nation's citizenry. Advancing the point that Jesus made in the Sermon on the Mount, recent theologians have attacked this tradition and called for a new social conscience. In their eyes, the widespread poverty of the third and fourth worlds is the harbinger of a fierce judgment day. Because we have distributed the world's goods so unjustly, the just Judge will cast us into outer darkness, where there will be weeping and gnashing of teeth.

Peruvian liberation theologian Gustavo Gutierrez has spoken lately of the historical force of the poor, claiming that it is only when we view human rights from the standpoint of the poor that we see the entire issue correctly.[7] His claim is pressing. The great burden of Christian social teaching, which but expresses the implications of Christ's Body, falls on the side of the right of all people to the goods necessary for life. From the standpoint of the poor, it is incontrovertible that human rights begin with funda-mentals. The result is a base-line social theory in which no person has the right to luxuries as long as any person lacks necessities.

That seems a simple enough sketch, a mere entailment from the equality of the branches on the vine, until one reflects on the hindrances it throws in the path of human greed, or even today's business as usual. In the God's-eye view opened by Jesus' grace, it places great brackets around the superstructure of the developed world's economy. Until the lower quarter of the world's population is assured of necessities, the rest of us accept our superfluities at our moral peril.

I am attempting to move through these concepts rather dispassionately, avoiding lurid side trips to the ghetto or to ethical intimidation. As open to question as my results may be, my intent is cool contemplation. For faith, God is the author of the goods of the earth, even though humanity has husbanded the earth with labor and sweat. The goods of the earth are for all the earth's people, because all the earth's people are children of God. At least potentially, and often actually, one group of people is bonded to another like one branch to another.

Thus in the deepest and highest perspectives, the criteria we regularly use to differentiate people pale into secondary significance. Our bloodlines, our brains, our nationalities, our religions, even our personal virtues and industries matter less than the gratuities we receive, less than our common status as creatures sprung from nothingness and friends called to intimacy by grace. But with such a common status, surely the similarities in our material fortunes should outweigh the divergencies. With such a common status, surely we should agree to assure necessities to all before we accord luxuries to some. Can one seriously make a case that Jesus would sketch a contradictory scenario? Does the proposition that Jesus wants some people to gorge themselves and others to starve deserve a moment's serious consideration?

So the poor are always with us as an index of our waywardness. As long as the earth shows itself capable of supporting our (properly restrained) human numbers, the crushing poverty of any significant number of human beings is like the gimlet eye of a hanging judge. This is truer today than ever before, because today we are better equipped than ever before to feed the hungry and clothe the naked. The plains of North America alone could solve the mortal problem of the world's saddest 450 million:

> Raising the food intake of the over 450 million severely undernourished to the level of their nutritional requirements would involve the equivalent of 40-60 million tons of wheat per year. This is no more than 3-5% of present world cereal consumption, or 10-15% of the cereals now being fed to livestock in the developed countries.[8]

No wonder people of internationalized conscience are saying (of North American livestock), Let them eat grass.

Therefore, when one is brought today to the margins of life by one's poverty, one is right to call today's human arrangements, today's international economy and politics, rotten to the core. By blundering and selfishness, we (the international all of us) have refused to accept or to honor the co-humanity of all homines sapientes. Against rather patent facts of biology and theology, and against any conscience of the slightest elevation, we have pseudospeciated (to barbarize Erikson) and denied that Indians of Calcutta, Africans of drought-stricken areas, slum-dwellers in Brazil, and the wretched of the Phillipines are complete human beings. Why have we done this? Mainly because the acknowledgment that there is only one species of us, that all we featherless bipeds make up a single block, would have forced us to look critically at the status quo, which those whom the status quo most benefits have resolutely refused to do. By fiats or by silly references to an invisible hand, they have insisted on free markets, on laissez-faire economies, relegating to a footnote the great bulge this attitude has produced at the margins of decent human life.[9] Somehow, faith suspects, economists' footnotes are God's chapter headings.

Race

In one of the stories about the Reagan budget in the fall of 1981, a note gave the unemployment rate among black Americans as about 16 percent, which was almost twice the figure for whites. (The rate for black youths was down from its summer high of almost 50 percent, but it was still more than four times the rate for white adults.) In a nutshell, the American dream was continuing to be a nightmare for blacks. Despite praiseworthy progress on some fronts, the drift of the economic mainstream still placed blacks on the margins. To be born a person of color (brown, yellow, or red, as well as black) was to be born with a significant handicap. Lyndon Johnson's Great Society was being put to rest long before it had given blacks equal access to the national cornucopia.

Black theology has utilized economic patterns such as these, but usually as ancillary to its main meditations. Like the corroborating data from the political, educational, and military sectors of American culture, the economic figures on blacks invite a quest for deeper causes. Beneath the factors of poor job preparation, erosion of morale through welfare, malnutrition, crime, and drugs, the theologians (and psychiatrists) have found a more frightening pathology. It goes by the name racism and points to the segregation of a group of people from the human mainstream merely because of their skin color. For having a different pigmentation, a different quotient of melanin, people of color have been considered nonhuman by some. If ever one needed a gross specimen of irrationality, racism would certainly supply it. Shylock argued that he was human because if one cut him, he would bleed. That argument has been crucial for blacks since they first came to the United States as slaves in 1619, a year before the Pilgrims landed at Plymouth Rock.

Through the 1960s, blacks struggled with the issue of power, and their theologians were quick to set this struggle in the context of biblical liberation.[10] Like the Latin American theologians of liberation, blacks found a special place in God's plan for the poor. Though marginal to American society, the people of the black ghettos were somehow the apple of God's eye. If Christ on the cross said anything, they thought, he said that black suffering could not be in vain. A God willing to embrace human pain, willing to fight against history's evils, must take to heart the legions of hopeless black children, enduring black women, and humiliated black men. (From slave times to the present, the nearly systematic racism of United States' culture has devastated the black family.[11] In some cases this has pulled children and parents closer together. In many others, it has warped the lives of all the family members.)

The black church, however, has gained some distinction from these circumstances. As one of the few institutions that blacks alone controlled, it often has become a sort of extended family. Blacks themselves now debate the advantages and disadvantages of the otherworldly orientation often taken by the black church, but few analysts of any stripe deny that church's crucial role in helping its people ward off depression. Through preachings and songs with African roots, the church has kept alive a joyous heritage. It has prepared many blacks for distinguished careers in music, fostered a notable black eloquence, and stood with athletics as a prime place in American culture where black talent has been manifest. If people could sing and preach and form communities with such vibrancy, they must be human far beyond the capacity to bleed.

But a still more profound meaning has lain in black Americans' experience, and theologians such as Vincent Harding recently have begun to probe it.[12] Reflecting on the sufferings blacks have endured in the United States, they see the possibility that blacks now hold the key to a future American culture worthy of our founders' best visions. We are all amateur Americans, Harding says, inexpert at predicting our culture, yet loving its best potential. We all have promises to keep, miles to go before we sleep. As distinguished witnesses, blacks could staff a new corps of prophets, to tell us where America has most gone wrong and what such wrong-going elicits from biblical Christianity. In our culture, the suffering servant has been black. So have the persons most enslaved, despised, rejected, formed by sorrow, and acquainted with grief. Any American Christian theology faithful to the "kenosis" *(emptying)* of Philippians (2:5-11) will make a great deal of these historical and cultural facts.

Harding summarizes the positive outlook of such a theology:

> Reaching out beyond itself, reaching out beyond its oppressors, reaching out beyond the religion of its oppressors, our religion has caught up all of the great human experiences of scattering, of defeat, of trial and tribulation, of hope and ecstasy. . . . Men and women who have come through, who have created such a spiritual crucible in the struggle for a humanizing freedom, have both earned the right and created the responsibility to participate centrally in the making of a new America, in the search for a new vision.[13]

Sex

America's women form another group that lately has come to realize its marginalization. Many women now intuit that the pathologies of sexism are somewhat parallel to the pathologies of racism. Whereas racism castigates a group simply because of its color, sexism castigates a group simply because of its gender. Economically, for example, a woman who has worked in our culture in recent times has earned about 59¢ for each $1 earned by a man. Politically, religiously, and professionally, women constitute far less than 50 percent of those in power. Many women sense in men a deep fear and opposition, much like the feelings many blacks sense in whites.

Further, the abuse of women (beatings, rapes, degradations by prostitution and pornography) suggests that American sexuality harbors a deep sickness. In ways that often implicate the Christian churches, American men have grown up troubled in their sexuality, aberrant and angry in its undertow. Our Christian theology has not done a good job of blessing sexuality, of making it shine with the grace of the Incarnation. Women have been subjected to much pain as a result, and many feminists now consider Christianity their enemy. Because of woman's ambivalent image in Christian theology, they say, women have failed to gain a humanity equal to that of men; they have been marginalized despite their numerical advantages.

The marginalization of women, both in American culture and throughout the world, illustrates especially vividly the social losses that occur when any group is denied participation. Because women have not been able to contribute directly to sizable portions of American life, those portions have risked imbalance and unrealism. We have already alluded to the contribution women might make to a saner national defense. Parallel contributions to a saner high finance, technology, higher education, and theology of sex (love, marriage, parenting) are now aglimmering. In most cases, a heavier contribution from women would tilt the scales toward less conflict and greater concern for people. Without pushing any sexual stereotypes, I find that women are better at mediating conflict and at keeping human suffering in view. I find them keener in social intelligence and more given to cooperation.

Consequently, feminist politics, social theory, and ecclesiology also glimmer attractively on the horizon. If the insights carried by women's experiences were transferred from the margins to the center, we might begin to see a better balance of payments. This is not to canonize women, or to make them carry the hero's share of our country's or of our church's future burdens. It is simply to look hopefully beyond women's present sufferings, as Vincent Harding looked hopefully into the future for blacks.

In Jesus' time, women were marginal to the going channels of political and religious power. Yet Jesus went out of his way to associate with women, as he went out of his way to associate with the poor. What was marginal to the society of his time was not marginal to him. Like the poor (of whom, of course, they often were a large percentage), women had fewer of the stakes one must pull up in order to follow the gospel. With little profit from the status quo, they tended to be more open to change. That is often the case today. While fear and advantages (economic, social, psychological) incline some American women to conservatism, others see the ironies and sicknesses of American life with a very discerning eye. Dorothy Dinnerstein has drawn the psychology of such women's condition quite artfully.[14]

My own sympathies lie with feminists who desire an androgynous human future, rather than those who want a future that separates women from men. While I see much merit in the work of separatists such as Adrienne Rich and Mary Daly, their radical lesbianism seems to me doomed from the start.[15] They should have the right to their own sexual preference and the right to define some of the terms on which they will participate in the culture at large, but to turn solipsistic or misanthropic (sexist in reverse, we might say) will not solve our general sexual problems. Men and women are relational, defined in part by their difference from and orientation toward one another. So while the T-shirts and bumper stickers that proclaim "a woman without a man is like a fish without a bicycle" have their humor and bit of truth, they are not a full feminist philosophy. Two margins that never meet cannot compose a book of life, let alone a saucy bed and breakfast.

Ideally, Christians now would embrace the mainline feminists' ambitions and so give the extremists less credibility.[16] Ideally, the churches now would rush to redress their centuries of benign or malignant neglect and so shield Jesus from abuse he does not deserve. As with the city placed upon a hill, the church has the responsibility to dramatize the full freedom possible when the branches are healthy on the vine. It has the responsibility to show, in all the dimensions of its own life, that in Christ there is neither male nor female, neither free nor slave. Extending its own performance to the worlds of work and politics, the church might then have a persuasive list of amendments to hasten the day of equal rights for all. So a church leadership without women is like a fish with only one eye, a bicycle with only one wheel. It is not the humanity God made in Genesis; it is not male and female making one flesh.

The New Right

Poverty, race, and sex have cast a majority of Americans and many citizens of the full world to the margins of social prosperity. Who, then, are the people occupying the center? In the main, they are affluent, white, and male. In our culture, power still flows more to white males above the median income than to other social groups. For the world as a whole, white males of the northern hemisphere still broker most of the power. Some of these people criticize the current political and economic structures, of course, and argue for changes that would make them more humane. But others dig in their heels to defend the status quo and argue that the current structures reward those who should be rewarded. I find this argument marginal to the centrist stream of Christian social teaching, so I propose a closer examination of the group that tends to advance it.

As it happens, this group came into overt power in the United States at the time of the 1980 elections. With or without allegiance to a form of evangelical Christianity, the New Right agreed on laissez-faire politics and economics. Free enterprise was perhaps their favorite hymn; socialism was perhaps their topmost opponent. Both free enterprise and anti-socialism, they claimed, were ingredient in the American way, the American tradition. On this they may well be right. They are certainly wrong, however, when they go on to infer or assume, as many of them do, that this American tradition is Christian. And when the final capping point of their argument holds up spokesmen such as William F. Buckley, George Will, and James Kilpatrick as representing Christian realism, the New Right stands revealed as naked foolishness.

Jesus is as far from the bib-and-tucker capitalism of the rightist chic as he is from the grubby terrorism of Yasser Arafat.

The central problem of the rightist chic is its idolization of money. Contrary to the biblical notion that money is the root of (all) evil, the gilded capitalists make lucre their first sacrament. The reason is simple enough: Money is the open sesame to the good life they covet—the designer gowns, country club dinners, and tax-deductible hideaways. While a defensible conservatism would argue that we should preserve individual freedoms because they offer the best conditions for creativity and service, the members of the rightist chic seems to argue that the past is venerable because it has brought to prominence those most worthy of America's riches—namely, themselves. In the case of godless sophisticates for whom history and society are all, this argument makes a certain warped sense. If there is no Lord of history, it is not absurd that we should account one group more patrician than another, so we might as well exalt those who have clawed their way to the top. If the cathedrals stand empty of influence, we might as well worship on Wall Street. In the case of purportedly Christian rightists, the argument is patently Pharisaic. It is easier for a camel to pass through the eye of a needle than for such rightists to enter the kingdom of God.

You cannot enter the kingdom unless you love God with your whole mind, heart, soul, and strength. You cannot enter unless you love your neighbor as yourself. And if you follow these two commands, you will take on some likeness to Jesus, who wandered in his time as a countercultural outcast, with no place to lay his head. Because Jesus loved his Father passionately, he refused to be called good, let alone mover and shaker. Because he loved his neighbor as himself, he had to mount the cross. It is very hard to imagine Jesus bending down from the cross to listen intently to E. F. Hutton. It is very hard to imagine him pursuing a social policy of nonentitlement to distributive justice. The goods of Jesus' earth were for all the people of the earth. The burden of Jesus' ministrations was to give sight to the blind, heal the lame, cleanse the leper, and preach good news to the poor.

Finally, underneath Jesus' conservatism, his concern that not a jot or tittle of divine justice be lost, lay a view of human nature deeply at odds with the American tradition to which the New Right appeals. Jesus invited all people, without distinction, to respond to the grace of the Kingdom. Before God's overwhelmingly generous offer of love, each person stood needy and blessed. If God were willing to make this offer, if God were so good that he would promise a new creation, Jesus could only offer himself utterly. So while Jesus knew the worst instincts of human hearts, he put himself out for human beings, arguing by his self-spending that the Christian call is to human nature's better instincts, to its joyous quest for honesty and love. This argument runs directly counter to the pessimism of such influential Americans as Alexander Hamilton, James Madison, John Adams, and Abraham Lincoln.[17]

Hamilton, for instance, spoke in the seventy-eighth *Federalist Paper* of "the ordinary depravity of human nature" and "the folly and wickedness of mankind." Generalizing on similar statements from America's founding fathers, Sidney Mead, perhaps the dean of historians of American religion, has delivered himself of the opinion that "the insight of the founders that gives them the rank of genius was that such stability in government as humankind is capable of producing must rest on human self-interest or, in Christian terminology, sinfulness."[18] That may be genius in the horizon of "Enlightened" or deistic pessimism, but it is folly in the horizon of the resurrection. For Christian faith rooted in the resurrection, where sin has abounded, grace has abounded the more. Worse than folly, though, is the use to which many of the New Right put this distortion of Augustinian theology. Arguing that all people are evil, they sanction a perpetual state of civil war, run by the motto Look Out for Number One. The result is a parody of Jesus' teaching, with the Beatitudes coming to rest on the rich and powerful, who are honored as realistic and virtuous by the mere fact of their success in the civil war they stimulate.

The Peacemakers

In Jesus' lexicon, the blessed are not those who stimulate civil war for their own profit, but those who make peace. For this present discussion, we may define peacemaking as *reducing marginalization.* As David Hollenbach has argued, a primary tactic of those committed to Christian social justice (and, we might add, to the avoidance of global war) should be to champion the participation of marginalized groups and oppose the political orders that exclude them.[19] It also should be to translate, under the influence of Christian views on the equality of the branches on the vine, the insights of management theories such as "Z," in which participation is the crux, since from participation comes mutual trust, and from mutual trust come a dozen hindrances to war.[20] The peacemakers of the next global era therefore probably will be those who make sure that participation is practical, both politically and economically. They will be those who drag such bodies as the United Nations and the World Council of Churches kicking and screaming into effectiveness.

Admittedly, this is a great challenge, a tall order. Most nations, like most American citizens, are not so mature that they can think beyond their own immediate interests. James Fowler's sketch of the maturation of faith suggests that only the few who have reached stages five and six of faith are in a position to grasp and advance the ingredients of tomorrow's peacemaking.[21] For only those quite mature in their faith are able to handle the complex both/and character of actual human reality (stage five) and then transcend even this complexity to unite themselves with a God at work everywhere, a humanity valuable in all its forms (stage six). Fowler exemplifies his stage six with such people as Gandhi, Hammarskjöld, and Mother Teresa—all consummate peacemakers. Along with such fellow visionaries as Martin Luther King and Thomas Merton, they challenge the acquiescence of the rest of us in the injustices of the present orders. So we tend to be ambivalent about people of great faith, radical peacemakers, as the Israelites were ambivalent about their greatest prophets.

However, perhaps a few further reflections on mature, peacemaking faith will make it seem more practical and less threatening. Practically, I do not interpret Jesus' blessing on peacemakers as an unqualified endorsement of pacifism. Certainly Jesus thought that those who live by the sword will perish by the sword, and certainly he saw the ultimate futility of war and violence. Until human beings become persuaded, convinced in the roots of their souls, that war-making is stupid and doomed to failure, they will continue to run in vicious circles, attacking and counterattacking like Pavlovian dogs.

In the presence of people unconverted to this pacifist core, however, prudence dictates that one weigh the likely operations of evil soberly—all the more so when the potential enemy possesses weapons of massive destruction such as hydrogen bombs. In such cases, it seems to me, one must develop a flexible stereoscopic faith, as in Fowler's stage five (perhaps leaving the higher vision of stage six to saints and martyrs, whom God raises beyond human prudence). In other words, one must be able to say both (1) "We want peace, and we are going to do these peacemaking things" and (2) "If you attack us, we will make you wish you had not." I have been persuaded by Solzhenitsyn that not to add (2) to (1) would be to wander in a dreamworld.

Solzhenitsyn also has expressed some grim views on American spinelessness—for instance, in his commencement address at Harvard—but it seems that more Americans have taken offense at his words than have taken stock of them.[22] From his experiences in the dreaded Gulag Archipelago, he has learned that one cannot underestimate the soullessness of the Soviet regime. Again and again the Soviets have shown themselves to abhor the light because their deeds are evil. Indeed, the cause of their great wrath at Solzhenitsyn has been his publication of the truth, his insistence upon the light. Were we to take stock of his experience, it might teach us the tactic we most need for effective peacemaking.

In essence, that tactic is to do our own business in the light, so that we can stand global scrutiny, and to challenge the Soviets (or Marxists of other stripe) to do the same. The problem of our recent foreign policy has been that we ourselves have not been able to stand global scrutiny. Our actions in Vietnam, Latin America, and other parts of the world have too often been works of darkness. Our motives have too often been impure, directing our foreign policy toward the profit of our conglomerates or the increase of our military power, rather than toward international justice.

So, to be peacemakers, we shall need to change so as to be able to withstand the valid part of the Marxist critique (the thesis that a group's socioeconomic position shapes a great deal of its ideology). This is but a more sophisticated version of the ancient cui bono *(to whom does the advantage go?)*. When we can say to the Marxists, "Here is our program, and here are our motives. We place them before public scrutiny. Let's see you do the same," we shall be able to consider our politics Christian. Then if we must go to war, the chances are good that our cause will be just. Until then, we Americans will not clearly have separated ourselves from the rest of the world's evildoers.

CHAPTER 13. *ONE EARTH*

Spare Living

If American foreign policy began to do business in the light, it would quickly run into ecological issues. For beyond even the question of distributive justice, which asks whether all the members of the global community are receiving a fair share of the world's goods, is the question of the life-styles the earth can support in the decades ahead. We shall consider below some indications that the earth cannot support the present life-style of the United States, or of the northern nations generally. Here the best link from our foregoing reflections seems to be consideration of the changes that would occur in the average American's life-style, were we to begin to live in light of the current global situation—economic, political, and ecological. My thesis is that it would underscore the judgment John A. Ryan made more than fifty years ago: "The only life worth living is that in which one's cherished wants are few, simple, and noble."[23]

Ryan's judgment did not repose on the facts of ecological crisis and widespread malnutrition that stare us in the face today. It reposed on his understanding of religion, with special sensitivity to social justice. Religion in itself inculcates a certain spareness, a certain freedom from "things." When she adds a simple look at the deprivations suffered by so many of her neighbors, the religious person quickly realizes that loving them as herself amounts to a second inclination to spareness.

For example, monasticism, both Christian and Buddhist, always has entailed a commitment to poverty. Ideally, both Christian monk and Buddhist monk have led lives simple in food, clothing, and shelter, which they secured either by the labor of their own hands or by begging. Both have fasted the body, that the spirit might fatten. Both have sponsored works of charity, whether motivated by Christian love or by Buddhist *mahakaruna (great compassion)*. A perennial call of religion, then, East and West, has been to spareness.

If ever a people needed to heed that call, it is the Americans of the 1980s. Despite all our moaning about the decline in our standard of living, we in the American middle classes are more in danger of drowning in our possessions than of seriously suffering want. Nor is our need for spareness applicable only to our physical possessions. Many of us are in danger also of having our minds cluttered with irrelevant information, our imaginations overstimulated by pictures of luxury. It takes great spiritual discipline to live religiously in our time, but there is little in our churches and schools to inculcate spiritual discipline. As more homes become equipped with electronic gadgets, the need for great discipline will only grow. People who can play simulated war games, football, baseball, and golf, as well as watch movies twenty-four hours a day, will have to *choose*, if they want better occupations. But they are not likely so to choose unless they sense the danger in constant distraction, constant pursuit of fun. Finally, this in turn depends on their having a treasure—something that superficial living really does endanger.

The treasures endangered by superficial living and approached by radical contemplation and radical politics are God and human community. To answer God's prevenient grace and pursue a joyous quest, one must descend from the superficial to the profound. As long as one skates on the thin ice of the surface, one does not even know there are pearls of great price in the depths. Any significant suffering can crack the thin ice, as can any significant joy, but the affluence and good fortune we Americans enjoy are such that we can exist for years without being forced beneath the surface.

Three cheers, then, for the parents who limit their children's hours before the television set, who restrict their children's access to electronic games. Twenty-seven cheers (three cubed) for those who study with their children and teach them to pray. The best antidote for wasting time on superficialities is to have better things to do. Children who find study a joyous quest, family prayer a healing love, and hard exercise a way to energy will be relatively safe from the depredations of Madison Avenue and Silicone Valley.

To pursue human community and ecological survival in the twenty-first century, a similarly positive ascesis will be necessary. Children who learn to regard themselves as citizens of the world, members of an international community, may think twice about luxurious living. Children who have first-hand acquaintance with wilderness lands, or even with nature that is transformed by human technology, may think twice about pollution and conservation.

The spirituality I see beckoning to us from the twenty-first century is an interlocking set of such attitudes. It aspires to be a whole by linking such matters as diet, study, prayer, social service, exercise, and creative work. If one thinks regularly about these matters in a daily examination of conscience, one begins to realize that they are interconnected.[24] Slowly, one comes to see that it is schizophrenic to treat one's body differently from one's mind, one's colleague differently from the earth. Each such "neighbor" asks us to deal with it gently, nurturingly, with a love such as we ourselves crave. Each whispers that things will prosper best when we cooperate, listen as well as speak, and keep our wants few. So we find ourselves asking our bodies for good health, and we find them answering, "Give us fifteen miles a week of hard running." We find ourselves asking our minds to broaden and deepen our "reality," and we find them answering, "Give us an hour a day of study and prayer." Neither request entails much money or matériel. Nor do the parallel requests we will hear from other people and from the earth. All these relationships ask and encourage only a life that is simple, spare, beautiful, a freedom like that of the Christ and of the Buddha.

Asian Religion

Mention of the Buddha reminds us that we share this one earth with billions of people who are not Christian and who bring a different philosophy to bear on global problems such as pollution and malnutrition. Often these people have been formed by traditions that are in closer touch with nature than Christianity recently has been. Through local shamanic traditions or such diffuse systems as Hinduism, Buddhism, Confucianism, Taoism, and Shintoism, many people of the East have seen nature as an object of reverence, not mainly as something to be subdued and exploited. Thus some commentators on the ecological crisis, stressing the link between modern industrialization (a major source of the crisis) and the Western cultures with biblical roots, have argued that Christian anthropocentrism is the great ecological culprit.[25] Whether or not biblical religion should have sponsored an almost rapacious attitude toward nature, Westerners often have used it to justify their exploitation of natural resources. Thus the critique has enough bite to prompt honest Christians to reexamine their theology of nature and to open their ears to the preachings of other religious traditions.

The Asian traditions have by no means sponsored ecological paradises, but there is much in their experience that can complement the more anthropo-centric orientation of the West. For in general, all the traditions mentioned above have kept their people closer to nature, more immersed in the cosmological myth, than has biblical religion. The "cosmological myth" is the storied expression of an intuition that minerals, plants, animals, and human beings are but different forms of a single stuff. The universe therefore is a sort of continuum, a many-sided dispersement of a single substance, and at any point in the universe, the sacred power of ultimate reality (*mana* or *orenda*) can break out. This being so, nature deserves great respect, perhaps even more respect than human beings deserve. In certain strands of Japanese Bud-dhism, for instance, the ideal of a spontaneous union with the whole of reality, out of a deep sense of its oneness, has led to the exaltation of vegetative nature. Trees and plants just "are." Their being is simple, its perfection unstrained. By contrast, human nature is complicated, struggling, burdened with consciousness, reflection, and decision. This attitude is quite contrary to our typical Western outlook, which exalts consciousness, reflection, and decision. Logically enough, it leads to a better appreciation of subhuman nature than does our Western outlook. Indeed, it often leads to a close association of subhuman nature with divinity.

It is but a short step from this association to an outlook that is richly ecological. Thus Japanese Buddhism and Shintoism have joined in sponsoring the landscape gardens, tea ceremonies, flower arrangements, and other aesthetico-religious rituals that stress the graceful flow of all reality, the dance of all the elements on emptiness.[26] Despite the fact that Tokyo is as polluted as Los Angeles, this aesthetico-religious outlook has something important to teach us about the one earth. All creatures, great and small, do form a whole, an interconnected entirety. To change any one creature is to change many others. Thus the massive intrusions we human creatures have made into nature through our advanced technologies ripple throughout the rest of creation. The food chain, for instance, shows that our chemicals pass a great circuit: They leave our industrial plants to enter the rivers, and then the oceans, and then the plant life of the oceans, and then the fish—only to return to us in mother's milk. Surely the religious implication is that we are less exalted above nature than we may have thought, more intimately called to find God in subhuman creation.

The Jains and Hindus of India have expressed their

intuitions about the oneness of creation through the concept of ahimsa, *nonviolence, not doing injury.* The Jains have sometimes carried this concept so far that they swept the path in front of them, so as not to tread on any microorganisms. Whatever the proper analogue for ourselves, it is clear that our attitude toward nature will have a lot to do with our future commitment to the preservation of the physical matrices of life. Our way of thinking about God's creation may be as important a factor in our commitment to clean up the air and the sea as the monies and technologies involved. As long as we think that nature exists only for our benefit, with no rights of its own, we will move toward ecological restoration only in the measure that it seems to be to our human advantage. That in itself should convince us to mount an urgent campaign, but the long-range survival of our planet demands even more.

With the Asians, we must draw from our native traditions a way to treat the earth compassionately, as a friend rather than as an object of exploitation. Ultimately, we must so appropriate the biblical doctrine of creation that we see all that exists as God's gift, something entrusted to our care rather than tossed out for our caprice. As the Jains offer all living things ahimsa, we must learn to offer all existents a certain respect and noninjury. We must teach our children that beautiful places are not to be defaced, living systems are not to be disrupted casually. Each move of human development into a natural setting might then be estimated in terms of its environmental impact, not simply in a biological sense, but also in a theological. This does not mean that we would never alter the face of nature. It does mean that we would reassess our ways in terms of whether they run with the natural grain or against it.

One Sky

Anyone who visits a major city of our country, or indeed of the developed world, knows that we have been working against the natural grain dramatically, where the air is concerned. Whereas Father Sky arched over archaic peoples, seeing all and blessing much, Smog Alert tells our children that pollution is in the heavens and a great deal is wrong with the world. To be sure, societies have had problems with air control for many centuries. Seneca complained of bad air in Rome more than 2,000 years ago, and in 1273, King Edward I of England passed a law forbidding the use of a particular type of coal. The poet Shelley wrote in the early 1800s that "hell is a city much like London, a populous and smoky city," and 1,150 Londoners died from the effects of coal pollution in 1911. (From this came the word *smog,* to denote the *mixture of smoke and fog* that fouled London's atmosphere.) In 1952, deadly air pollution in the same city killed more than 4,000 people, prompting a massive effort at air control, and as a result, London's air is cleaner today than at any time during the past century.[27]

One could document the situation in the United States with similar stories, though perhaps not with a similarly optimistic conclusion. The fact is that each human being needs about 30 pounds of relatively pure air each day. This must come from the troposphere, the fairly thin layer of air that extends five to seven miles above the earth's surface. Recently, from the United States alone, the troposphere has received about 548,000 tons of air pollutants each day. That averages out to about 4.8 pounds from each American! It is no wonder we have a hard time finding 30 pounds of pure air per person.

Carbon monoxide has been the number-one air pollutant, and the automobile is by far the major source of carbon monoxide. However, more dangerous to human health than carbon monoxide are sulfur oxides and particulates. This leads to the following estimate of air pollution sources: "In terms of air pollution sources, stationary fuel combustion (primarily at fossil fuel power plants) is the most dangerous, with industry (especially pulp and paper mills, iron and steel mills, smelters, petroleum refineries, and chemical plants) and transportation in second and third places, respectively."[28] Thus the reforms necessary to reverse the recent trends of air pollution must target such massive ingredients of our present life-style as our energy production, our heavy industry, and our love affair with the automobile. It is obvious from the economic and political consequences of such reform that environmentalists often seem to be striking at the heart of the status quo. To ask this major change of our energy producers, our heavy industries, and our automobile manufacturers is to ask for a conversion to a new philosophy of nature.

It is all the more encouraging, then, that the Clean Air Act of 1970 has proved relatively effective. By 1980, over 80 percent of the major stationary air pollution sources had complied, with the result that between 1965 and 1979 sulfur dioxide levels in the United States decreased 62 percent, particulates 31 percent, and lead levels 35 percent. (However, ozone levels showed little change, and nitrogen oxides probably increased.) Ecologists estimate that progress in this period saved about 14,000 lives and $21.4 billion. They were greatly distressed, therefore, at signs that the Reagan administration might take the teeth out of the 1970 legislation. A great deal remains to be done, and it

seems extremely short-sighted to sacrifice environmental health to the supposed needs of the American
economy.

Among the major things remaining to be reversed is
the health trend that air pollution, combined with
smoking, has lately been setting. In 1980, one in five
American men between the ages of 40 and 60 suffered
chronic bronchitis, and emphysema has become our
fastest growing cause of death, killing almost as many
people as lung cancer and tuberculosis combined. The
figures on lung cancer alone, however, show the lethal
impact of air pollution. Urban nonsmokers are now
three to four times more likely to develop lung cancer
than are rural nonsmokers.[29]

Another major problem is acid rain, and it is
growing. Acid rain results when sulfur and nitrogen
dioxides in the atmosphere are converted into sulfuric
and nitric acids. Since the sulfur dioxides come from
coal-burning power plants, factories, and metal
smelters, and the nitrogen dioxides come from cars
and fossil-fuel power plants, the sources of acid rain
are major factors of our national economy. It is
incontrovertible, though, that acid rain and snow now
threaten equally major factors: food crops, trees,
materials, buildings, and aquatic life. The United
States, Canada, western Europe, Scandanavia, and
Japan—the frontiers of the Western life-style—all find
their future clouded by acid rain.

The United States has planned to build about 350
coal-burning power plants between 1979 and 1995.
This could lead to a 10 to 15 percent increase in acid
rains. The results can be foretold from the present
condition of the lakes in the northeastern United
States and Canada. More than 300 lakes in the
Adirondacks have become so acidified that they no

longer support fish, and Canadian scientists predict that 48,000 lakes in Ontario will be devoid of life in 20 years if acid rains continue to fall there.

Therefore, unless we wish to begin our Lord's Prayer with "Our Father who art in heaven, sour be thy name," we Christians must start to redeem the one sky from the forces that poison it. In the future, Christian salvation, the condition that Easter really seals, must indeed become a matter of life and breath.

One Water Supply

The increasing acidity of our rain illustrates the interconnectedness of such ecological systems as air and water. Scientifically, it is feasible to improve the quality of one system only by working also on the other systems with which it meshes. However, we probably each have a favorite ecological niche, one to which we spontaneously gravitate, and mine is the system of our waters. This is not a disjunctive, either/or gravitation, of course. I doubt that I shall ever forget a night in the Grand Tetons, when the air was so clear and crisp that the stars were like diamonds on a wrap of sable. No doubt others can report similar experiences in the desert, or even in the jungle.

But my habitual ecstatic reaction to the splendors of nature emerges at the sea. Be it watching the otters playing off Point Lobos, or body-surfing at Gloucester's Good Harbor Beach, I find the ocean a constant source of recreation and beguilement. On a bright day at Good Harbor, the water sparkles with a shocking clarity. Nearby it crashes against the famous Bass Rocks, sending spray thirty feet high on a blustery day. At such times, I believe completely that we humans crawled forth from the sea and that the sea must always remain our mother. I can no more conceive of polluting the sea than the American Indian Smohalla could conceive of putting the blade of a plow into the bosom of his mother the earth.

Yet we are polluting the sea and all the earth's other waterways. We are fouling the waters and killing the marine life. The fishermen of Gloucester, set upon in the late 1970s by the Moonies, have a more formidable enemy in the coalition of government and petroleum forces that intend to open Georges Bank to oil exploration. Georges Bank is one of the richest fishing areas in the world—literally an irreplaceable seafood resource. But, in what would seem to be economic as well as ecological folly, the maws of government and industry are preparing to devour it whole. The same applies to the waters off the coast of Southern California. They too are up for leasing, about to be sacrificed to our lust for oil.

The reader may well feel that I have little objectivity in this matter, and the reader may well be right. When I look at a wasteful economy on the verge of ruining natural systems both beautiful and crucial to the biosphere, I feel the sort of outrage one associates with sacrilege. In my view, my incarnational religion, we human beings do not have the right to foul the nest God has given us. We are not such lords of creation that destruction is our birthright. One day, if we persist in this sacrilege, our arrogance will deliver the tragic backlash we deserve. Already the signs are on the horizon, the prophet has data aplenty.

For example, all but a very few of the 246 water basins in the United States have become somewhat polluted. Topsoil erosion, the worst cause, now is such that each year the eroded earth would fill 18 freight trains, each long enough to reach around the world. One-third of the soil on our croplands has eroded in the last 200 years, and a major reason is agricultural greed:

> Many farmers are more interested in maximizing short-term crop yields than in conserving the soil. Heavy and increasingly expensive applications of fertilizer and pesticides to maintain high yields merely hide the fact that the natural fertility and productivity of U.S. soils are being depleted at an alarming rate. Until soil erosion can be sharply reduced, sediments will be the major source of water pollution from nonpoint *[diffuse]* sources.[30]

Industrial and municipal discharges also contribute greatly to water pollution, accounting for between 50 and 75 percent of the 400 to 500 fish kills reported each year. As many as two-thirds of all American lakes (80 percent of all our urban lakes) have developed serious pollution problems, although intensive efforts seem to be turning things around in some places (for instance, the Great Lakes). Electric power plants now account for about 25 percent of all water used in the United States annually (this could increase 650 percent by the year 2000), and the result is serious thermal pollution: Heating a body of water above its natural temperature endangers its ecological balance.

Nor are the oceans, the ultimate basins of our water systems, immune from similar pollution. Just as the crux of air pollution is a fragile zone (the troposphere) close to the earth, so the crux of marine pollution is the neritic zone (the 10 percent of the ocean area closest to land) that contains about 90 percent of all sea life. And the neritic zone, including both the estuarial waters and the waters out to the continental shelf, is obviously the area most directly affected by our discharges of chemicals, human wastes, industrial sewage, and such.

After many years of work, in 1980 the United Nations Conference on the Law of the Sea approved a draft of a treaty to prevent both ocean pollution and overfishing. In 1981 the Reagan administration indicated that it wished to renegotiate the entire treaty, so we may expect that such pollution as the seven million tons of oil and petroleum added to the oceans each year will continue. Standard operating procedures (river and urban runoff; intentional discharge from tankers) account for 61 percent of this pollution. Dramatic accidents, such as the breakup of the Amoco Cadiz off the coast of France in 1978 (which released 67 million gallons of oil and polluted 200 miles of coastline) probably will be but dirty frosting on an increasingly dirty cake.[31]

The Right to Life

One could match the pollution of the land to that of the air and the seas, as such nefarious incidents as the Hooker Chemical Company's pollution of Love Canal in Niagara, New York, show all too soberingly. True, we have yet to learn the full effects of the body's accumulation of such nondegradable substances as cadmium, lead, and mercury, but the Japanese experience at Minamata Bay, where the methyl mercury discharged from a chemical plant entered the local fish and caused severe brain and nerve damage in the human beings who ate them, gives little cause for optimism.[32] If we human beings and the other living things of the land are to continue to exercise our rights to life, we must severely reduce our chemical discharges and other pollutants.

As I reflect on the social theology implicit in these ecological forays, it emerges that we should suggest an extension of the second commandment to our mother the earth. In view of today's knowledge of the intimacy with which we human beings live with the earth, participate in its ecosystems, it becomes increasingly clear that we shall have no peace with nature until we begin to love it as we love ourselves. Environmentalists have suspected this for some time, but theologians by and large have remained impervious to environmentalists' insights. For example, Pope John Paul II's 1981 encyclical on labor, *Laborem Exercens,* built much of its case for the dignity of work on a reading of Genesis' "subdue the earth," which paid scant heed to the earth's rights to reverence. That is especially unfortunate (but not unrepresentative of recent Roman Catholic social theory[33]), because the encyclical is a wonderful defense of human beings' rights to dignity and nonexploitation. Had it accorded nature but a small portion of such rights, it would have been a papal landmark.

How might we persuade theologians to be more sensitive to ecological issues? Perhaps through their concerns with war and abortion. For example, the ultimate threat in nuclear proliferation is the destruction of the earth's biomes. This would be the final sacrilege, even beyond the destruction of millions of human beings, for it would say the definitive No! to creation. Modern war therefore is a highly ecological issue.

Abortion is a highly emotional issue and a very complex one. It seems to me, though, that in their concern with reverence for life, antiabortionists have pushed forward a principle capable of wide ecological extension. Within the confines of the abortion debate itself, the principle spotlights the rights of the unborn, reminding us that conception is a wonderful gift. By extension, however, it also reminds us to ask about the quality of life that a child and its family will enjoy. These further questions should not shade the primary issue of basic physical existence, but they should receive a fair hearing, especially in consideration of such circumstances as genetic defects, congenital disease, rape, incest, economic hardship, and so on.

The only fully Christian solution to the abortion controversy, I suspect, would be for all parties to collaborate and so progress toward the day when far fewer unwanted children are conceived. Reverence for life then would result in far better birth control, so that abortion no longer would be a prime contraceptive. ("After the Pill and prolonged lactation, abortion is the most widely practiced form of birth control in the world today."[34]) It also would result in more generous adoption procedures and better education of our people as to the inability of the earth to sustain our recent rates of population growth.

So ecological considerations turn out to be highly germane to some of our most pressing moral problems. Unless or until we find ways to reason together under the (properly sophisticated) banner of reverence for life, we shall fail to link our peacemaking, defense of the unborn, concern for hard-pressed parents, support of women's development, and struggles to safeguard the environment. These issues all beg to be treated with a certain consistency, a certain organic outlook, and their interconnection suggests that any single-issue morality or politics is hopelessly simpleminded.

Of course, ecology does not imply that nature itself is fully reverential toward life. In the long view, evolution has been a terribly painful and inefficient process, full of detours and disappointments. Human evolution has left many groups nasty and brutish for long periods, and human wars have been as destructive to the noosphere as plagues have been to the biosphere. So the nature we reverence is far from having been consistently kind or gentle. At many times it has shown itself cold, uncaring, and mindlessly destructive. The second commandment, though, urges us to humanize nature, rather than pay it back in its own worst coin. If "subduing the earth" were translated in this sense, it might be acceptable to ecological theologians.

The final thesis of an ecological theology might be that conviviality should obtain between us and nature. Lewis Thomas has expressed this marvelously in a story about visiting the Tucson zoo. He was so taken out of himself in joy at the sportive play of some otters and beavers that he wondered whether kinship with them was not set in his very genes: "I am coded, somehow, for otters and beavers . . . for feeling exaltation and a rush of friendship [in their presence]."[35] But friendship, as I need remind only the slow, entails a love of the other as oneself. This implies that we will have one good earth only when we have truly come to love all the earth's creatures as we love ourselves.

CHAPTER 14. *ONE ECONOMY*

Steady-State Economics I

A number of economists sensitive to ecological considerations have begun to push the thesis that we must change our tacit expectations of ever-continuing economic development and begin to think in terms of steadier economies. Arguing that there are inbuilt limits to the earth's fund of natural resources, they emphasize renewable resources and a better balance between what nature can supply and what human beings realistically demand. Many of the notions associated with this steady-state position were popularized by E. F. Schumacher, who furnished quite an impressive spiritual rationale.[36]

For example, Schumacher spoke of a Buddhist economics, based on some observations he made while working in Burma, which stressed simplicity, the worker's creativity, and the working group's cooperation. Whereas the West tends to think of clothing, for instance, in terms of accumulating a wardrobe of many garments, Schumacher's Buddhist economics thinks in terms of a few garments that are versatile, simply cut, easily produced, graceful, and durable. Whereas the West tends to view workers as human cogs in a machine to produce goods, Buddhist economics considers the worker's self-mastery and self-expression more important. Finally, whereas the West tends to focus an entire enterprise on the financial profits one can expect, Buddhist economics stresses that the best work is a cooperative effort for a common good—an activity that reenforces the people's social bonds and fulfills a genuine (as opposed to a falsely stimulated) social need.

As most of Schumacher's writings indicate, the adjective *Buddhist* attached to this economic outlook is relatively unimportant. Schumacher saw at least the seeds of such an economics in Burma, so he developed it under the Buddhist banner. But any world-view that places importance upon simplicity, self-discipline, self-expression, cooperation, and so-cial service can generate a similar set of economic convictions. Certainly Christianity can. As its long line of saints who embraced poverty suggests, Christianity can conceive life as best ordered when the spirit is predominant over the body. Thus when the body's basic needs—food, clothing, shelter—have been met, the major portion of a society's energies can be put into higher culture (scientific, artistic, religious).

Further, the crafts that meet the body's basic needs can develop into truly humane works, so that cuisine, clothing design, and architecture all flow from a religious and humanistic spirituality. The Buddhist robe made of plain but good cloth, cut simply but elegantly and serving many uses for many years, is an ideal Christian garment. If the eye of the Christian mind is simple, the purity of the Christian heart is, as Kierkegaard urged, "to will one thing." The same applies to the food we prepare, the housing we build.

Clearly, in the context of the current Western tendency toward fast foods and tract housing, less could be much more.

Similar reflections emanate from *self-discipline* and *self-expression*. In Schumacher's ideal economics, an artisan or an intellectual labors for much more than a paycheck. Assuming a just wage and a social service, the main goal of human work should be the schooling it gives the worker's mind and body, the creativity it nurtures. When we have the opportunity to learn work skills well and to practice them at a humane pace, our work become our great teacher. So a carpenter who makes tables or a teacher who prepares lessons becomes increasingly sensitive to the "requests" made by the wood or by a lesson's materials. If one honors such requests through the years, one develops a perception and art like that of Chuang Tzu's famous ox-carver: "There are spaces in the joints; the blade is thin and keen: When this thinness finds that space, there is all the room you need. It goes like a breeze! Hence I have this cleaver thirteen years as if newly sharpened."[37]

The advantages of humane work for the worker are complemented by its advantageous effects in human sociability and service. In a Buddhist economics, people work together—cooperate, rather than compete destructively. Japanese industry is now teaching the United States some of the higher "efficiencies" possible when a firm conceives of itself as a family rather than as a free-for-all. Granted that Japanese work patterns are far from perfect, they do seem capable of finer tuning, more effective cooperation, than most American work patterns. Human interactions in work, as elsewhere, are amazingly subtle and indirect, so that genuine cooperation is a wonderful achievement, a fine translation of *community.*

Finally, with community, not only is a splendid goal attained, but also the basic condition necessary for the stimulation of work that produce goods and services we really need, rather than superfluities and trash. Neither the United States nor Japan is close to solving this final problem, which admittedly is a tall order. How *do* we shift from an economy dependent on the constant buying of nonessentials to an economy targeted toward real social needs and services? What would happen were we to stop the engines that produce trashy food, trashy clothing, trashy furnishings, trashy entertainment? Could the moguls of Detroit and Madison Avenue conceive of an economy not predicated on planned obsolescence? Could the dictum that less is more rouse them to anything other than a frown? Perhaps yes, but more than likely no—and this illustrates the enormity of the task that lies before Buddhist economists and steady-staters.

Steady-State Economics II

For those who are left cold by the spiritual rationale of an E. F. Schumacher, some figures from Herman E. Daly may be more germane. Speaking to the 1979 World Council of Churches Conference at Massachusetts Institute of Technology, Daly argued for the ecological and moral necessity of limited economic growth.[38] The basic framework of his argument was a ground-level analysis of the two things necessary for a sustainable economy: a renewable resource base; and a scale of consumption within the sustainable yield of that resource base. In other words, we must keep producing life's necessities; and we cannot consume them at a higher rate than we produce them. The basic systems on which humankind has always lived are the forests, fisheries, grasslands, and croplands. Recently we have increased the short-run productivity of each of these systems with subsidies of nonrenewable fuels and minerals. Nonetheless, there is evidence that each system has reached its peak of global per capita productivity and is now declining.

By Daly's calculations, forest productivity peaked in 1967; fisheries in 1970; grasslands for wool in 1960, for mutton in 1972, and for beef in 1976; and croplands peaked in 1976. Since per capita production of oil seems to have peaked in 1977, it is unlikely that increased expenditures of oil will help to boost the per capita productivity of any of the four systems in the future. One of the many conclusions that one can begin to draw from these figures is that it is futile for the whole world to aim to reach an economy like that of the United States, which has a "high mass consumption." Specifically, it takes about one-third of the world's annual production of mineral resources to support the 6 percent of the world's population that resides in the United States. To bring the entire world up to this country's standard of living, it would be necessary to increase the world's flow of resources by a factor of six to seven times the current production levels.

From these simple facts, Daly moves to some moral inferences. First, if we set today's resource problems in the light of tomorrow's needs, we arrive at an ecological version of the fifth commandment of the Decalogue: In interpreting "Thou shalt not kill," we must further enjoin, "Thou shalt not destroy the capacity of creation to support life." In other words, our race needs to learn to live within a reasonable, finite set of renewable resources. Rather than multiplying shopping centers and suburban developments, we must begin to view the development of our resources in the context of the world's future needs for food, clothing, and shelter.

Insofar as both capitalism and communism think in terms of continued economic growth, neither system presently is realistic ecologically, and so neither appears viable for the future. Only a system that falls between communism and capitalism, joining their respective strengths (supposed concern for the general welfare; personal initiative) to a spirit of spare living and ecology, seems realistic from a radical point of view.

The good news is that there are many signs that, granted a redirected set of economic attitudes toward the earth, human genius could provide the global community with the essentials for a spare and healthy life. Barbara Ward's *Progress for a Small Planet* gives realistic and hopeful surveys of most of the problems a future global economy would need to solve.[39] The bad news is that a sane global economy will require major readjustments, while a just global economy will require wholesale conversions. Desirable as either may be spiritually, their political demands are daunting indeed.

As the figures cited above show, it is folly to speak of bringing the rest of the world up to the standard of living that Americans, or members of the northern nations generally, now enjoy. Even if the gap between the rich and poor nations were not widening; even if we were gaining control of worldwide population growth; even if our defense budgets were declining so that all nations were putting more of their resources to productive use, we would still need sacrifice on the part of all nations—but especially the wealthy—to come close to a just distribution of the goods needed for a spare but decent life-style for all people. When one thinks of the inertia of the present systems, let alone their greed and corruption, such a conversion can seem only miraculous—outside the realm of reasonable expectation.

The place to begin is obviously with the rich nations, but even if those were converted, massive problems would remain. The poor nations, understandably enough, think mainly of developing to the level of the rich nations. With them, any talk of a steady-state economy goes down hard for it seems to deny them their place in the sun.[40] Thus many liberation theologians seem almost to block their ears to speeches about the ecological facts of the future, with the result that many of their hopes are sadly unrealistic. Parallelwise, the poor nations emulate the rich nations' diversion of resources to military arms more than they repudiate such action:

> In today's world, 1.5 billion people lack access to professional health services. Over 1.4 billion people have no safe drinking water. More than 500 million people suffer from malnutrition. But world governments spend twice as much on armaments as on health care. Although 700 million of their adult citizens are illiterate and 500 million (more than half) of their children do not attend school, today's developing nations are importing the most sophisticated conventional arms at a rate of $6 billion a year. In our modern arms economy, military research consumes the creative efforts of over 500,000 scientists and engineers worldwide and gets more public funds than all social needs combined. Over half the scientists in the U.S.A. are employed

by the military-industrial complex. And despite the much-publicized "energy crisis," energy research and development in the U.S. still gets only one-sixth as much funding as weapons research.[41]

So such a "simple" proposal as the need to live within nature's budget in order to give all the world's people a fair chance for a spare good life becomes a call for a completely new global economy.

Energy

Central to any future global economy will be the problem of generating sufficient energy. However, one no sooner enunciates such a sentence today than ecologists pounce with the questions, What is *sufficient* energy? Sufficient for what? So energy production is inextricably bound up with the question of life-style. The best "solution" to the energy problem, most ecologists agree, is conservation: to make much more efficient use of the resources we now have, the resources we now spend. Assuming some firm population controls and a steady shift from non-renewable to renewable energy sources, strict conservation could put the United States in good energy health in fifty years. Each of those three ingredients, however, will require a change of heart on the part of America's citizenry, industry, and government. Religious people who read the signs of the times therefore will begin to hone their two-edged swords.

Figures are a penny a dozen in energy matters, but the wise prophet always has a meaningful store. For example, in the last few years, the average American has used about 125 times the 2,000 kilocalories needed for primitive survival. This is equivalent to the use of 91 pounds of coal each day, or 16.5 tons of coal each year. "This means that 228 million Americans use enough energy each day to provide the survival energy needs for 28 *billion* people—about six times the present population of the world."[42] In 1975, the more developed nations, which contained about 25 percent of the world's population, used about 80 percent of the energy consumed in the world. To meet even the current world demands for oil, it would be necessary to discover the equivalent of a set of Mexican or Saudi Arabian fields every five years. And even if we could find oil equal to four times the present world reserves, it would add only about 25 years to the moment when, at current usage rates, the world's oil and natural gas supplies will be exhausted.

Perhaps the greatest tragedy in the sort of economy we have built in the United States is the energy *waste* it has made us consider normal. About 85 to 90 percent of the energy we have used recently was wasted (used so inefficiently it did not get from the source to the work intended). The inefficiency of our cars and the underinsulation of our homes are major culprits, but a prodigal style has ruled throughout. Each year we Americans have been wasting more fossil-fuel energy than was used by two-thirds of the world's population. Even Japan and the industrialized nations of Europe, which are most comparable to us in terms of their economies, have been using only one-third to one-half the per capita energy we use. Experts such as Amory Lovins claim that we could cut our average per capita energy use 90 percent without sacrificing our quality of life, if we were to remedy our present inefficiency.[43] There might be debate about Lovins' definition of *quality*, but he certainly envisions no threat to adequate health, nutrition, clothing, shelter, education, or social services.

Analysts often discuss this question of energy efficiency in terms of two basic laws. *First law energy efficiency* has to do with the ratio of useful energy produced to total energy received. Thus an energy-conversion device is more efficient if it requires less input and generates more output. An incandescent light bulb, for example, is only 5 percent efficient, because 95 of every 100 kilocalories it produces are degraded to heat, rather than converted to light. The introduction of newer, more efficient bulbs (which would use 70 percent less electricity) in all homes in the United States could save the equivalent of 500,000 barrels of oil *each day*. Similar examples abound. In terms of the first law, the conventional internal-combustion engine is only 2 percent efficient, the typical hydroelectric plant is only 12 percent efficient, and all energy used in the United States in 1979 averaged about 32 percent efficiency. This means that almost two-thirds of that energy went out into the environment as low-grade heat instead of being used effectively.

Second law energy efficiency refers to the minimum amount of energy theoretically necessary for a given task in ratio to the amount actually used to perform the task. This law spotlights the high standard at which we should be aiming: maximum efficiency through the best possible design. Some recent percentage estimates of second-law efficiency among major energy systems in this country include: air conditioning, 4.5; refrigeration, 4; automobiles, 8-10; power plants, 33; steel production, 23; and oil refining, 9. For all United States energy systems combined, the estimate is 10 to

15 percent.[44] (These seem to be the figures that led to the judgment that our energy waste is as high as 85 to 90 percent.) One can see, therefore, why environmentalists and many energy experts wax eloquent about conservation (increased efficiency). Conservation lessens our harm to the environment as it decreases our need for energy.

A full-scale energy program in the United States will need to provide for some new production, since it will take considerable time to approach anything like maximum conservation/efficiency. The best ecological strategy, and perhaps the best economic strategy as well, would seem to be to promote production of energy from such renewable souces as sun, wind, and water. The United States probably should target a stable population of about 250 million by the year 2015 (between 1955 and 1978, 38 percent of our increased use of energy was due to population growth), and begin to seriously consider the ramifications in housing design, transportation systems, and the like that are necessary for an earnest effort at conservation.

For theologians, the obvious contribution consists of helping to muster the popular will for such change. Once again, this emphasizes that it is religiously desirable to live simply and to look upon the rest of the world's citizens as one's equals in rights to the globe's resources.

Beyond Luxury

The global economy demanded by a realistic assessment of the future is spare and essentialistic. As though God were speaking to us through evolution, it beckons as a worldwide system in which no one has a

right to superfluities as long as anyone lacks necessities. In a contrary scenario, chapters on war, revolu-
tion, starvation, environmental pollution, and other
tragedies would be added. The forces of history,
including our own successes in technology and
medicine, have brought us to the point where we
simply must change our consumerist life-styles. If we
continue to treat the earth as we have treated it for the
past hundred years, our grandchildren will be forced
to pay a terrible price.

A Jewish friend of mine recently bought a splendid
used car. It cost more than he had planned, but the
white leather upholstery and the sturdy ride broke
down all his defenses. The car was middle-sized,
getting about twenty miles to the gallon, but he
reasoned that it would not bankrupt him. Besides, it
would be a step up, a little reward after his lean years as
a graduate student. Those years had taken him to
several parts of the United States and to Israel for a
goodly time, but they had not brought him a sense of
the ecumene, of the single world that we human
beings increasingly share. So he made no significant
connection between his purchase of a somewhat
luxurious car and the critical poverty now devastating
the southern nations. So he, like most of us, let the
rules of the local market dictate his economic outlook,
forgetting the global issues of conservation and future
survival.

My friend comes from a religious tradition that is
ambivalent toward wealth and luxury, as most religious traditions are. On the one hand, his tradition
centers life in the Lord God, before whom all earthly
treasures pale. Theoretically, it most honors scholars
of God's teaching, whom it paints as poor and ascetic,
and its Law traditionally has provided for a humane

treatment of creation (for example, animals) like that of the friends-of-the-earth philosophy we have sketched above. On the other hand, his tradition has not been strong on an afterlife, and so it has tended to accept wealth as a blessing and encourage the enjoyment of this world's goods. It has stressed the social obligations that come with wealth, the need for alms to the poor and contributions to local works of charity, but it seldom has urged material sacrifice and lean living. Despite the fact that its people have been scattered to the ends of the earth, the attacks they have suffered have rendered Judaism somewhat suspicious of the global community. Sufficient for the day has been the survival of its own people—the survival of the world could wait for another, more peaceful day.

I am using my friend and his tradition simply as a springboard to launch a critique applicable to all of us in the developed world. Since he exhibits many traits now typically American, yet comes from a tradition somewhat marginal to the American mainstream, he throws an uncommon light on our common problems. That light, in my view, illumines our need of a solid basis for sacrifice. If we in the wealthy nations are to do what must be done for the global future, we shall need good reasons for changing our life-styles in ways that many will find sacrificial, at least initially. For we will be asked to reduce our consumption to levels that will enable the whole world to survive decently. Before long, sweet reason will wake up and spring the surprise that a sane standard of living, applicable to the whole world, falls far below American luxuriousness, but far above African starvation.

In such a sane global standard of living, there will be no place for cars like my friend's Chrysler, homes of ten or more rooms, empty skyscrapers that light the night with fluorescent discharges. There will be no place for grain-fed cattle, mountains of throwaway containers, chemical or nuclear pollution. Unless we affluent peoples possess more in our souls than our present habituation to comfort, we shall find these verdicts very difficult. Indeed, many of us are likely to fight them tooth and nail, if not laser and bomb.

From my friend's tradition, charity and social sensitivity step forward to nourish the soul. From Christian tradition, Resurrection and the Parousia step forward as well. We Christians have no lasting city on this earth. But contrary to some politicians who think it best to develop this earth most rapidly, I hear the good Christian of the future saying, "Therefore I shall pass through the earth lightly, neither stamping nor grabbing."

In the Creation and the Incarnation, the biblical religionist should hear a command to love the world and his own body, to call them good as God has called them good. In the Resurrection and the Parousia, she should hear a command to place this-worldly life in the context of somethiing more, something named *heaven* and *beatific vision.* If heaven is real to us, we need not gorge and gather with the heathen. If heaven is real, we can travel lightly, aiming only to beautify the world and serve its needy. From the way a great many modern Christians live, one would say that heaven is not very real. For stressing prosperity so greatly in this life, they, of all believers, are most to be criticized. It is up to other believers, therefore, to show the world the centrality of the Resurrection by the sacrifice and hope it provides. If we prepare our food, build our homes, and transport ourselves at anywhere near the spare standards demanded by the global future, resurrectional hope will become as tangible as tofu, as simple as a one-bedroom apartment. That is hardly a heroic level of sacrifice, but Jesus may find it a beginning— enough to call us peacemakers and children of God.

Beyond Profit

Part of the Christian rationale for championing conservation, therefore, is based on its contribution to peacemaking and the revelation of God. By cutting back on our consumption, we affluent nations would offer underdeveloped peoples a more just share of the global pie and thereby remove some of the main triggers of violent conflict. We would show, if only modestly, that we are willing to sacrifice in order to demonstrate our goodwill. Thereby we would conjure, if only subliminally, the way our God has demonstrated his good will. Contrary to classical Marxists, for whom economic disparity among peoples is the basis for an almost intrinsic class warfare, Christians should prize the solidarity of the human family more than their own material advantage. They should prove the Marxist axiom of class warfare false by their incarnation of the biblical invitation "Come let us reason together." By throwing off antiquated notions of favored status and developing current notions of God's universal grace, they should consider all people at least anonymous children of Jesus' Abba.

Applied to economics, this sort of theology offers a horizon in which the capitalistic peoples might begin to move beyond their reputation as bête noires who pivot their cultures on financial profit. Far too frequently and far too deeply, our Western economies are dominated by a profit motive no more sophisticated than the accountant's bottom line. If a venture does not bring a hefty cash reward, we account it a failure. So true is this that we stigmatize even schools and churches, quintessentially "nonprofit" ventures, if any quarter finds them running in the red. Perhaps latent in capitalism there are more sophisticated possibilities, the development of which could make it viable in the global future that lies ahead. At present, however, capitalism seems destined to go the way of the dodo.

That is not to say, of course, that those who champion capitalism do not proclaim some important truths. Human beings *do* need incentives, there *should* be economic accountability, and the wrong kind of giveaway programs *do* sap industriousness. The problem is the narrow interpretation that apologists for capitalism usually place on such terms as *incentives*, the way money (mammon) directs so much of their thinking. Jesus, the great executive, told his managers and crack sales personnel, "You cannot serve God and mammon." Not even Milton Friedman or the wickedly clever writers who turn out the Mobil ads have managed to pirouette around that one.

You cannot be religious in any genuine sense and crave money, creature comforts, matériel, status, and the pride of life they all engender. You cannot be religious and find yourself enjoying the power structure of a materialist economy or culture. It simply does not compute. If the mainstream is flowing toward mammon, religion will take you against the mainstream. If God is your great treasure, you must define profit in humanistic, rather than simply fiscal terms.

What, then, is a simple American, still fascinated by the national dream of working hard and making it big, to do? Perhaps he should begin with those parts of capitalism, as the conservatives popularly portray it,

that he can endorse. For example, he could begin with
the call to balance the budget. It does seem the
antithesis of responsibility (and spare living) to pay
interest on a national debt of over one trillion dollars.
It does seem a profligacy like that of the son in Luke's
story. But let us consider the national debt a little
further. We castigate it because it is inefficient, making
us pay far more for government than we should have to
pay. Why, then, do we not cast a similarly dark eye on
the whole usurious slant of modern western economies, which add so much to the cost of our homes, our
cars, our food?

From basic banking to current credit cards, all sorts
of people and companies are now prospering like
Shylock, taking pounds of lucre by no more title than
their lending of money. The power of such people
seems clearly to designate money, or mammon, as
lord of the West. Perhaps the religions could justify
such idolatry when mammon was a small god,
charging 5 percent and paying 3. When the prime rate
hits 20 percent, though, mammon obviously has
ousted God, and the sense of human solidarity given
by God, from the shrine of human buying and selling,
human needing and fulfilling.

In my view, the churches now face a massive
challenge to attack mammon and reassert God. They
have lain down before money and banking for far too
long, because it so often has profited their institutional
selves. Beginning with an ascesis to purify their own
sight, the churches might become credible to their
people as prophets of the new era that is clearly
dawning by making themselves the avant-garde of
tomorrow's ecological converts. In other words, they
might become credible by actually demonstrating that
in the new era of human responsibility, people would

value the good an enterprise serves more than the money it earns. They would hold it accountable—not in terms of how richly it rewards its stockholders, but how greatly it advances global justice.

In *Laborem Exercens*, Pope John Paul II lashed out at capitalists who would vilify such a new accountability, reminding them that Christian social teaching limits the rights of private property in view of the common human good. He indicated the priority of labor over capital, since labor represents people who do the consummately human thing—they develop the earth. By contrast, capital is but an impersonal part of human work, lesser in dignity, and it should never be allowed to run roughshod over an economy. Thus we ought to measure the good that investments can accomplish in terms of humane services, adding today the needs of the billions of the world's suffering. Beyond profit, then, lies the kingdom of God, the horizon of workers and managers who try to achieve God's priorities.

CHAPTER 15. *RADICAL POLITICS*

Redeeming Religion

To love our neighbors well, we Christians must see them in terms of God's priorities. When we begin to do that, the kingdom of God will become meaningful, a matter of at least slight experience. As long as we refuse to admit the radical implications of Jesus' second commandment, we will continue to gouge the earth, pollute the skies, and run our economies for profit rather than for service.

The place to begin the political program for which the future seems to call, therefore, is right at home. Until our churches have ousted mammon from their own reckoning, we will hear little preaching that carries conviction in view of the suffering peoples of the world. Religious politics, religious strivings for human relationships that are upbuilding and just call for the redemption of many current religious practices from much that is unbiblical, un-Christian.

In the previous chapter, I was hard on the politics of economic growth, energy waste, luxury, and profit. Without taking back any of that critique, I wish to assure the reader that I understand at least some of the practical limitations under which ordinary Americans now labor and that I realize how little a global horizon impresses most of middle America. If I ever had forgotten this, a night at a college football game recently would have brought it back vividly. Watching the enormous squads of huge players, the cheerleaders, the marching band, the spectacular fireworks display, and (above all) the crowd, summoned the tempter's mocking laugh to my soul again, reviving for the nth time his counsel to despair. "You are so much the dreamer," the tempter always says. "Look at this crowd, see what it wants." I wonder how much aberrant religion results from the tempter's plausibil-ity. I wonder how many preachers come to feel in their hearts that Dostoevski's Grand Inquisitor was right.

The Grand Inquisitor, you may recall, accused Jesus of being a dreamer. Midst the disordered human passions that litter *The Brothers Karamazov*, the inquisitor argued quite plausibly that Jesus offers people more freedom than they want. People want direction, orders, to be taken care of, he said. They want distractions, fireworks, bread and games. Jesus offers freedom, but thereby responsibility. He offers depth, spiritual adventure, ecstasy toward God, but only at the price of facing the world's chaos, of suffering dark nights when God's otherness sears the soul. American sports (entertainment, politics, subur-ban living) are a monumental witness that Jesus is as far from our hoi polloi as the heavens are from the earth. Sunday morning religious television to the contrary, Jesus gives no cheap grace, no baptism of our football, our barbecues, our old-boy politics.

When the tempter laughs his mocking laugh and points to the rollicking stadium, one must retreat to a better news analyst. In the tempter's analysis, what we see is what there is, what we see is what we get. Jesus analyzes the news differently. What we see is just a fraction of what there is, no reliable guide to what we may get. It all depends on our outlook, the interpretational frame in which we set the data of our senses. Were we to use a text such as Matthew 6:19-34 as our interpretational frame and listen to Jesus rather than to the tempters of Sunday morning television, we would find protection against a religion of football, fireworks, and marching bands. Were we to take this text and the other parts of the Sermon on the Mount to heart, we would move beyond luxury and profit to Jesus' steady state, Jesus' house built upon rock.

"Do not lay up for yourselves treasures on earth, where moth and rust consume and where thieves break in and steal, but lay up for yourselves treasures in heaven" (Mt 6:19-20). If Jesus' God is real, this-worldly goods—football and mammon—lie under a great burden of proof. To spend much time or many resources on them, to consider them of much account, is quite dubious, quite untenable. Indeed, not to consider them somewhat one's enemy is to miss Jesus' plain meaning: "No one can serve two masters; for either he will hate the one and love the other, or he will be devoted to the one and despise the other. You cannot serve God and mammon" (Mt 6:24).

But what about our need to consider money, food, clothing, recreation? What about decent profit, the body, and all the other things that make ordinary life go? Doesn't the Incarnation itself show their importance, their rightness? Yes, the Incarnation is a great proof that God knows we need these things, that God has them as part of her plan. But see where Jesus places these things, see how Jesus weighs them in the heavenly scale:

> Therefore I tell you, do not be anxious about your
> life, what you shall eat or what you shall drink, nor
> about your body, what you shall put on. Is not life
> more than food, and the body more than clothing?
> . . . The Gentiles seek all these things; and your
> heavenly Father knows that you need them all. But
> seek first his kingdom and his righteousness, and all
> these things shall be yours as well. (Matthew 6:25,
> 32-33)

To do well by Christ in the future, we desperately need to rescue our Christian religion from mammon and bring it back to God's righteousness. We desperately need a reassertion of God's priorities. Only then will we be poised to execute a truly radical politics, a truly believing obedience to Jesus' second command.

Reconciling the Religions

When a people sets its face to seek God's righteousness, it makes itself available to God for ministries of reconciliation. The great obstacles to peace are the disordered human passions that set idols in the place reserved for God. The place reserved for God is the sanctuary of the heart. "God" should be the light and love we seek from the very center of ourselves. Mysterious, otherworldly, prescribing few answers, the true God stabilizes the pure heart in unknowing. Again and again, the Spirit of the true God teaches us negatively: not this species of dishonesty, not that form of selfish loving. For now we see only in a glass darkly, not face to face. Now we have only the call to light and love, the restless but joyous quest, not the sureties of heaven.

Still, this call can be enough for us. It can glaze our vessel to become lovely humanity, the imaging of God that the Creator had in mind. When we add the paradigm of Jesus' expressions of honesty and love, there is sufficient iconography to move human affairs wisely, to manage human history well. Jesus' art shows us the causes of our wars and alienations, the reasons we continue to bloody the map. Knowing these causes, we can begin to accept the law of the cross, Jesus' demanding plan to reverse our human disorders.

In the realm of Christian ecumenism, the law of the cross implies that all parties to the church's current divisions must sacrifice more than they hitherto have been willing to do. In the realm of world affairs, the law of the cross inplies that all parties to the globe's divisions must sacrifice similarly. This is obvious enough on one level—almost a platitude. When the negotiations start, however, it usually goes out the door. Pride and "victory" having entered in, the negotiations degenerate into blustering, bluffing, and the many other forms of egotism. False gods having usurped the place of the sole Absolute, moderation scatters to the winds and bloody hatred blows in. One learns this all too intractably when one considers Ireland and the Middle East.

In Ireland three traditions of Christianity spotlight the diabolical strain in Christian division. Because their forebears ate grapes of pride and possessed the will to power, the children of Northern Ireland now have their teeth set on edge.[45] There are no heroes among the belligerent politicians of Northern Ireland. Both Ian Paisley and Bernadette Devlin have mistaken their hatred for religious passion. Both have sought a species of self-righteousness, rather than the righteousness of the true mysterious God. Paisley's thunderous harangues could be right out of Dante's hell, all sulfurous and foul-smelling. He opens his mouth and there wafts the stench of a sickened soul. Devlin has been worse, if possible, so clever and calculating. "God will be on the side of the victor," she has said, showing how far cynicism has carried her. Might is right and power is all. Little good will come to the Irish people if that sort of socialism gains control.

Nor is it hard to lash the British, who bear the ultimate responsibility for Ireland's endless time of troubles. The vaunted British highmindedness quickly becomes a sham when one probes the way they have handled imperialism closest to home. The Irish have every right to hate the British, in terms of human history. British greed and contempt have twisted a poetic people on a grimy mercantile rack. So the nose-in-the-air words from Ten Downing Street are as tainted as the ranting of Paisley and Devlin. Anglicans, Presbyterians, and Roman Catholics all have colluded in a terrible botching. Together, they reveal the faith of the leaders of England and Ireland to have been little more than a veneer over worldliness and religious corruption.

Things seem quite analogous in the Middle East. The one ray of hope in the past forty years was Sadat's peace initiative, his moment of prophecy. When Begin insisted on playing lawyer to Sadat's prophet, the ray of hope tarnished, Sadat was set for martyrdom. Israelite hawkishness so blinded Begin and his followers that they ignored simple demographics. The world houses 600 million Muslims and 15 million Jews. How could sane people, realizing this, prefer "an eye for an eye" to "Come, let us reason together"? So the cynicism or irreligion of too many Jews faces the

murderous irreligion of many more Muslim fundamentalists. So plagues keep falling on all houses, as
surely as acid rain from clouds of chemical pollution.

Last, we must not fail to note that, from lack of faith
and vision, the United States has tolerated this case
study in wrongheadedness. It has not understood the
dangers of Qur'anic simplemindedness, has not
owned up to the Western powers' injustices to the
Palestinians, and has not forced Begin and his like to
foreswear their biblical foolishness, exposing their
claims to Zion as a fundamentalism almost as stupid as
that of Muslim extremists.

Of course, this is very hard talk, and it prescinds
from immense complexities. I thump it down deli-
berately, though, to clear some space for theological
reflection, for going deeper than current diplomacy
seems capable of doing. We will not solve problems
like those of Ireland and the Middle East until we bring
the people concerned to reconciliation: confessions
of foolishness and sin, movements toward mutual
forgiveness, sacrifices, and new beginnings all
around. This may never happen. Mutual forgiveness
and sacrifice may prove beyond ordinary human
beings, at least in their national forms. But we should
see the demands of peace clearly, not deluding
ourselves that power-politics has ever accomplished
anything lasting. Peace demands good people, genuine religion, perhaps even sanctity. Being humane
demands being more than human, demands being led
by the Spirit of God.

Citizens of the World

As the foregoing examples are meant to suggest, the
radical politics demanded by the future will be

international. In the face of so many peoples' immersion in chauvinistic nationalism, Christians are called to be citizens of the world. With the communications networks, economics, sets of war machines, and ecology that exist today, there is little place for nationalistic or ethnic mine and thine.

To be sure, people will always cluster in like-minded groups. They will always need small communities of significant others, communities of faith at the grass roots. But not to place these sources of identity in the context of the global whole will be to misread the forces of current history. Not to subordinate the demands of these sources of identity to the demands of the global common good will be to reject the one thing necessary for our planet's peace.

As a single planetary tribe, we have sufficient natural resources to feed, clothe, and shelter all the earth's current peoples. We even have enough to provide for a modest, controlled population growth. The question is whether we have sufficient human resources. Will our stores of compassion, insight, sacrifice, and reconciliation prove equal to the task of humanity's survival?[46] From the time of recorded history, which reports only a small fraction of our tribe's experience, we consistently have fallen below the demands of peacemaking and justice. In the 10,000 years or so since the rise of the first towns, the 5,500 years or so since the invention of the wheel, we have been slow to appreciate the passing of tribal culture. It may be that tribal culture was more peaceful and just than "civilization" has proved to be. Life was short and hard in those days, however. Nature was a mythic field, and we knew little of the earth's proportions, much less those of the universe. For all its problems, civilization has been an offer we could not refuse.

In an evolutionary sense, it is somewhat under-
standable that we are still fumbling the ball. We are, at
best, in our race's adolescence, powerful enough to
do great damage but not wise enough to deploy most
of our power constructively. Today one of the most
urgent crises of our adolescence lies in our educational systems. In most of the West, wisdom has been
dropped from the curriculum. As a result, we are
reducing education to a collection of technical skills,
dispensed from Clark Kerr's "multiversity." Little
peace will come from this.

The main task "higher" education faces today is the
task that traditioning has always faced. How can elders
pass on to youngsters the lessons life has taught them?
How can people over fifty (the age Aristotle demanded
of ethicists) hand on enough of their practical wisdom
(phronesis) to enable the next generation to perceive
the tasks of being human clearly enough and with
enough hope and resolution to transport our race
across its next generational threshold?

It is fashionalbe today for students of religion to
speak of *liminality*. Liminality is precisely *threshold
time*, phases of life when, through transition, it is
natural to confront deeper things. Since prehistoric
times, deeper things have been holy things. Imme-
morially, the holy and the actual have been one. Today
our larger evolutionary threshold consists of transition
to a global culture. Owning up to the effects of
communications and economics on human consciousness, we must ease our collective 4.5 billion into
enough maturity, enough sense of life's holiness, to
keep our fingers off the nuclear buttons. More
hopefully, we must translate the splendor of God into
a wide-reaching Esperanto, a language for all with ears
to hear. "There is no God but God," we Christians

must translate, "and Muhammad can be his prophet. There is no heaven but moksha or nirvana, so East and West can be one."

Of course, not all will be agreement during the honest colloquy a worldwide Esperanto might make possible. There will need to be a place for the differences between Muslim jihad and Christian war that is just, between Buddhist great compassion and Marxist class warfare. But if we agree that ultimate reality calls all human beings to a joyous quest for light and love, we can cushion these differences with a stronger hope for honesty and goodwill. If we agree that God has witnesses everywhere, that Jesus and the Buddha manifest a universal grace, we can relegate our differences to the second rank, the lesser station they deserve.

For all of us 4.5 billion are, first of all, human beings. All of us, first of all, can think and choose, need bread and wine. We all have sinned and fallen short of God's glory. We all can see merit in the critiques of honest atheists, the doubts of honest agnostics, the theocentrisms of honest Western religionists, the yogic peace of honest Eastern religionists. We can all do these things, see these things, because they demand only honesty and love, the basic openness that "humanity" itself asks of us.

A person is human in the measure that he or she is honest and loving. Humanity is as simple and as radical as that. Radical politics is merely a matter of being honest and loving together. It concerns only the means to make and the obstacles to hinder the making of cities of light, neighborhoods of love. It depends only on whether the light shines in all darknesses, whether the love has abandoned no human consciousness that still takes breath. Radical politics is therefore as close as the pulse at our throats, as solid as the groan of the Spirit in our prayer. If we hear its voice today in agonized cries from Ireland, from the Middle East, and from other places of anachronistic tribalism, let us harden not our hearts.

People of Few Wants

If we Christians must have something to harden in the future, let it be our ascetic wills. Globally, perhaps the most important demonstration of our faith will be our incarnation of the spare servant living that the transition to a just planetary ecumene will demand. Most helpful, therefore, will be interpretations of Christian spirituality that highlight the qualities of a simple, good life. Then, desiring only these few necessities, Christians may be better able to sacrifice their many superfluities. In the process, the legions of the Christian privileged who have found no joy in their wealth and status may get a second chance at Jesus' glad tidings.[47]

What are those few necessities? They are the bare needs of the body: food, clothing, shelter, exercise, basic health care; the bare needs of the mind: ongoing education, challenging work; the bare needs of the soul: faith, hope, and love; the bare needs of the human community: radical politics, honesty, and love. We need little more than survival, culture, and community. Each of these can expand, be embellished, push out roots in a hundred directions, but the core of each is relatively simple. Nourishing food, for example, is simpler than gourmet cuisine, though today perhaps harder to find. Durable, attractive clothing may, in the future, be as simple as homespun, much less complicated than the polyester on the racks. Earthen houses, warm in winter and cool in summer, probably will be more like the simple Mongolian yurt than the suburban split-level. With decent diet and health care, the way to a vigorous body will remain as simple as finding a place to run or a waterway (clean enough) to swim in. We do not really need half the things we now produce—the luxuries and injurious distractions.

Of course, to focus cultures on essential human needs and to emphasize the spiritual among those needs implies a thorough reconsideration of human work and economics. Education and religious contemplation demand leisure, as do science and art. Leisure is the creative basis of culture; art and religious contemplation are closely related to play. To achieve cultural vitality, therefore, work cannot be all. Work must serve the worker more than it serves an extrinsic accountant, the community's needs more than the needs of the fat cats. So let us begin to create technologies of small and intermediate scale, proportioned to the indigenous capabilities of a people, proportioned to their local ecology.[48] Let us begin to stress common planning and common sharing of burdens and rewards. Then perhaps we will enjoy our poets, revere our teachers and doctors, honor our research scientists more than we listen, hushed, to our bankers and brokers. Then perhaps we will move again in the direction of spiritual health. Christian spirituality ought to push us in that direction vigorously. It ought to call with a stentorian voice for worship rather than for dissipative "fun," social justice rather than the high life advertised in The New Yorker.

But, my svelte brothers and sisters, you may say that education and culture depend on a great deal of money, flourish only in lands of capitalistic freedom and enterprise. I find that opinion a dubious reading of the past and a hopeless prescription for the future. Historically, most significant education has not depended on high infusions of capital. It has depended on the reflective capacities of the tribe's shamans, the contemplative skills of the polis' sages, the eloquence of the nation's prophets.

This has not changed significantly today. Poets still need only access to beautiful nature, experience of significant human relationships, and space to sit at the feet of artists more mature. Give them these, part-time work for board and bed, paper, a nonelectric typewriter, and they should produce good work, if they really are poets. If they are panderers, needing a chic superstructure, their loss at the hands of simplified living will be of little matter.

We may say the same of teachers, doctors, scientists, musicians, monks, and genuine artisans. The number of decent occupations that demand much capital investment, much high voltage technology, are few. A computerized age may dispute this, but that is because a computerized people is slow to realize how little their silicon chips have to do with essential humanity. If Aeschylus did not know more about essential humanity than 95 percent of today's computer programers, I will turn in my writer's badge. If Einstein's main instrument was not his own imagination, I will put away the candles I have been lighting at his shrine.

The future I foresee and before whose shrine I light my prophetic candles may have a place for computers, as it may have a place for nuclear medicine and shuttles through space. I do not mean to foreclose any particular technology or veto any sort of imaginative creativity out of hand. Rather, I mean to make them all pay their way in terms of their contributions toward humanity's basic requirements, the first-order needs of the bodies, minds, souls, and communities of the one global race.

I suspect that the one global race will need to be a people of few wants, of deep rather than collateral desires, if we are to survive and reach distributive justice. I suspect technology will need to become more servant than it has been lately, if saints, artists, and scientists are to regain their traditional status. And I account this a democratic suspicion, far more populist than the current cost accounting, which promotes an elitism as superficial as money or notoriety. Each of us can be a saint, a human being of deep honesty and love. Many of us can be artists, making things of beauty; scientists, pursuing reality with minds vowed to integrity. If we but think of board and room, friends and work, before we think of guns and butter, a new humanity may begin to take shape. If we can but become a people of few (but deep) wants, Jesus' icons may have fewer frowns.

Ecumenical Implications

Can we boil down the implications of radical politics (in which religion is redeemed, the religious are reconciled, citizens of the world and people of few wants are formed) for the common agenda of the churches? Do these implications add anything to the ecumenical task itself? In this final section, I would like to brood on these questions.

First, questions such as these undercut most of the bases for division. Our new situation, in which we are placed by ecology, communications, and the other features of an increasingly planetary culture, shatters most historic Christian provincialism. The first response I would hope to find in ecumenical circles, therefore, is an acknowledgment that the new age makes Christian division acutely embarrassing. As long as ecumenical work for reunion claims to root itself in the truth, it must face such entailments honestly.

For in evolutionary terms, most of the historic divisions of the church *are* passé They make no sense at all to the 3.5 billions of the world who are not Christian, and they make very little sense to perhaps half of the 1.0 billion Christians—those who are somewhat mature. Against the backdrop of world history, what the people who confess Jesus to be Lord and Savior hold in common is far more significant than what they hold separately. The audacity of their faith, which claims that this man from Nazareth holds the key to all evolutionary time, should hush all their squabbles about trivialities of doctrine and church politics. Thus the radical politics set on the horizon by current history challenges Christians of all stripes to come to a deeper grasp of their true beliefs. Only if we separate the wheat from the chaff of our confessions will we be ready for the kairos God seems to be preparing.

Second, a blazing faith, riveted on what Kierkegaard called the moment (of the Incarnation), ought to express itself in a more profound contemplation and praxis than one finds upon glancing around. The churches have asked much too little of their members, so they have spawned a *massa damnata* of mediocre believers. Neither hot nor cold, these believers give the moment of the Incarnation a bad name. The Word of God supposedly has become flesh in human history—and most of our benches sniffle and yawn. They ought rather to be challenged to put their whole minds, hearts, souls, and strengths to this wonderful paradox. They ought to be shown that it is an inexhaustible subject of contemplation, never failing to nourish the deepest soul. And their leaders should become their prime examples.

For instance, the signs of the Johannine Jesus give us a golden humanity, filled by the Spirit of God. The glory of the Johannine Jesus gives us a scandalous humanity, revealing God's love as flesh torn on a cross. We, Jesus' brothers and sisters, are made of similar flesh. The glory and the scandal pertain wholly to all of us. How silly, then, to seek wisdom from the gurus of godless humanism, profit from the preachers of cheap grace. We should seek wisdom from our own center as a Christian people, our own Scriptures and sacraments. Were we to understand the meaning of our Scriptures and sacraments, we would find our hearts burning within us, as did the disciples on the road to Emmaus.

Third, by taking Jesus this seriously, by lashing and gentling our minds and spirits with his momentous Incarnation, death, and resurrection, the Church ecumenic could put the sword to all stupid fundamentalism. The Word of God, contemplated and treasured, is an energy for the mind, an encouragement for the soul's restless yet joyous quest, and it brands fundamentalism—lazy literalism about Scripture or tradition—as a blasphemous affront both to God's plan and to God's major sacrament, our own humanity. So clever about communications and finance, today's popular fundamentalists are so ignorant of Christian truth, its dynamic inheritance from the Spirit, that they cannot be children of the light. Indeed, their flight from the light of study and critical reflection is so gross a fugue that their deeds probably are evil.

I would like the Church ecumenic to make such statements in the near future—kindly but firmly. In the face of massive threats from fundamentalism in Islam and other religions, I would like the Church to proclaim that God has given us minds with which to study, intellects with which to think, precisely because God is a God of light, in whom there is no darkness at all; precisely because God is a God of love, who wants us to be adult, not childish.

Fourth, the Church ecumenic ought to speak kindly but firmly also about its radical political obligations, making it clear that Christian faith is not a matter of comforting the comfortable. There are comforts in Christian faith, to be sure, and all of us, weak and ignorant, need them. But in a healthy faith, they are more oblique than direct. Directly, healthy Christian faith seeks God and service of neighbor, not its own comforts. Directly, a healthy Christian faith is selfless, self-losing. Granted the psychological caveats concerning the need to possess a self before one tries to lose it and the place of a proper self-love, the point remains that God and neighbor are objective realities toward which we should be outgoing. They reside in us, demonstrating that objectivity and subjectivity coincide in mature spiritualities, but they do not encourage our narcissism, ought not to give us the vapors. If human beings fully alive are God's glory, as Irenaeus intuited, Christians should be people of live minds and live hearts, of fire and ice in all their varieties, all their subtleties of application.

The summary implication, then, is that the Church ecumenic should demand more of itself. We the people should ask ourselves for more fire and more ice, a faith more biting and more profoundly soothing. Today we dither about too many nonessentials. Tomorrow, let us go to the roots, tear up what is rotten (especially our divisions), and plant good seed: high Christology, deep prayer, and wide political action.

CONCLUSION

Jesus: Order for the Self

Once more, let us repair to the heart of the Christian matter, removing ourselves from the infarcts of ecumenical congestion. First, let us focus on Jesus' order for the self. It is a function of the twofold commandment, and I think it is well expressed in a radical contemplation and a radical politics.

A person is a Christian because of Jesus. Through the paradoxical congruence between Jesus' life, death, and resurrection, and a person's experience, Jesus becomes a savior of power and might. For the Christian of lively faith, there breathes the dearest freshness in Jesus. He is a thesaurus, a treasury, never to be emptied. From cradle to grave, his mysteries shine golden with Johannine grace, glint green and white with Pauline grace aligned with springtime and Passover.

When we contemplate Jesus, we see something of the Father, for Jesus is the icon of the Father. When we pray as Jesus prayed, we open to the Spirit's instructions in the life of the Father, the boundless life of love. When the Spirit groans in our depths, making us cry "Abba, Father," we step out of ordinary reality, become ecstatic toward the God who always has been our heart's great known unknown. The first time our eyes opened in wonder, we sensed the presence of God's great mystery. Philosophy begins in wonder, Aristotle said. The love of wisdom is always wonderful, thaumaturgic.

As it wonders about God, grows more and more in love with Jesus' mysterious Father, the self gains a strong protection against the depradations of the world, the flesh, and the devil. It has things to do, things whose very doing proves their worth, so it is innoculated against most idleness, boredom, and superficiality. Were we to teach our children to contemplate, we might halve their personal problems. Awakening their minds, sensitizing their hearts, we could set them on the right path, the path all good Muslims seek from Allah. Though most of their peers will grow up uncontemplative, with selves living on the periphery, our children would have a chance to deepen, gradually to ripen an interiority. Though most of their peers will be almost defenseless against money, pleasure, and fame, our children would have a start toward a stable center, an interior castle safe from at least the grosser seductions.

Jesus' order for the self therefore begins with a passionate love of God. Nothing worldly captivates Jesus' heart, so nothing worldly should captivate the heart of Jesus' follower. Order, health, come to the Christian's soul as workings of the Spirit poured forth, workings of the divine life of faith, hope, and love. These theological virtues develop the koinonia, the community with God, which "grace" primarily ought to import. We best nourish these virtues by good prayer, study, and liturgical worship. Much of the

Christian's active self-definition comes from the relation to God that such contemplation can nurture. As Kierkegaard especially emphasized, the self is a relation to the Absolute. The human person is the being whose "I" is a project, a restless but joyous quest into Mystery.

So much for the solitary side of Christian selfhood, which no sociology of religion, however sophisticated, must be allowed to deprecate. Whitehead was only half right when he said that religion is what one does with solitude, but he was half right. The social side of Christian religion stands epitomized in Jesus' second great commandment, which I find to be well obeyed through a radical politics. For good order, the Christian self must try to relate to its neighbors as to so many other selves. It must try to love them, to promote their good, just as it tries to promote its own good. Not to regard other people this way is to fall into some form of pseudospeciation. To neglect Jesus' teaching about the vine and the branches is to think that only a part of the race is worthy of God's salvation. Manifestly, Jesus did not think or act in that way. Manifestly, he chose a Samaritan to teach his followers, his Church, how they were to regard even their reputed enemies.

What happens to the self when it takes up this Christian socialism?—an ascetic stripping of many pretensions, many privileges; a compensating relief from many burdens, many uneasinesses. It is finally untrue to pretend that any one of us is more unlike than like the rest of us. All of us born of woman and headed for the grave enjoy a radical equality. As the medieval danse macabre portrayed it, cardinals and beggars all join hands when the dance is in human time.

Further, our basic equality calls into question all

gross disparities in wealth and opportunity, so that those of sensitive conscience like Francis of Assisi and Simone Weil grow increasingly uneasy with their inherited wealth, find themselves drawn more and more strongly to serve the poor. That serving gives order to their lives, joy to their selves, because it allows them to honor ground-level realities. At ground level, we all know that the really poor—the ragged kids of Cairo, Delhi, Bangkok, Sao Paolo—suffer unjustly. The servant saints are those who do something about that injustice. The rest of us in the ecumenic Church ought at least to do what we can, turn ourselves around as much as we are able, lest the servant saints be utterly alone.

Jesus: Order for Society

In the evolutionary view of current history that I find persuasive, few of us human beings are going to be utterly alone in the twenty-first century. Ecologically, politically, economically, and unfortunately, through our engines of war, we are likely to be brought face to face more and more frequently. What does Jesus' social teaching sketch for the good order of this global future? Where do Jesus' love of God and service to neighbor place Christians who would be people of a truly ecumenic future?

Jesus' love of God places his reflective followers beyond dogmatism. However defensible the notion of dogma, of Christian truth officially declared, dogmatism, holding rigidly to one's conceptions, is ill-fitting in the face of Jesus' God. For no one has ever seen Jesus' God, and the declarations in space and time of the Only Begotten of the Father suffer the limitations of all spatiotemporal communication. So Christian theology, especially in the East, has been drawn to an important negative moment, an important kinship with wordless prayer. If a community were to conduct its liturgy, sponsor its study, and orient its polity in this mood, it might find great resources for modeling the flexible, cooperative interaction that at least the proximate phases of our planetary culture seem sure to demand.

Consider, for instance, the case within the church itself. If our theologians, leaders, and ordinary faithful were to quiet the clatter of their tongues and minds before the mystery of Jesus' God, they might be more amenable to the proposition that many of their differences could be complements rather than antagonisms. The general designations I suggested— Protestant prophecy, Catholic wisdom, and Orthodox worship—were inadequate, but even more precise designations could first receive an open, unsuspicious hearing, first be greeted as potential enrichments rather than dreaded as potential threats.

Tradition by tradition, geographic locale by geographic locale, Christians have striven to penetrate the Lordship of Jesus and live out its implications faithfully. Now well, now poorly, they have interacted with the particular conditions of their environment, have adapted both their faith and that environment in pursuit of a good life. As a result, all communities have learned some valuable lessons, and each community has something distinctive to contribute to the Church ecumenic. My emphasis on the heart of the Christian matter, the bedrock experiences of Christian faith, is meant to facilitate the sharing of these richly diversified resources, not to bulldoze them away in a futile search for one level ground. By searching more deeply, I contend, we may find a still point that makes the many divergences of the churches' faith more acceptable than they traditionally have been. By contemplating more deeply, so that the One of God comes more closely into view, the many of our religious experiences could be more attractive, more harmonizable, than they previously have been.

At least, this has been my personal experience. By seeking the heart of the Christian matter, I have found myself able to enjoy, in what I hope is a highly religious sense, the varieties of Protestant prophecy and biblicism, the varieties of Catholic wisdom and ceremonial, the varieties of Orthodox worship and ethnicity. I shall never be able to leap out of my own skin, genes, and history, of course, but I can grow more universal, more sympathetic, more ecumenic, in spirit. I can let the silence of my radical contemplation express itself in diverse forms of worship, theology, and social service. As I do, I find the churches' dissensions, their refusals to commune with one another (especially at the Lord's Supper), less and less tolerable.

For Christian society, then, radical contemplation of the One God could make the many diversities more tolerant and more tolerable. I think it could do the same, analogously, for world society at large. Even more pressing for world society than radical contemplation, however, is a radical politics that will take dead aim on the world's injustices. Peacemaking, ecological, servant and spare in its life-style, this radical politics strives to embody Jesus' love of neighbor as self, strives to turn social institutions toward truly fraternal/sororal paths. Respecting ethnic and religious differences, it yet calls people to a humanism that will undercut all that is disruptive and hateful in such differences. It yet calls people, also, to live out a oneness that allows manyness to be a benediction rather than a curse.

"God's will is that we do justice," the liberation theologians chant in a mesmerizing refrain. God desires effective mercy and compassion, not ornate sacrifices. There is no mystery about the first items on the planetary society's current agenda. Unless we reduce the arms build-up, convert to a more ecological life-style, and turn the world's economy toward a strict distributive justice, we shall scarcely get the next phase of human history off the ground. Radical politics is the only Christian response to this situation that I can accredit. It is the only response that is consonant with both the current facts and Jesus' lovely bearing, and so is able to pass my (actually rather undemanding) muster. The social heart of the Christian matter, the order it offers us humans collectively, is that we set our faces toward loving sacrifice, trusting that the un-known God will make herself more fully known if we but strive to love our enemies as ourselves.

NOTES

Introduction

1. See Lawrence Cunningham, *The Meaning of Saints* (San Francisco: Harper & Row, 1980); James W. Fowler et al., *Trajectories in Faith* (Nashville: Abingdon, 1980).

2. See Patrick Henry and Thomas Stransky, eds., *God on Our Minds* (Philadelphia: Fortress Press, 1982).

Part One: Jesus

1. Shusaku Endō, *A Life of Jesus,* trans. Richard A. Schuchert (Ramsey, N.J.: Paulist Press, 1978; reprint, paper, 1980). On different impressions of Jesus over the centuries, see Dennis C. Duling, *Jesus Christ Through History* (New York: Harcourt, Brace, Jovanovich, 1979); Aiden Nichols, *The Art of God Incarnate* (Ramsey, N.J.: Paulist Press, 1980); (for the twentieth century) John H. Hayes, *Son of God to Super Star* (Nashville: Abingdon, 1976).

2. Robert Funk, *Jesus as Precursor* (Philadelphia: Fortress Press, 1975), p. 67. For more New Testament interpretation along this line, see Sallie TeSelle, *Speaking in Parables* (Philadelphia: Fortress Press, 1975); Paul Ricoeur, *Essays on Biblical Interpretation* (Philadelphia: Fortress Press, 1980). For a broader overview of recent New Testament trends, see Patrick Henry, *New Directions in New Testament Study* (Philadelphia: Westminster Press, 1979).

3. Jeremias, *New Testament Theology* (New York: Charles Scribner's Sons, 1971), p. 147.

4. *Ibid.*, p. 148.

5. See José Miranda, *Marx and the Bible* (Maryknoll, N.Y.: Orbis Books, 1974).

6. Raymond E. Brown, *The Community of the Beloved Disciple* (Ramsey, N.J.: Paulist Press, 1979). For a somewhat parallel look at the sociological background of the other Gospels, see Howard Clark Kee, *Christian Origins in Sociological Perspective* (Philadelphia: Westminster Press, 1980).

7. A good exposition of this point is Stephen Neill's *Jesus Through Many Eyes* (Philadelphia: Fortress Press, 1976).

8. Terrien, *The Elusive Presence* (New York: Harper & Row, 1978).

9. See Vladimir Lossky, *The Mystical Theology of the Eastern Church* (Crestwood, N.Y.: St. Vladimir's Seminary Press, 1976).

10. Lucas Grollenberg stresses this in *Jesus* (Philadelphia: Westminster Press, 1978), esp. pp. 111-13.

11. Rahner, *Foundations of Christian Faith* (New York: Seabury Press, 1978), esp. chs. 3, 4, 5.

12. See André Lacocque, "Job or the Impotence of Religion and Philosophy," *Semeia* 19 (1981): 33-52.

13. See Karl Rahner, "Thomas Aquinas on the Incomprehensibility of God," *The Journal of Religion* 58/Supplement (1978): S107-25. On the implications of viewing biblical revelation and classical Greek philosophy as the two (compatible) cultural events in which human consciousness (and consequently much of theological predication) was decisively clarified, see Eric Voegelin, *Conversations with Eric Voegelin* (Montreal: Thomas More Press, 1980). For a counterview, which views God as finite, see John B. Cobb, Jr., and David Ray Griffin, *Process Theology: An Introductory Exposition* (Philadelphia: Westminster Press, 1976).

14. See James B. Pritchard, *Ancient Near Eastern Texts*, 3rd ed. (Princeton, N.J.: Princeton University Press, 1969), pp. 405-7.

15. Percy, *The Second Coming* (New York: Pocket Books, 1981); Hazzard, *The Transit of Venus* (New York: Playboy Paperbacks, Playboy Press, 1981).

16. Potok, *My Name Is Asher Lev* (New York: Alfred A. Knopf, 1972), p. 330.

17. Exhaustive background and analysis of those times are available in Edward Schillebeeckx, *Jesus* (New York: Seabury Press, 1979); *Christ* (New York: Seabury Press, 1980).

18. See Bernard Lonergan, *Method in Theology* (New York: Herder & Herder, 1972), p. 106.

19. Pirsig, *Zen and the Art of Motorcycle Maintenance* (New York: Bantam Books, 1975).

20. R. M. French, trans., *The Way of a Pilgrim* (New York: Seabury Press, 1965).

21. For a beginning, see Stephen Neill, *A History of Christian Missions* (Baltimore: Penguin Books, 1964).

22. Schillebeeckx, *Ministry: Leadership in the Community of Jesus Christ* (New York: Crossroads Books, Seabury Press, 1981), p. 5. See also Bernard Cooke, *Ministry to Word and Sacraments* (Philadelphia: Fortress Press, 1976).

23. Rahner, *The Shape of the Church to Come* (New York: Seabury Press, 1974), p. 56.

24. See, e.g., Emilie Griffin, *Turning: Reflections on the Experience of Conversion* (Garden City, N.Y.: Doubleday & Co., 1980).

25. See, e.g., Robert McAfee Brown, *Creative Dislocation—The Movement of Grace* (Nashville: Abingdon, 1980).

26. Kingston, *The Woman Warrior* (New York: Alfred A. Knopf, 1977).

27. See E. F. Schumacher, *A Guide for the Perplexed* (New York: Harper & Row, 1977).

28. Solzhenitsyn, *The Gulag Archipelago* (New York: Harper & Row, 1974ff.).

Part Two: Loving God

1. Tillich, *Systematic Theology*, vol. I (Chicago: University of Chicago Press, 1967), p. 227.

2. Erikson, *Gandhi's Truth* (New York: W. W. Norton & Co., 1969), pp. 431-33.

3. Leo O'Donovan, S.J., "The Mystery of God as a History of Love: Eberhard Jüngel's Doctrine of God," *Theological Studies* 42/2 (June 1981): 252.

4. See Niebuhr, "Sin," in *A Handbook of Christian Theology*, ed. Arthur A. Cohen and Marvin Halverson (Nashville: Abingdon Press, 1958), pp. 348-51.

5. F. L. Cross, ed., *The Oxford Dictionary of the Christian Church* (New York: Oxford University Press, 1966), p. 833.

6. Marty, *The Public Church* (New York: Crossroad Publishing Co., 1981).

7. Brown, *The Spirit of Protestantism* (New York: Oxford University Press, 1965), pp. 171-85.

8. See Vincent Ferrer Blehl, ed., *The Essential Newman* (New York: Mentor Books, New American Library, 1963), pp. 115-55.

9. Stanley L. Jaki, *The Road of Science and the Ways to God* (Chicago: University of Chicago Press, 1978).

10. See David Tracy, *The Analogical Imagination* (New York: Crossroad Books, Seabury Press, 1981).

11. See William M. Thompson, *Jesus: Lord and Savior* (New York: Paulist Press, 1980).

12. See the study of this epigram in the appendix to Gaston Fessard, *La Dialectique des Exercices Spirituelles de Saint Ignace de Loyola* (Paris: Aubier, 1956).

13. See Ignacio de Loyola, *Obras Completas*, ed. Ignacio Iparraguirre, S.J. (Madrid: Biblioteca de Autores Cristianos, 1963), pp. 203-18.

14. See William R. Burrows, *New Ministries: The Global Context* (Maryknoll, N.Y.: Orbis Books, 1980).

15. Meyendorff, *The Orthodox Church*, 3rd ed. (Crestwood, N.Y.: St. Vladimir's Seminary Press, 1981), p. 67.

16. Sergius Bolshakoff and M. Basil Pennington, *In Search of True Wisdom* (Garden City, N.Y.: Doubleday & Co., 1979), p. 171.

17. See Aiden Nichols, O.P., *The Art of God Incarnate* (New York: Paulist Press, 1980), p. 88.

18. Alexander Schmemann treats Orthodox church/state relations intermittently in *The Historical Road of Eastern Orthodoxy* (Crestwood, N.Y.: St. Vladimir's Seminary Press, 1977).

19. On nature, see Joseph Sittler, *Essays on Nature and Grace* (Philadelphia: Fortress Press, 1972).

20. Robert G. Stephanopoulos, "Denominational Loyalties and Ecumenical Commitment: A Personal View," *Journal of Ecumenical Studies* 17/4 (Fall 1980): 640.

21. Bolshakoff and Pennington, *In Search of True Wisdom*, p. 106.

22. For the best short analysis of Voegelin's work, see Peter J. Opitz, "Rückkehr zur Realität: Grandzuge der politischen Philosophie Eric Voegelins," in *The Philosophy of Order*, ed. Peter J. Opitz and Gregor Sebba (Stuttgart: Klett-Cotta, 1981), pp. 21-73. See also Stephen A. McKnight, ed., *Eric Voegelin's Search for Order in History* (Baton Rouge, La.: Louisiana State University Press, 1978).

23. Voegelin, *Order and History*, I: Israel and Revelation; II: The World of the Polis; III: Plato and Aristotle; IV: The Ecumenic Age (Baton Rouge, La.: Louisiana State University Press, 1956; 1957; 1957; 1974).

24. See T. S. Eliot, "Burnt Norton," in *The Four Quartets* (New York: Harcourt, Brace, & World, 1943), pp. 15-16 (11. 60-75).

25. Gilkey, *Reaping the Whirlwind: A Christian Interpretation of History* (New York: Seabury Press, 1976).

26. Julian N. Hartt, *Theological Method and Imagination* (New York: Seabury Press, 1977).

27. For a contrary view on the outcome of history, see Lewis S. Ford, *The Lure of God* (Philadelphia: Fortress Press, 1978), pp. 113-19.

28. For explanation of *communicato idiomatum*, see Karl Rahner and Herbert Vorgrimler, *Theological Dictionary* (New York: Herder & Herder, 1965), p. 90.

29. See J. P. de Caussade, *Holy Abandonment* (New York: Benziger Brothers, 1952).

30. Smith, *Towards a World Theology* (Philadelphia: Westminster Press, 1981).

31. See Richard G. Cote, *Universal Grace: Myth or Reality?* (Maryknoll, N.Y.: Orbis Books, 1977).

32. See Karl Rahner, "The One Christ and the Universality of Salvation," in *Theological Investigations,* 16 (New York: Seabury Press, 1979), p. 219.

33. See Kelsey, *The Other Side of Silence* (New York: Paulist Press, 1976).

34. See William Johnston, ed., *The Cloud of Unknowing* (Garden City, N.Y.: Doubleday & Co., 1973).

35. A good introduction to recent adaptations of *The Cloud,* in terms of "centering prayer," is Thomas Keating et al., *Finding Grace at the Center* (Still River, Mass.: St. Bede Publications, 1978).

36. See Erikson, "Reflections on Dr. Borg's Life-Cycle," in *Adulthood,* ed. Erik Erikson (New York: W. W. Norton & Co., 1978), pp. 1-31.

37. Vatican II, "Decree on Ecumenism," no. 11.

Part Three: Loving Neighbor

1. Geertz, *The Interpretation of Cultures* (New York: Basic Books, 1973), pp. 412-53.

2. For one sad tally, see Arnold Toynbee, *Mankind and Mother Earth* (New York: Oxford University Press, 1976).

3. See Sergio Torres and John Eagleson, eds., *The Challenge of Basic Christian Communities* (Maryknoll, N.Y.: Orbis Books, 1981). See also *Christianity and Crisis* 41/14 (September 21, 1981).

4. See Cardenal, *The Gospel in Solentiname,* 3 vols. (Maryknoll, N.Y.: Orbis Books, 1978-1979).

5. See, e.g., Penny Lernoux, *Cry of the People* (Garden City, N.Y.: Doubleday & Co., 1980).

6. Solzhenitsyn, *East and West* (New York: Harper & Row, 1980), p. 36.

7. Gutiérrez, *La Fuerza Historica de los Pobres* (Lima, Peru: Centro de Estudios Y Publicaciones, 1979), p. 151.

8. Diego de Gaspar, "Economics and World Hunger," in *Faith and Science in an Unjust World: Plenary Presentations,* Vol. 1, ed. Roger L. Shinn (Philadelphia: Fortress Press, 1980), p. 227.

9. E.g., see Adam Smith, *An Inquiry into the Nature and Causes of the Wealth of Nations,* 2 vols., ed. R. H. Campbell (London: Oxford University Press, 1976).

10. See Gayraud Wilmore and James Cone, eds., *Black Theology* (Maryknoll, N.Y.: Orbis Books, 1979).

11. See J. Deotis Roberts, *Roots of a Black Future* (Philadelphia: Westminster Press, 1980).

12. See Harding, "Out of the Cauldron of Struggle," *Soundings* 61/3 (Fall 1978): 339-54.

13. *Ibid.,* pp. 351-52.

14. Dinnerstein, *The Mermaid and the Minotaur* (New York: Harper & Row, 1977).

15. Rich, *The Dream of a Common Language* (New York: W. W. Norton & Co., 1978); Daly, *Gyn/Ecology* (Boston: Beacon Press, Harper & Row, 1978).

16. I am especially influenced here, as throughout this section, by Denise Lardner Carmody, *Feminism and Christianity: A Two-Way Reflection* (Nashville: Abingdon, 1982).

17. See Sidney E. Mead, "Religious Pluralism and the Character of the Republic," *Soundings* 61/3 (Fall 1978): 320-24.

18. *Ibid.,* p. 321.

19. See Hollenbach, *Claims in Conflict* (New York: Paulist Press, 1979), p. 204.

20. See William Ouchi, *Theory Z* (Reading, Mass.: Addison-Wesley Publishing Co., 1981).

21. See Fowler, *Stages of Faith* (San Francisco: Harper & Row, 1981), pp. 184-213.

22. Solzhenitsyn, *East and West,* pp. 37-71.

23. Ryan, *Distributive Justice* (N.Y.: The Macmillan Co., 1927).

24. In Carmody, *Reexamining Conscience* (New York: Seabury Press, 1982), I essayed a lay spirituality in terms of the examination of conscience.

25. See David Spring and Eileen Spring, eds., *Ecology and Religion in History* (New York: Harper & Row, 1974).

26. See Frederick J. Streng, *Emptiness* (Nashville: Abingdon Press, 1967).

27. See G. Tyler Miller, Jr., *Living in the Environment*, 3rd ed. (Belmont, Calif.: Wadsworth Publishing Co., 1982), p. 407.

28. *Ibid.*, p. 409.

29. *Ibid.*, pp. 420-21.

30. *Ibid.*, pp. 395-96.

31. *Ibid.*, p. 392.

32. *Ibid.*, pp. E33-38.

33. Note the low visibility of "environment" in Joseph Gremillion's *The Gospel of Peace and Justice: Catholic Social Teaching Since Pope John* (Maryknoll, N.Y.: Orbis Books, 1976).

34. Carl Djerassi, *The Politics of Contraception*, vol. I (Stanford, Calif.: Stanford Alumni Association, 1979), p. 23.

35. Thomas, *The Medusa and the Snail* (New York: Viking Press, 1979), p. 9.

36. See E. F. Schumacher, *Small Is Beautiful* (New York: Harper & Row, 1973), *A Guide for the Perplexed* (New York: Harper & Row, 1977), *Good Work* (New York: Harper & Row, 1979). The essay on Buddhist economics appears in *Small Is Beautiful,* pp. 50-58.

37. Thomas Merton, *The Way of Chuang Tzu* (New York: New Directions Publishing Co., 1965), pp. 46-47.

38. See Daly, "The Ecological and Moral Necessity for Limiting Economic Growth," in Shinn, *Faith and Science,* vol. 1, pp. 212-20.

39. Ward, *Progress for a Small Planet* (New York: W. W. Norton & Co., 1979).

40. See, e.g., C. T. Kurien, "A Third World Perspective," in Shinn, *Faith and Science,* vol. 1, pp. 220-25.

41. Helen Caldicott, *Nuclear Madness* (Brookline, Mass.: Auburn Press, 1978), p. 76.

42. Miller, *Living in the Environment,* p. 255.

43. *Ibid.*, pp. 259, 290-92.

44. *Ibid.*, p. 265.

45. See Robert Coles, "Ulster's Children," *The Atlantic Monthly* 246/6 (December 1980): 33-44.

46. Robert L. Heilbroner, *An Inquiry into the Human Prospect* (New York: W. W. Norton & Co., 1980) provides a sober estimate of this task.

47. See Robert Coles and George Abbott, "The Religion of 'The Privileged Ones,'" *Cross Currents* 31/1 (Spring 1981): 1-14.

48. I recommend the monthly *Sojourners* as an impressive expression of radical Christian politics.

ANNOTATED BIBLIOGRAPHY

The following books, together, should illumine the next level of complexity in each of the three areas we have treated.

Part One: Jesus

Grollenberg, Lucas. *Jesus*. Philadelphia: Westminster Press, 1978. A readable, winning portrait by a Dutch Roman Catholic scholar of Scripture who stresses Jesus' humanity and Jewish religious background.

Henry, Patrick. *New Directions in New Testament Study*. Philadelphia: Westminster Press, 1979. A fine survey of recent trends by an academic of Protestant formation but ecumenical sympathies.

Kee, Howard Clark. *Christian Origins in Sociological Perspective*. Philadelphia: Westminster Press, 1980. A Protestant scholar of Scripture gives a clear exposition of the new light that the social sciences now offer on the background of the early Christian communities.

Machovec, Milan. *A Marxist Looks at Jesus*. Philadelphia: Fortress Press, 1976. A stimulating and appreciative view of Jesus by a Czech Marxist who finds many of Jesus' ideas about human authenticity and social justice akin to the best in Marxism.

Neill, Stephen. *Jesus Through Many Eyes*. Philadelphia: Fortress Press, 1976. A readable introduction to the many theologies of the New Testament by an Anglican bishop of wide historical learning and deep missionary experience.

Nolan, Albert. *Jesus Before Christianity.* Maryknoll, N.Y.: Orbis Books, 1978. A study by a South African Roman Catholic priest, which focuses on Jesus' own message and finds many themes that disturb the powerful and comfort the adherents of liberation theology.

O'Collins, Gerald, S.J. *What Are They Saying About the Resurrection?* New York: Paulist Press, 1978. A brief exposition by a Roman Catholic theologian of the recent findings of Scripture scholars and theologians on this central point of New Testament Christology.

Sobrino, Jon, S.J. *Christology at the Crossroads.* Maryknoll, N.Y.: Orbis Books, 1978. A full-scale Christology by a Catholic theologian in El Salvador, illustrating the pointed political implications of the liberation brought by Jesus.

Terrien, Samuel. *The Elusive Presence.* New York: Harper & Row, 1978. A lengthy study by a mature Protestant Scripture scholar of the notion, central to both Testaments, that God is present to his people, but in ways we cannot control.

Vermes, Geza. *Jesus the Jew.* London: Wm. Collins & Co., 1976. A rather technical study by a Jewish Scripture scholar, focusing on the Jewish background contemporary to Jesus, in terms of which much of the New Testament was cast.

Part Two: Loving God

Brown, Robert McAfee. *The Spirit of Protestantism.* New York: Oxford University Press, 1965. A readable overview written with great ecumenical sensitivity, offering an inside view of the Protestant pulse.

Gilkey, Langdon. *Message and Existence.* New York: Seabury Press, 1979. An introduction to Christian theology from a scholar rooted in the Protestant and process traditions.

Hellwig, Monika K. *Understanding Catholicism.* New York: Paulist Press, 1981. A lucid overview of current Catholic faith from a centrist position.

Johnston, William. *The Inner Eye of Love.* San Francisco: Harper & Row, 1978. A fine exposition of contemplative prayer from a Catholic and internationalist viewpoint.

Macquarrie, John. *Principles of Christian Theology.* London: SCM Press, 1977. A clear exposition of mainline Christian theology from a Heideggerian point of view.

McBrien, Richard P. *Catholicism.* Minneapolis: Winston Press, 1980. A two-volume work that organizes recent Catholic theology into a clear impressive statement on all aspects of Christian faith.

Meyendorff, John. *The Orthodox Church.* 3d rev. ed. Crestwood, N.Y.: St. Vladimir's Seminary Press, 1981. A good introduction, blending history and doctrine.

Saliers, Don E. *The Soul in Paraphrase.* New York: Seabury Press, 1980. A lyric view of prayer and religious affections by a leading Protestant liturgist.

Smith, Wilfred Cantwell. *Towards a World Theology.* Philadelphia: Westminster Press, 1981. A most stimulating study by a Christian scholar of Islam, sketching the new context of interreligious dialogue and theology.

Ware, Timothy. *The Orthodox Church.* Baltimore: Penguin Books, 1964. A standard introduction, still readable and valuable.

Webb, Eugene. *Eric Voegelin: Philosopher of History.* Seattle: University of Washington Press, 1981. A good introduction to the leading philosopher of history of our time.

Part Three: Loving Neighbor

Abrecht, Paul, ed. *Faith and Science in an Unjust World: Reports and Recommendations.* Vol. 2. Philadelphia: Fortress Press, 1980. Quasi-consensus statements from the subsections of the World Council of Churches' 1979 conference at M.I.T., covering most of the salient problems in the arms-energy-food-justice complex.

Anderson, Bernard E. et al. *American Indians, Blacks, Chicanos, and Puerto Ricans. Daedalus* 118 (Spring 1981). Essays on various aspects of the lives of minority Americans.

Baker-roshi, Richard et al. *Earth's Answer: Explorations of Planetary Culture at the Lindisfarne Conferences.* New York: Harper & Row, 1977. Essays that explore many of the salient issues of the emerging planetary spirituality.

Barnet, Richard J. *The Lean Years: Politics in an Age of Scarcity.* New York: Simon & Schuster, 1980. The political future as forecast by one who takes the energy crisis seriously.

Bolshakoff, Sergius, and Pennington, M. Basil. *In Search of True Wisdom.* Garden City, N.Y.: Doubleday & Co., 1979.

Explorations of Orthodox spirituality and monasticism that offer much on the internationalist, spare living the future seems to portend.

Gremillion, Joseph, ed. *Food/Energy and the Major Faiths.* Maryknoll, N.Y.: Orbis Books, 1978. Papers from the 1975 Interreligious Peace Colloquium held at Bellagio, Italy.

Häring, Bernard. *Free & Faithful in Christ.* Vol. 3. New York: Crossroad Publishing Co., 1981. Reflections on bioethics and the healing of public life by a leading Roman Catholic moral theologian, one of the first to take ecology seriously.

Heilbroner, Robert L. *Marxism: For and Against.* New York: W. W. Norton & Co., 1980. A balanced assessment of Marx's economics and social philosophy by a liberal economist who is well aware of tomorrow's international problems.

Miller, G. Tiller, Jr. *Living in the Environment,* 3d ed. Belmont, Calif.: Wadsworth Publishing Co., 1982. A basic text in ecology, full of pertinent information and wonderfully illustrated.

Rifkin, Jeremy. *Entropy: A New World View.* New York: Bantam Books, 1980. A popular presentation of the facts and implications of the energy crisis.

Sale, Kirkpatrick. *Human Scale.* New York: Coward, McCann, & Geoghegan, 1980. A full, leisurely exploration to explain why small is beautiful—socially, economically, and politically.

Schumacher, E. F. *A Guide for the Perplexed.* New York: Harper & Row, 1977. The philosophy of the best single guide to the economic and ecological sides of a radical Christian politics.

INDEX

297